SIGNS

OF

HIS

COMING

SIGNS
OF
HIS
COMING

David Allen Lewis

New Leaf Press

First printing: May 1997

ISBN: 0-89221-347-7
Library of Congress Catalog Number: 97-65169

Cover design by Janell Robertson

Dedicated to

Dr. Stanley M. Horton

teacher, mentor, friend

Contents

Chapter 1

SIGNS
OF THE
TIMES

What shall be the sign of thy coming? (Matt. 24:3).

And God said, Let there be lights in the firmament of the heaven to divide the day from the night; and let them be for signs, and for seasons, and for days, and years (Gen. 1:14).

He delivereth and rescueth, and he worketh signs and wonders in heaven and in earth (Dan. 6:27).

The signs of His coming are very apparent and meaningful to believers. But there is a different word to the scoffers.

The Pharisees also with the Sadducees came, and tempting desired him that he would shew them a sign from heaven. He answered and said unto them, When it is evening, ye say, It will be fair weather: for the sky is red. And in the morning, It will be foul weather to day: for the sky is red and lowring. O ye hypocrites, ye can discern the face of the sky; but can ye not discern the signs of the times? A wicked and adulterous generation seeketh after a sign; and there shall no sign be given unto it, but the sign of the prophet Jonas. And he left them, and departed (Matt. 16:1-4).

Knowing this first, that there shall come in the last days scoffers, walking after their own lusts, And saying, Where is the promise of his coming? for since the fathers fell asleep, all things continue as they were from the beginning of the creation (2 Pet. 3:3-4).

1. Sign of Looking Ahead

Sign number one is humanity's desire to know the future. The disciples Jesus had chosen wanted to know the future, just like you and I want to know the future. They asked Jesus what signs would indicate that the end of the age (Gr. *aion*, translated "world" in the KJV) was at hand. We are not looking for the end of the world, but of this age or world system. Jesus rebuked the scorners of His day who demanded a sign from heaven to prove himself, as Matthew records. But when the disciples asked Jesus about the signs of His coming, He proceeded to give them an extensive discourse on prophecy, including many signs. Other New Testament writers also wrote of many signs of the end of this age.

The bewildered world outside of Christ turns to psychic hot lines, via "900" phone numbers, to try and get glimpses of tomorrow. The most revealing TV commercials for psychic services are those that urge, "Don't pay any attention to those phony psychics on other hot lines. Use our services. We have the real psychics!" At best they are all phony, at the worst, demonic.

Christians respond, "We don't need a psychic bag of tricks when we can go to the source of all truth. In prayer we contact the sovereign Creator, omniscient God of the universe, from whom all truth issues forth. God alone knows and reveals the future."

The disciples asked Jesus what signs would indicate that the end of the age (*aion*) was at hand. We are not looking for the end of the physical world but we know there will be an end of this age or world system. After the close of this era, there will be a 1,000-year visible manifestation of the kingdom of God on this earth. We call the coming age the Millennium.

2. Sign of Dying World System

> And there shall be signs in the sun, and in the moon, and in the stars; and upon the earth distress of nations, with perplexity; the sea and the waves roaring (Luke 21:25).

Signs! Distress! Confusion! Commotion! Sign number two is the apparent decay of society and the inevitable collapse of the world system. Never has chaos and confusion ruled as today. A few decades ago we did not have the massive problems of drug usage; abortion; pornography; rampant taxation; inflation; family breakup; children rebelling, assaulting, killing and raping other children; weapons of mass destruction; cults and false prophets; false christs; occult invasion of the New Age movement; satanism; wicca; violence in the streets; terrorism; UFO deception; euthanasia; suicide increase; human slavery again (Sudan); Mars rocks and government-sponsored Search for ExtraTerrestrial Intelligence (SETI); increase of knowledge; the worldwide web; inability to discern reality from fantasy; Hollywood and TV moral corruption; Gulf War disease (now thought to be contagious); AIDS; pestilence; weird weather; increased earthquake activity; and on and on the list could go. This doomsday scenario is the black background against which sign number three shines so brightly.

3. Sign of Hope

Sign number three is the sign of hope. After enumerating the dire conditions afflicting the world system at the end of the age, Jesus offered hope to believers, saying, "And when these things begin to come to pass, then look up, and lift up your heads; for your redemption draweth nigh" (Luke 21:28).

Ours is not a message of doom but of hope in Jesus Christ. Indeed, we are "Looking for that blessed hope, and the glorious appearing of the great God and our Saviour Jesus Christ" (Titus 2:13). Sign number three is the sign of a new beginning. Jesus is not coming back to wreck the earth, but to fix it. There will be a complete disassembly of the physical universe, for complete cleansing, then the restoration of a perfect world, spoken of as the new earth in prophecy. This will take place right after the Millennium. Second Peter 3:10-13 describes the meltdown of the earth, not the annihilation of its elemental components. The earth is to be redeemed, not destroyed.

The end is the beginning! Yes, the end of this age and this doomed anti-God world system signals the beginning of the millennial Kingdom and then the dawn of eternity which features a new heaven and a new earth!

4. Sign of the Acceleration Factor

Are the signs really signs? Wars? Famine? Pestilence? Earthquakes? The skeptic asks, "What kind of signs are these? These are conditions that have always been with us."

Yes, these are valid signs of the times, for at least two good reasons. First, there is the saturation factor, or you can call it the acceleration factor. This is the sign of exponential increase.

It is true that there have always been wars, but now for the first time mankind has the weapons capable of destroying all life on earth. There have always been earthquakes but now the incidence of earthquakes is rapidly increasing. Pestilences have devastated masses of people in the past but now we must cope with AIDS and other incurable sexual diseases. We must contemplate the horrors of biological warfare, nerve gas, and germ warfare. And the threat is increasing as whole nations gain new weapons technology. Nations dedicated to terror as a means of de-stabilizing other nations stand poised to wreak havoc on the entire world.

Let's illustrate the concept of exponential increase. Suppose you had a really big piece of paper. Fold it in half, doubling its thickness with each fold. Keep folding it fifty-four times. How thick will your piece of paper be? Ten feet? A mile? How far is it from the earth to the sun? Answer: 93 million miles. After the fifty-fourth fold, your piece of regular twenty-pound bond paper will reach from earth to the sun two and one-half times. That is how the signs of the times are. Accelerating! Saturation! Exponential increase! Sign #10 deals with exponential population increase.

But the skeptic still says, "Okay, so there has been incredible increase in the alleged sign factors, but they are still relative."

That is why the next reason is so important in proving that we are living in the last days. There is one sign that is not relative. One day it was not and the next day it was. I refer to the rebirth of the nation of Israel in 1948.

5. The Great Sign — the Fig Tree

Jesus said, "Now learn a parable of the fig tree; When his branch is yet tender, and putteth forth leaves, ye know that summer is nigh" (Matt. 24:32).

The fig tree is Israel. Jesus said, "Learn a *parable* of the fig tree." The word parable indicates that He was not referring to a literal fig tree, but was speaking in a symbol. All symbols have a literal meaning. We must allow the Bible to interpret its own symbols. In every passage in the Bible where figs or the fig tree is used as a symbol, and where the context defines the meaning of the symbol, without exception, it means Israel. See Jeremiah 29:17, Hosea 9:10, Jeremiah 24:1-8, and Joel 1:6-7. God's dealing with Israel is a key sign. If you get Israel in the right place in your prophetic scenario everything else will fall into place. Get Israel wrong and you have nothing but confusion.

You might conclude that the other signs are relative, but not the sign of the fig tree. Before May 15, 1948, there was no nation of Israel to relate to anything. In 1948 a nation was born in a day (Is. 66:8). In 1925 Frank M. Boyd, one of my teachers in Bible college, wrote a book titled *The Budding Fig Tree,* in which he confidently predicted that the Jews would establish a nation in Palestine, as the land was called under the British Mandate. For Professor Boyd to make this declaration clearly demonstrated his faith in God's Word. It seemed highly unlikely at that time that the prophecy could ever be fulfilled.

Rev. Boyd taught classes in prophecy, the Book of Revelation, and the Book of Daniel from 1923-1929 and 1948-1963, at Central Bible College in Springfield, Missouri. He lived to see Israel become a nation in his lifetime. God's Word is absolute and always unerring in its accuracy.

In Luke's recording of the Olivet Discourse, Jesus says, "And he spake to them a parable; Behold the fig tree, and all the trees" (Luke 21:29). The fig tree is Israel, all the trees are all the rest of the nations of the world. Israel is God's centerpiece and nations are judged by how they treat Israel. Moses understood this when he wrote, "When the most High divided to the nations their inheritance, when he separated the sons of Adam, he set the bounds of the people according to the number of the children of Israel" (Duet. 32:8).

The tragedy of the nations is when they come against Israel. "For I will gather all nations against Jerusalem to battle; and the city shall be taken, and the houses rifled, and the women ravished; and half of the city shall go forth into captivity, and the residue of the people shall not be cut off from the city" (Zech. 14:2).

This brings on the battle of Armageddon. Think about it. Jesus does not come back in His open revelation to save the Church. That has already taken place in the earlier event known as the Rapture. HE RETURNS TO DELIVER AND SAVE ISRAEL. The nations will gather to destroy Israel. It is not by accident that the Antichrist will lead his coalition of armies into the Middle East. Armageddon is the war for Israel, the fig tree nation. Following are more signs that relate to Israel. Also, the next few chapters will expand on Israel's relation to end-time prophecy, and how the Church relates to Israel.

6. Sign of Israel's Temple

It was Jesus' prediction that the temple of His day would be destroyed that shocked the disciples and prompted them to inquire about the sign of His coming and of the end of the world (Matt. 24:1-3).

The temple was destroyed in A.D. 70 by the Roman armies, but that is not the end of the temple in prophecy, for there will be a temple in our future. In fact there will be two temples in the future. The first is of short duration, and will be defiled by the Antichrist halfway through the Tribulation. Jesus spoke of this evil event as "the abomination of desolation" (Matt. 24:15-16): "When ye therefore shall see the abomination of desolation, spoken of by Daniel the prophet, stand in the holy place, whoso readeth, let him understand. Then let them which be in Judaea flee into the mountains." (Also see Dan. 9:27, 11:23, 12:11, and 2 Thess. 2:3-4.

The preterist interpreter of prophecy who says that Jesus came back a second time around A.D. 70 is self-deceived. Did every eye behold Him in or around A.D. 70? I should say not.

The next temple is approved by God since Jesus calls it the *holy place,* and both Paul and John describe it as the *temple of God.* In the Book of Revelation, written in A.D. 96 while John was imprisoned on the Island of Patmos, we read of a *future* temple:

> And there was given me a reed like unto a rod: and the angel stood, saying, Rise, and measure the temple of God, and the altar, and them that worship therein. But the court which is without the temple leave out, and measure it not; for it is given unto the Gentiles: and the holy city shall they tread under foot forty and two months (Rev. 11:1-2).

The first temple was built by King Solomon on Mount Moriah (2 Chron. 3:1), and was dedicated in 953 B.C. It was destroyed by the Babylonians during the time of the youthful prophets Daniel and Ezekiel. The second temple which also stood on Mount Moriah in Jesus time was the focus of the prophecy of Matthew 24:1-3. It was destroyed in A.D. 70 by the Romans.

For a photo-illustrated account on how the Jewish people are actually preparing to build the next temple, read chapters 10 and 11 in my book *Prophecy 2000.*[1] The future third temple disappears from view at the end of Daniel's 70th week, the tribulation of seven years duration.

Jesus will come back with the raptured church in His entourage and He will oversee the building of the fourth and final temple. This will be a house of worship for all nations during the Millennium. "And it shall come to pass, that every one that is left of all the nations which came against Jerusalem shall even go up from year to year to worship the King, the Lord of hosts, and to keep the feast of tabernacles" (Zech. 14:16). Zechariah also spoke of a temple built by Messiah (the Branch). "And speak unto him, saying, Thus speaketh the Lord of hosts, saying, Behold the man whose name is the Branch; and he shall grow up out of his place, and he shall build the temple of the Lord: Even he shall build the temple of the Lord; and he shall bear the glory, and shall sit and rule upon his throne; and he shall be a priest upon his throne: and the counsel of peace shall be between them both" (Zech. 6:12-13).

The temple sign is powerful, and is at the very heart of the key prophetic sign, the nation of Israel. Not all Israelis are enthusiastic about the temple being rebuilt, but there are many dedicated persons in a multi-faceted temple movement that vigorously pursues the goal of a rebuilt temple on Mount Moriah.

Stanley Goldfoot heads up the Jerusalem Temple Foundation. Gershon Solomon, who has a cornerstone for the next temple, is the leader of the Temple Mount Faithful. Several Yeshivas (Jewish seminaries) pursue the training of the known descendants of the tribe of Levi with a view to the reviving of the priesthood. The best known of these seminaries is Yeshiva Aterit Cohanim, located on the Via Dolorosa street in Old Jerusalem. The Agudat Shmirat HaMikdosh Society (see *Prophecy 2000*) maintains a computerized listing of all known Levites and Cohens. The Cohens are the priestly family of the tribe of Levi. All Levites are temple servants, but only the Cohens qualify for the priesthood.

Rabbi Ariel and Rabbi Richmond head up the Temple Institute at #24 Rehov Misgav Ladach in the Old City. They and their workers are responsible for the manufacture of the implements for the future temple. These are serious people. They are not playing games. You can see the implements in a facility open to the public, and while in that area also see the temple models at #29 Misgav Ladach. These are outstanding displays, not to be missed when you are in the Holy City.

7. Sign of the Red Heifer and the Kalal

For temple worship to begin again a perfect red heifer must be located to fulfill the instructions for purification found in Numbers 19. Ideally her ashes should be mingled with the ashes from the last red heifer sacrifice performed before the destruction of the temple in A.D. 70. Vendyl Jones, Gary Collette, and others have been searching in different locations for the kalal (urn) which contains the ashes of the last sacrifice of the red heifer.

But whether the kalal is ever found again, it could be possible to start the Numbers 19 process all over again. The problem is where to find a heifer that is totally red and without blemish, suitable for the sacrifice.

The Pentecostal Farmer and the Red Heifer

She has been found. On a farm in Mississippi, Clyde Lott, a Pentecostal Christian man, has been breeding cattle with the hope of producing a pure red heifer. I have talked to Mr. Lott on the phone. He has been certified by the Temple Institute to provide the red heifer for the next Jewish temple in Jerusalem! A rabbi from the Temple Institute has visited the farm in Mississippi to examine the first red heifer. She has been approved. She will soon be flown to Israel.

My associate evangelist, Rev. Chuck Heidle, recently made two trips to Mississippi to interview Clyde Lott and to photograph the red heifer. Chuck reports that Clyde will be allowed to import cattle to Israel to start up a beef cattle industry. At present Israel has a world-famous dairy cattle industry, but raises almost no beef cattle. Mr. Lott has been chosen not only to supply the red heifer, but to start a much-needed new farm product in Israel.

The red heifer will not be sacrificed since she is over the required age for a heifer, but she will very likely be the mother or grandmother of the heifer to be used in the sacrifice.

8. Sign of False Christs and False Prophets

The disciples asked Jesus, "What shall be the sign of thy coming?" Jesus is about to deliver the longest prophecy message He ever gave. The Olivet Discourse is found in Matthew chapters 24 and 25. This sweeping, panoramic view of the future is full of eschatological truths, exciting insights, warnings to sinners, and hope for believers.

It seems peculiar that He introduced the Olivet message with a somber warning: "And Jesus answered and said unto them, Take heed that no man deceive you. For many shall come in my name, saying, I am Christ; and shall deceive many" (Matt. 24:4-5). Also read verses 11 and 24. In dealing with end-time prophecy we must be wary of corrupt prophetic voices.

Many New Age leaders speak of a paradigm shift slated to take place around the year 2000. They will release so much psychic energy that all human minds will be changed and a new reality will be perceived. They claim that a "Christ" figure will appear and lead us to world peace, New World Order, world religion, and a new economic system. The new Christ will not be Jesus, but will be revealed as the Avatar, the Cosmic Christ, the Lord Matraya, the World Teacher, etc.

> Then if any man shall say unto you, Lo, here is Christ, or there; believe it not. For there shall arise false Christs, and false prophets, and shall shew great signs and wonders; insomuch that, if it were possible, they shall deceive the very elect. Behold, I have told you before. Wherefore if they shall say unto you, Behold, he is in the desert; go not forth: behold, he is in the secret chambers; believe it not (Matt. 24:23-26).

We will enlarge on the sign of the New Age and cultism later.

9. Sign of War

Weapons of mass destruction now in existence could expunge the very memory of mankind from the face of the earth. Atomic bombs, fission and fusion bombs, the 5-pound red mercury neutron atomic bomb, chemical warheads and ballistic missile delivery systems, disease bombs, and a host of other monster weapons are already operational.

Bizarre weapons like the super cannon, invented by the Canadian scientist Gerald Bull, are now being built in Russia. Saddam Hussein had these huge weapons in readiness for the Gulf War. If the U.S. stealth bombers had not destroyed them, they would have wreaked havoc on Saudi Arabia and Israel. The scud missiles were tinkertoys by comparison. Bull's super gun had a barrel 487 feet long and a bore of one meter (39 inches). It was capable of delivering a projectile weighing 3,000 pounds a distance of a thousand miles. The super cannons were mentioned briefly in American weekly news magazines, accompanied by very small photos. Iraq was a client state of Russia, but no secular journalist bothered to raise the question, "Where did the plans and technology go after the alleged defeat of Saddam Hussien and the armies of Iraq?" Our intelligence sources indicate that the super guns are being built in Russia, the new CIS (Commonwealth of Independent States), which replaced the old Soviet Union (USSR).

Briefcase A-Bomb — 5 Lbs.
A Terrible Threat to All Humanity

> This know also, that in the last days perilous times shall come (2 Tim. 3:1).

In June 1995 we printed the following brief article in our publication, the *Jerusalem Courier and Prophecy Digest*.

> According to a recent Associated Press report, "Russia has produced a miniature neutron bomb using the mystery substance red mercury, according to a British television documentary broadcast."
>
> The AP report cited Yevgeny Korolev, a former Soviet nuclear physicist, "and some nuclear experts are quoted as saying that the miniature neutron bomb exists — and several said the tech-

nology is being sold to states without nuclear capability."

Theodore B. Taylor, an American nuclear weapons designer, said that Western governments should take it very seriously.

The American inventor of the neutron bomb, Sam Cohen, stated that the British documentary confirms his own perspective, that the Russians have used red mercury to manufacture miniature neutron bombs based on fusion technology. This would be the first time that fusion power was used for a weapon of this nature.

The most startling aspect is that the bomb could weigh less than five pounds. Think of that. It could be carried, hidden in a paper sack, and be used for "tremendously terrifying" consequences.

The neutron bomb differs from regular atomic and hydrogen bombs. The current bombs rely on fission-fusion combination, do great physical destruction, and spread radioactive debris (fallout) over a large area. This deadly radiation lasts for a long time.

The neutron bomb produces massive radiation in a limited area, does little damage to buildings and structure, but kills humans and animals in the sphere of its influence. Its radiation has a short life. This allows the enemy to move in and use the buildings and equipment left standing, shortly after the explosion of the neutron bombs.

It is conjectured that a bomb or a couple of bombs, well placed, could wipe out the entire population of a major metropolis like Minneapolis, Dallas, Atlanta, Chicago, Los Angeles, or New York. Most of the buildings would not be damaged, and the after-effects of radioactivity would soon dissipate, allowing conquerors to march in and loot the place or use the city for their own purposes. Now think of these words written by the apostle John on the Island of Patmos in the Aegean Sea in A.D. 96:

> And the nations were angry, and thy wrath is
> come, and the time of the dead, that they should be
> judged, and that thou shouldest give reward unto
> thy servants the prophets, and to the saints, and
> them that fear thy name, small and great; and
> shouldest destroy them which destroy the earth
> (Rev. 11:18).

Now this information is no longer read only in the
Jerusalem Courier. The mainstream media is finally paying
attention. We have seen recent TV reports showing pictures
of the so called "brief case A-bombs." The great fear is that
these weapons are or soon will be in the hands of renegade
nations that sponsor terrorism against the USA and Israel.

Military intelligence informs us that over 25 percent of
earth's nations are now involved in war. Arms dealers are
some of the richest Commu-Capitalists on the face of the
earth. Getting ready for Magog and Armageddon is big
business.

> And ye shall hear of wars and rumours of
> wars: see that ye be not troubled: for all these
> things must come to pass, but the end is not yet.
> For nation shall rise against nation, and kingdom
> against kingdom (Matt. 24:6-7).

10. Sign of Famine

Harsh images of skeletal, starving children flicker
across the TV screen daily. Famine is a specter casting its
evil shadow over vast regions of the world. Care, World
Vision, Pat Robertson, Don Jones Mission, Church mission
boards, Larry Jones, Save the Children Fund, and many
other charitable organizations raise millions of dollars to aid
the unfortunate little ones. But the problem goes on in spite
of our best efforts.

The problem is many-faceted. World population has
increased exponentially. In Jesus' day world population was

only about 250,000,000 people. It was in 1840 that the figure rose to one billion. By 1900 the number stood at two billion. The skyrocketing graph in 1940 showed earth's inhabitants to be three billion. The end of 1995 registered five and a half billion, and at the end of 1996 it was reported that 5.9 billion men, women, and children occupy this planet's habitable lands. World population is increasing steadily at a rate of 90,000,000 per year.

God has given us an earth that can easily support 10 to 15 billion people. Israel has demonstrated that deserts can be transformed. There are crops that will grow with salt water from the seas. Other desert lands have been cleansed and are watered by highly efficient drip irrigation. Sea water can be desalinated using solar energy, as demonstrated at the Dead Sea. The Dead Sea is mined for vast quantities of potash and other minerals vital for fertilization of crops. This world now produces enough to feed all the hungry people. The problem is greed, lust for power, bureaucratic red tape, and political ineptitude. Neither capitalism nor socialism has the answer. If they have, they should stop hiding it. Politics cannot deal with the human sin factor — only Jesus can deal with evil like a cancer, eating at the vitals of humanity.

11. Sign of Pestilence

Ebola, flesh eating bacteria, HIV-AIDS, and now warnings are being sounded regarding the Gulf War pestilence. Tens of thousands of our soldiers were exposed to chemical and biological weapons. The newspapers are full of it. Congressional hearings were recently aired on this dreadful subject. A chiropractic doctor here in Springfield, Missouri, told me that there is evidence that the Gulf War Syndrome diseases are contagious. Family members are catching it from our suffering returned veterans of the war. The doctor told me of reports that it is spreading in epidemic proportions on at least one army base here in the Midwest. Jesus said that one of the signs of the end of the age would be pestilence (Matt. 24:7).

12. Sign of Earthquakes

> And, Thou, Lord, in the beginning hast laid
> the foundation of the earth; and the heavens are
> the works of thine hands: They shall perish; but
> thou remainest; and they all shall wax old as doth
> a garment; And as a vesture shalt thou fold them
> up, and they shall be changed: but thou art the
> same, and thy years shall not fail (Heb. 1:10-12).

This has been the greatest century of earthquake activity in all earth's history. I read recently that there have been more earthquakes in the last 50 years than in the previous 1,500 years. Checking the most recent *World Almanac* indicates the truth of that statement.

> [God's] voice then shook the earth: but now
> he hath promised, saying, Yet once more I shake
> not the earth only, but also heaven. And this word,
> Yet once more, signifieth the removing of those
> things that are shaken, as of things that are made,
> that those things which cannot be shaken may
> remain" (Heb. 12:26-27).

Earthquake activity is on the increase. Jesus said that there would be earthquakes "in divers [various] places" (Matt. 24:7).

One of the most devastating earthquakes struck, not in California or Japan, but in the state of Missouri, in the very center of the United States of America! In 1811, on the 16th day of December, the earth heaved and shook in the heartland of the nation. From December 1811 through February 1812 there were three major quakes. The one in December was the worst ever to take place in America. The epicenter was in New Madrid, Missouri, but the effects were felt for hundreds of miles around. I have read that it rang church bells in Boston, shook Washington, DC, did structural damage in Kansas, and formed a new lake in Tennessee.

Both this quake and the two that followed in 1812 would measure 8.0+ on the Richter scale. There were thousands of aftershocks, felt as far away as Quebec City, Canada. Historians record that the Mississippi river backed up for a hundred miles, and when the earth dams formed by the quake broke loose the flood damage equaled the quake damage.

Some scientists claim that the New Madrid fault has major activity approximately every 175 years. Other experts put a longer interval between quakes. At any rate, we are due for a real shake up very soon. In 1990 Dr. Iben Browning predicted that a major earthquake in the Mississippi Valley, where the New Madrid fault lies, would happen on December 3, 1990. While we note the risk of setting a date for the quake, we nevertheless note a scientific article predicting a major New Madrid quake by the year 2000. In our local public library I found several books and essays in technical journals describing the necessary rebuilding that will be required after the next Missouri quake.

God has often used earthquakes as a form of punishment upon rebels. "Thou shalt be visited of the Lord of hosts with thunder, and with earthquake, and great noise, with storm and tempest, and the flame of devouring fire" (Isa. 29:6).

The many references in the Book of Revelation project the idea that earthquakes are very significant in the end times. In Revelation 16, John records: "And the seventh angel poured out his vial into the air; and there came a great voice out of the temple of heaven, from the throne, saying, It is done. And there were voices, and thunders, and lightnings; and there was *a great earthquake, such as was not since men were upon the earth, so mighty an earthquake, and so great.* And the great city was divided into three parts, and the cities of the nations fell: and great Babylon came in remembrance before God, to give unto her the cup of the wine of the fierceness of his wrath. And every island fled away, and the mountains were not found" (Rev. 16:17-20; emphasis added).

As awesome as the New Madrid quakes of 1811-1812 were, they were not the worst in terms of loss of life. In A.D. 476 a powerful earthquake destroyed the city of Rome, but it was not the worst. The year A.D. 526 saw the loss of 250,000 lives in the earthquake of Psidian Antioch in Asia Minor (Now Turkey), but it was surpassed in killer power by one other earthquake. The worst of them all took place in China when 830,000 died in the devastating quake of January 24, 1556.

The most destructive, the most terrifying, will be a future globe-shaking quake prophesied in the Book of Revelation. Mighty fissures will open in the earth's crust and entire continents will be ripped apart. Mountains will be thrown into the air and will fall like bombs on major cities. Great coastal cities will slide into the seas. The islands will be shot like torpedoes against the remaining land masses of the planet. There will be no hiding place from this fearsome judgment on rebellious mankind.

I suspect that when the great worldwide quake shakes the earth, there will not be an instrument with scales high enough to measure the intensity of the *great earthquake, such as was not since men were upon the earth, so mighty an earthquake, and so great.*

13. Sign of Terrorism and Violenc e

But as the days of Noe [Noah] were, so shall also the coming of the Son of man be (Matt. 24:37).

The earth also was corrupt before God, and the earth was filled with violence. And God looked upon the earth, and, behold, it was corrupt; for all flesh had corrupted his way upon the earth. And God said unto Noah, The end of all flesh is come before me; for *the earth is filled with violence* through them; and, behold, I will destroy them with the earth (Gen. 6:11-13; italics added).

On March 20, 1995, members of the Aum Shinriko (Supreme Truth) Cult released toxic nerve gas in the Tokyo subway system, killing 12 people and injuring another 5,500.

The cult was founded by Shoko Asahara who proclaimed in a television interview that he was a "living god," an equal to "Lord Shiva." and declared: "I intend to become a spiritual dictator — a dictator of the world." He later consummated his self-deification by publishing a book unblushingly titled *Declaring Myself the Christ.*

New American magazine records that "Under the guidance of founder Shoko Asahara, Aum members built a community near Mt. Fuji to prepare for an apocalyptic world war that would supposedly begin with a U.S. attack on Japan. Aum headquarters included laboratories to manufacture LSD, methamphetamines, and a crude form of truth serum that was used to control the cult's communicants — as well as explosives, chemical weapons, and biological warfare agents such as anthrax cultures. Asahara also dispatched followers to Zaire to collect samples of the Ebola virus for possible use as a biological weapon. Other Aum operatives made arrangements to import military hardware from Russia."

The weapon of choice for the subway attack was the deadly nerve gas sarin. Japanese authorities revealed that Aum had the capacity to produce enough sarin to kill four million people.

New American author William Norman Grigg observes the liberal media spin put on the Tokyo incident:

> It would seem nearly impossible to shoehorn Aum into the familiar role of "right-wing extremist group" — yet the media's misinformation mavens proved equal to the task. The Tokyo nerve

gas attack — which came just weeks before the Oklahoma City bombing — has been treated as a cautionary tale about the dangers of religious extremism, particularly of the "fundamentalist" or "right-wing" variety.

In the immediate aftermath of the Tokyo subway attack, *Newsweek* described Aum as representative of "terrorist groups driven by religious rather than political zealotry," and compared them to Western groups ranging from "Christian white supremacists and messianic Jews to Islamic fundamentalists. . . ."

Terrorist "expert" Bruce Hoffman, of the Center for the Study of Terrorism and Political Violence at Scotland's St. Andrews University, declared that with the Aum atrocity, "We've definitely crossed a threshold. This is the cutting edge of high-tech terrorism for the year 2000 and beyond. It's the nightmare scenario that people have quietly talked about for years coming true. . . . Whenever religion is involved, terrorists kill more people."[2]

Americans are not used to terrorist acts. But that all changed with the bombing of the World Trade Towers in New York City and the bombing of the federal building in Oklahoma City. England and Ireland have shaken under the bomb attacks that have been endured for decades. Africa is well-acquainted with violence. In fact, the whole world is an open target to terrorists.

In the Middle East there have been continued acts of violence for hundreds of years and for the past 50 years or so there has been an escalation of outright terrorism. No country has been more ravaged than Lebanon, Israel's northern neighbor.

When I testified for the Senate Foreign Relations Committee in the early 1980s, Senator Percy held up a copy of my book *Magog 1982 Canceled — Did Israel Prevent the Third World War?* with a show of hostility. He challenged my conclusions regarding Israel's invasion of Lebanon in 1982. In my response to Senator Percy I faulted the United States State Department for putting undue pressure on Israel to conduct the war in a fashion that was detrimental to Lebanon, Israel, and the United States of America. I told the committee that the State Department was wrong to force Israeli General Ariel Sharon to stop pursuing the PLO terrorists in Beirut. This resulted in the debacle of the PLO fighting among themselves and slaughtering each other. Caught in the middle, our Lebanon Marine base was car bombed, resulting in the unnecessary loss of the lives of over 200 of our Marines.

One of the senators vigorously protested my assertion that Sharon should have been permitted to drive the PLO out of Beirut. He said, "But that would have caused the deaths of innocent civilians." I simply replied, "And what do you think is going on now? Every military analyst I have talked to thinks that it would have saved far more civilian lives than would have been lost. It would have shortened the war and could have prevented Syrian domination of Lebanon." In fact Israel's invasion of Lebanon in 1982 opened a window of opportunity in which Lebanon could have pulled itself together after its civil war stretching from 1975 to 1982. The policies of the United States State Department slammed that window of opportunity shut.

Attorney Leonard Horwin, in a privately circulated memorandum, hails Ariel Sharon as one who stands head and shoulders above all others in having the necessary creativity, boldness, and steadfastness to recognize and put an end to "terror," while promoting peace with deterrence.

Leonard Horwin sums up the terrorist situation as follows, listing major terrorist incidents of recent times.

1. A bombing out of existence of the realistic Beshir Gamayal government of Lebanon, U.S.

Embassy and U.S. Marine barracks in 1982;

2. The consequent unrealistic U.S. prevention of peace between Israel and Lebanon in 1983;

3. The consequent withdrawal of the United States from Lebanon with its "tail between its legs," leaving the terrorist PLO to transfer its goons and terrorist operations to Tunis;

4. The consequent interference of Syria/Iran in Lebanon, preventing peace between Israel and Lebanon, assuring to the Hezbollah ("Party of God") freedom to kidnap, hold hostages, and use them to advance the "terror process" in the Middle East;

5. The consequent emboldening of Saddam Hussein of Iraq to make the Gulf War necessary;

6. The consequent emboldening of Iran and Libya to advance the "terror process to the Sudan, Egypt, and through World Trade Center bombing and near bombing of the Holland and Lincoln Tunnels and FBI headquarters, to terrorism in the United States;

7. The consequent example and instruction to internal U.S. terrorists, as at Oklahoma City, in how to truck-bomb buildings.

The time has come, indeed, to "put an end to this terror process!" We must do all we can in this regard, and I have a Friend who is coming back one day, and rest assured He will "rule with a rod of iron," and violence will not be tolerated in the millennial reign of the Lord God Messiah.

Are These Signs of the Rapture or of the Second Coming?

There are no primary signs of the Rapture. Nothing has to take place before Jesus comes to resurrect the righteous dead and rapture the living Church (1 Thess. 4:16-18). *However, every sign of the Second Coming is a sign of the Rapture.* For if the Second Coming is close at hand, then the Rapture is even closer!

It is important to know that the Rapture is imminent. It may take place at any moment. The date of the Rapture cannot be pinpointed. "Take ye heed, watch and pray: for *ye know not when the time is*" (Mark 13:33; italics added).

After the Rapture, Israel's prophetic time clock starts ticking again. The exact timing of certain events including the Second Coming can then be calculated. For example, after the Roman Prince, Antichrist, signs a false covenant with Israel, it will be exactly 1,260 days until Israel's next temple will be defiled (Dan. 9:14-37). From that point it will be exactly 1,260 days until Jesus comes back and stands on the Mount of Olives (Zech. 14:1-4), in visible manifestation to the whole world. "For as the lightning cometh out of the east, and shineth even unto the west; so shall also the coming of the Son of man be" (Matt. 24:27).

14. Sign of the Persecution of Believers

The Church will go through general tribulation in the Church Age. The Church has endured martyrdom and oppression in various areas of the world throughout the past 1,900+ years. Jesus said, "These things I have spoken unto you, that in me ye might have peace. In the world ye shall have tribulation: but be of good cheer; I have overcome the world" (John 16:33). Hence, no one can accuse pre-trib Rapture believers of teaching escapism. While you believe in a pre-Tribulation Rapture you also know that there can be pre-Rapture Tribulation, as Jesus said in John 16:33. The safest position to take is, "I have determined to live for Jesus regardless of the cost, be it good times or bad, affluence or poverty, liberty or oppression. Praise God, whenever the first load goes, pre-, mid-, or post-, I plan to be on board!"

After careful consideration I have concluded that the undatable Rapture will take place before the seventieth week, the seven-year tribulation. If I am wrong, it is no problem — by His grace I will fight the good fight, oppose the Antichrist, and take a stand for Jesus. The Church has always come through in times of trouble. On the other hand, the pre-trib position leads one to look for Jesus, not Antichrist. We can believe God for revival even in the midst of apostasy. Anticipation of the blessed hope of the Rapture leads us to live a responsible lifestyle in this present age:

> For the grace of God that bringeth salvation hath appeared to all men, Teaching us that, denying ungodliness and worldly lusts, we should live soberly, righteously, and godly, *in this present world;* Looking for that blessed hope, and the glorious appearing of the great God and our Saviour Jesus Christ; Who gave himself for us, that he might redeem us from all iniquity, and purify unto himself a peculiar people, *zealous of good works* (Titus 2:11-13; italics added).

Secular World Intolerant

In a recent magazine article it was noted that being religious could be a serious stumbling block to career advancement. Although Dr. Levin is Jewish, this is a good illustration of the attitude of the secular world regarding religious people, whether Jewish or Christian.

Modern Maturity magazine, not noted for either a conservative or a religious bias, sounds a note of alarm. From excerpts found in an *Aging Today* article by Dr. Jeffrey S. Levin, Ph.D., M.P.H. we learn that being religious can hinder one's career in the academic world. While doing research in this subject Dr. Levin was encouraged by a professor to "find a more acceptable area of expertise. He took me aside, just as in the famous 'plastics' scene in *The Graduate,* and sagely advised, 'Jeff, you need a disease.' Another professor, curious over my weekly visits to a synagogue and amazed that a scientist could profess religious faith, once inquired, 'You mean you believe in Jesus and Mary and the Bible and all that?' "

Modern Maturity records, "The editor of a pre-eminent

epidemiology journal rejected a paper on the health effects of religious attendance and informed us that not only was our manuscript unacceptable, but that the mere *idea* of it was 'execrable.' "

That is a statement of pure prejudicial hatred!

Jesus said, "Marvel not, my brethren, if the world hate you" (John 3:13). "If the world hate you, ye know that it hated me before it hated you" (John 15:18).

15. Sign of the Mark

> And he [the Beast] causeth all, both small and great, rich and poor, free and bond, to receive a mark in their right hand, or in their foreheads: And that no man might buy or sell, save he that had the mark, or the name of the beast, or the number of his name. Here is wisdom. Let him that hath understanding count the number of the beast: for it is the number of a man; and his number is Six hundred threescore [and] six (Rev. 13:16-18).

When I was a little boy I heard an evangelist describe in gory detail how the Antichrist's henchmen would brand the number 666 on the forehead or hand of hapless humans who lived in the time of his worldwide domain. Then other ideas arose as to what the mark might be.

Up until a few years ago, people were saying, "It will be an invisible laser tattoo which will show up only under an ultraviolet light." Anyone who has visited an amusement park like Disneyland is acquainted with the invisible rubber-stamped date which allows one to come and go in and out of the park for that day.

Now that is old stuff. Technology changes continually and we cannot be sure how the mark will be applied. Nowadays we hear a lot about an implantable chip. Well, if the Antichrist (the beast) were to come to power very soon, perhaps the chip would be it. But if it is a ways off in the future, who knows if a more refined technology would make the chip outdated. It is dangerous to try and interpret God's unchanging Word, by man's everchanging technology. Here, nevertheless are some interesting comments from *Midnight Call* magazine:

A Chip in Every Child?

Think of it as a bar code for your pet. It's the Trovan electronic identification tag — a miracle of technology similar to Destron's Life Chip. It measures about 1 centimeter long and just a few millimeters in diameter. Implanted under the skin with a simple, handheld tool, each chip contains a unique 64-bit identification code, readable at a distance of about a foot. And because the chip is passive (meaning it works without batteries), it'll last as long as your pet does.

For $25 (lifetime charge) and a veterinary cost, you can store your pet's identification code, as well as your name, address, and phone number, in a national database operated by InfoPet Identification Systems Inc. of Burnsville, Minnesota. Organizations like the ASPCA in New York City, San Diego County in California, and the cities of Minneapolis and Saint Paul, Minnesota, are buying readers. So if you lose Fido in one of these locales, there's a pretty good chance you'll get him back.

But why stop with pets? InfoPet markets the implantable transponder for pigs, sheep, cows, and horses. Besides being computer-readable, the chips are less painful than the eartags, brands, or tattoos they replace. Even better, a trained farmer can implant more than 200 animals in an hour.

Animate objects are by no means the limit. According to Trovan's distributor, Santa Barbara-based Electronic Identification Devices Ltd., the Australian Wool Corporation has used the system to identify bales of wool, and in England, Yamaha dealers will happily chip your motorcycle. For less than UK65 (about $100 in U.S. currency), you can have an ID chip implanted into your bike's frame, wheels, tank, and seat. If the bike is stolen or stripped, the parts can still be tracked.

Of course, the burning question is — what about people? There would be no technical problem, says Barbara Masin, director of operations for Electronic Identification Devices, in implanting the chips in humans. But to avoid a public relations nightmare, the Trovan dealer agreement specifically prohibits putting chips under the skin. [For now].

A writer for *Midnight Call* magazine, published by Arnold Froese, commented: "Only 50 years ago, such technology did not exist. Thus, Revelation 13:16-17 was a far-out prophecy. In the meantime, these chips are no longer considered new technology because the electronic communication and identification industry is virtually exploding. What Daniel wrote almost 2,800 years ago is coming to pass in our day: 'But thou, O Daniel, shut up the words, and seal the book, even to the time of the end: many shall run to and fro, and knowledge shall be increased' " (Dan. 12:4).

Biometrics in Future Banking

Visa, Master Card, and Europay all seem to be committed to smart card-based credit and debit transactions by the turn of the century. Now they are also taking an interest in biometrics as a preferred method of secure identification.

The reasoning is obvious. First of all, identification based on a personal characteristic is much more secure than the Personal Identification Number system which is now widely used. Secondly, biometric identification would be much more convenient for customers than trying to remember a PIN for all the different credit/debit cards used by the consumer.

With the added convenience, consumers would be more likely to use credit/debit cards for their transactions, virtually eliminating the need for cash and checks, as the financial industry would eventually like. To this point, the financial industry has not been greatly interested in biometrics because the technology has been too expensive, or it has not been perfected enough to ensure that a client would not be falsely rejected by the system. But the technology has vastly improved in both these areas and banks and credit card organizations are now beginning to take an interest.

According to a report on smart cards in the August 24 to 30, 1995, edition of *The European*, "In the long term, biometric techniques should prove the answer to card security." *Midnight Call* commented, "The foundation stones for the eventual mark of the beast system are being established."

16. Sign of Revival and the Great Commission

Do you really want to understand prophecy? Then we should ask the question, "Which of the prophecies are near to the heart of God?" I believe that the two greatest prophecies have to do with the evangelization of the whole world (Matt. 24:14) and the ultimate, victorious survival of the Church (Matt. 16:13-18). See the chapter in this book on end-time revival.

17. Sign of Immorality

And the rest of the men which were not killed by these plagues yet repented not of the works of their hands, that they should not worship devils, and idols of gold, and silver, and brass, and stone, and of wood: which neither can see, nor hear, nor walk. Neither repented they of their murders, nor of their sorceries, nor of their fornication, nor of their thefts (Rev. 9:20-21).

And because iniquity shall abound, the love of many shall wax cold (Matt. 24:12).

Mortify therefore your members which are upon the earth; fornication, uncleanness, inordinate affection, evil concupiscence, and covetousness, which is idolatry (Col. 3:5).

This could well be identified as the era of rebellious immorality. Television flaunts every degrading and immoral act as if it were the normal way of life. Public schools pass out condoms to children. The government re-defines the family and contributes to the destruction of the biblical concept of family.

For this is the will of God, even your sanctification, that ye should abstain from fornication (1 Thess. 4:3).

Murder-rape, violent attack rape, "friendly" date rape, seduction-drug rape, and gang rape make life unsafe for both sexes, but especially women.

Flee fornication. Every sin that a man doeth is without the body; but he that committeth fornication sinneth against his own body (1 Cor. 6:18).

Certain forms of popular music like acid rock, hard rock, "hip hop," and "gangsta rap," have lyrics including profanity, vulgarity, and promotion of violence, rape, immorality, drug usage, and murder.

Being filled with all unrighteousness, fornication, wickedness, covetousness, maliciousness; full of envy, murder, debate, deceit, malignity; whisperers (Rom. 1:29).

Fraudulent claims to first amendment rights are used to

protect these destructive social forces. Television pundits make the ridiculous claim that violence and sex themes do not influence people to carry the drama into real life. Purveyors of music glorifying fornication, adultery, rape, and abuse expect us to believe the outrageous notion that no action is promoted by the music. But it is from what is in the heart or inner man that actions proceed. Pornography does entice participants to do evil deeds.

> Woe unto them that call evil good, and good evil; that put darkness for light, and light for darkness; that put bitter for sweet, and sweet for bitter! Woe unto them that are wise in their own eyes, and prudent in their own sight! (Isa. 5:20-21).

I once heard a public speaker say, "Thoughts are things, and dreams come true, the daydreams of today may become tomorrow's realities." Another wise person said, "Sow a thought, reap an action. Sow an action and reap a habit. Sow a habit, reap a destiny." One thing does lead to another.

> For out of the heart proceed evil thoughts, murders, adulteries, fornications, thefts, false witness, blasphemies (Matt. 15:19).

The media, both print and TV, are given to slandering conservative religious people, portraying them as being beleaguered with outdated morals, hopelessly behind the times, low class ignoramuses.

> Woe unto them . . . which justify the wicked for reward, and take away the righteousness of the righteous from him (Isa. 5:22-23).

The divorce rate soars. Teen sex and illegitimate births increase. Abstinence, the only safe sex for the single person, is scorned, The societal powers that be, tell lies about "safe sex." The fact is that there is no safe sex outside the parameters set by the Bible: If a non-diseased man marries a non-diseased woman, if they remain faithful to each other and refrain from doing drugs with dirty needles, there is very slight chance of their being infected with a sexually transmitted disease. The way to prevent AIDS, syphilis, gonorrhea, and chlymadia is simple: Don't fornicate! Don't commit adultery! Don't live a homosexual lifestyle! Also, teach your childen that "virgin" is not a dirty word! Alas, the fruit of wild vines has been put in the soup and now "there is death in the pot" (2 Kings 4:38-40).

> Therefore as the fire devoureth the stubble, and the flame consumeth the chaff, so their root shall be as rottenness, and their blossom shall go up as dust: because they have cast away the law of the Lord of hosts, and despised the word of the Holy One of Israel (Is. 5:24).

The final breakdown of society into anarchy is at hand. It is a sign of the times.

18. Sign of the Social Engineers

Charley Reese wrote the following in the *Orlando Sentinal* of December 22, 1996:

> No amount of social engineering will make a stupid man smart. . . . I think that social determinism is folly, and $5 trillion worth of social engineering won't make a lazy man industrious, a stupid man smart, or turn a killer into a priest. . . . I have observed that, despite trillions of dollars and tens of thousands of bureaucrats, the social engineering schemes have, by any reasonable measure, been a failure in effecting real changes in human behavior.
>
> The old-time religion appears to be right. Call it original sin or human nature, but humans

appear to be incapable of perfection. . . . The liberal says to a "D" student, "I'm going to find some way to make you an 'A' student." The conservative says, "Okay, you're a 'D' student. So what? Let's find a place for you in this economy." That is a huge difference. Marxist and Nazi social engineers in this century have been mass murderers on a scale unprecedented in history.

Author Jean Rael Isaacs describes liberal social engineers as "coercive utopians," and demonstrates that their tactics will not work, except to bring society under their control. The devil's last ditch effort to subjugate humanity under his evil thrall will also end in failure. The Antichrist is the loser of all time!

In spite of what these conservative writers say, there seems to be a forgotten factor. By God's grace and power, people *can* change, improve, and even strive for perfection.

Out of the darkest time of his despair, Job the sufferer asked, "Who can bring a clean thing out of an unclean? not one" (Job 14:4). Job was both right and wrong. Right that in the sphere of human ability, no one can bring forth that which is clean from that which is unclean. No scientist can take a rotten apple and transform it into a good apple.

But God can take a broken, sin-marred, lost person and transform him or her, by the cleansing of His shed blood, into a new person. Jesus said, "The things which are impossible with men are possible with God" (Luke 18:27).

"Therefore if any man be in Christ, he is a new creature: old things are passed away; behold, all things are become new" (2 Cor. 5:17). That is what Jesus was talking about when he told Nicodemus, "You must be born again" (John 3:3-7).

The best way to overcome a bad environment or flawed genetics is described by the apostle Peter as, "Being born again, not of corruptible seed, but of incorruptible, by the word of God, which liveth and abideth for ever" (1 Pet. 1:23).

> Brethren, I count not myself to have appre-
> hended: but this one thing I do, forgetting those
> things which are behind, and reaching forth unto
> those things which are before, I press toward the
> mark for the prize of the high calling of God in
> Christ Jesus (Phil. 3:13-14).

The transformation principle applies not only to the spiritual life of a person, but touches every aspect of need. I once knew a young man of 18 years, a junior in high school who was functionally illiterate. When he accepted Christ as his Saviour there was born in his heart a desire to read the Bible. He asked me to help him learn to read. I obtained some simple first grade reading books and started there.

We made progress, but not like I wanted to see. After much prayer for guidance, I took this man to a local university where we got the help of Dr. White, a remedial education specialist. She discovered that a second grade teacher had ridiculed Everett, calling him stupid and telling him he would never learn. One day that teacher shamed him by forcing him to stand in front of the class with an open book. She said, "Everett, you are going to stand there until you read that page." Everett could not read the words, and was so scared and nervous that he wet his pants in front of the class. The children laughed and from then on teased him merci-lessly. Everett knew he was stupid and would never learn to read. Everett had repressed these painful memories, but by the grace of God and the kind ministrations of Dr. White, along with my help, Everett became an excellent reader and graduated from high school. He went to a Bible College where he made the dean's list of honor students in his first semester. (Names have been changed in this true account).

The Teen Challenge (Christian) centers, started by my college classmate David Wilkerson have taken hopeless drug addicts, and with prayer, Christian care, and counseling, have transformed their lives through the liberating power of the Holy Spirit. My wife Ramona and I have two relatives who had fallen into the vortex of serious drug addiction, but were set free by the power of prayer and faith in God. Both of these men have been drug free for years, and are productive members of the Church. One found Christ through a television ministry, the other went through the rehabilitation program in a Teen Challenge center.

19. Sign of Spiritual Warfare

For though we walk in the flesh, we do not war after the flesh: (For the weapons of our warfare are not carnal, but mighty through God to the pulling down of strong holds;) Casting down imaginations, and every high thing that exalteth itself against the knowledge of God, and bringing into captivity every thought to the obedience of Christ; And having in a readiness to revenge all disobedience, when your obedience is fulfilled (2 Cor. 10:3-6).

While the following passage will be finally fulfilled in the Tribulation, even now we are in the throes of the end-time war that will be close to Armageddon's culmination when Revelation 12:12 is fulfilled:

Therefore rejoice, ye heavens, and ye that dwell in them. Woe to the inhabiters of the earth and of the sea! for the devil is come down unto you, having great wrath, because he knoweth that he hath but a short time (Rev. 12:12).

Put on the whole armour of God, that ye may be able to stand against the wiles of the devil. For we wrestle not against flesh and blood, but against principalities, against powers, against the rulers of the darkness of this world, against spiritual wickedness in high places. Wherefore take unto you the whole armour of God, that ye may be able to *withstand in the evil day,* and having done all, to stand (Eph. 6:11-13).

20. Sign of the Rapture

Some speak of a *secret* Rapture of the church. But how secret can the sudden disappearance of about 500,000,000 (conservative estimate) born-again, blood-washed believers be? This will be a spiritual shock-quake producing almost unimaginable trauma in the terrified minds of those who are left on earth. The fear of the great unwashed masses will drive many to insanity, and many more to suicide. Those with some command of their mental faculties will angrily turn to political leaders, scientists, and apostate religious leaders for an explanation.

A host of witnesses, 12,000 from every tribe of Israel, will be redeemed and sealed for service shortly after the Rapture. They and those they convert will give the true explanation that the Rapture has taken place and gives the final warning to humanity that the openly manifested second coming of Jesus Christ will shortly take place. John records that as a result of their witness, "After this I beheld, and, lo, a great multitude, which no man could number, of all nations, and kindreds, and people, and tongues, stood before the throne, and before the Lamb, clothed with white robes, and palms in their hands" (Rev. 7:9).

21. The Stones Cry Out

Writing for the Associated Press, December 7, 1996, author David Briggs said:

> Amnon Ben-Tor is an archeologist who doubts anything he can't dig up. He takes nothing in the Bible on faith. Yet, standing in a trench on a hot, barren mountainside, he stares into the fire-blackened stone and sees an army destroying the

Canaanite city of Hazor 3,200 years ago. Just as it says in the Book of Joshua.

The deeper the spade of the archaeologist goes, the greater is our proof that the Bible is historically and scientifically accurate. David Briggs continued:

> From the northern hills of Israel to the desert of Yemen, a string of recent archaeological discoveries have provided the first hard evidence for a number of biblical figures and events, many of which had been widely dismissed as myths and moral tales. Individually, the discoveries are important. Together, they are shaking the field of biblical archaeology and buttressing words believers have taken on faith.

The rediscovery of the Roman metropolis of Sepphoris, just three miles from Nazareth where Jesus lived most of His earthly life, has brought expanded understanding of His life and times.

Liberal skeptics have long doubted that King David ever existed, or if he did, that he had a kingdom as described in the Bible.

As Israel celebrates the 3,000th anniversary of the establishing of Jerusalem where David reigned over united Israel, it is interesting to note that Seymour Gitin of the W.F. Albright Institute of Archaeological Research in East Jerusalem called recent discoveries at Tel Dan in northern Israel "one of the greatest finds of the 20th century."

In 1993 archaeologists dug up a chunk of a stele, or ancient monument. An inscription on the stele, chiseled in archaic Aramaic spoke of both "King of Israel" and "House of David." This rattled the scorners of the Bible so that they hastily declared it to be either a fake or a mistranslation. In 1994, however, more fragments of the monument with further inscriptions referring to King David augmented the argument for biblical text reliability.

Now scholars are forced to agree that David was a real person. Ronny Reich of the Israeli Antiquities Authority said that it is known that David was real *not because the Bible says so,* but because "archaeology has found it." I beg to disagree Mr. Reich, it is quite the opposite way around.

Did we not know that Pontius Pilate was a real person even before the discovery of the now famous "Pilatus Stone" uncovered at Caesarea Maritima proved to the secular and religious doubters that the Bible was right?

Recent excavations and findings at Shechem, Ekron, Hazor, and Megiddo all bear new evidence in favor of the Bible. In the hot summer of 1996 a wine jug with the name of King Herod was found. This is the first evidence outside the Gospels that Herod existed. The Bible is right again, and the higher critics bite the dust once more.

Proof of King Solomon and the first temple of Israel is evidenced by an ivory pomegranate bearing the inscription, "Holy to the priests, belonging to the temple of Yahweh." This artifact from Solomon's Temple sold for $550,000 in 1988. It was purchased by the Israeli government.

> That this may be a sign among you, that when your children ask [their fathers] in time to come, saying, What mean ye by these stones? (Josh. 4:6).

22. Signs in the Skies

> And great earthquakes shall be in divers places, and famines, and pestilences; and fearful sights and great signs shall there be from heaven (Luke 21:11).

> And there shall be signs in the sun, and in the moon, and in the stars; and upon the earth distress of nations, with perplexity; the sea and the waves roaring (Luke 21:25).

> And I will shew wonders in heaven above,
> and signs in the earth beneath; blood, and fire, and
> vapour of smoke (Acts 2:19).

Comet Hits Jupiter on Tisha Be' Av

God has allowed us to see a celestial display, one which demanded the attention of all the earth as pieces of a broken comet struck the huge, distant, planet Jupiter with a force greater than the biggest nuclear explosion on earth. In fact, if this bombardment were hitting earth it would be the end for us all. The Book of Revelation tells that an object will strike the earth during the Great Tribulation. The May 23, 1994, issue of *Time* magazine devoted its front cover to the Shoemaker-Levy Comet that pounded the surface of Jupiter. The article beginning on page 54 was headlined: "COLLISION COURSE — Jupiter is about to be walloped by a comet. The cataclysmic explosion will serve as a warning to Earth: It could happen here."

The comet was discovered on March 25, 1993. Now hear this Word of the Lord, for these end times, from the New Testament:

> But the heavens and the earth, which are
> now, by the same word are kept in store, reserved
> unto fire against the day of judgment and perdi-
> tion of ungodly men (2 Pet. 3:7).

> For a fire is kindled in mine anger, and shall
> burn unto the lowest hell, and shall consume the
> earth with her increase, and set on fire the founda-
> tions of the mountains (Deut. 32:22).

If the first bit of the comet that hit Jupiter fell on earth it would cause an explosion of over ten million megatons of force. If it landed between Washington D.C. and Baltimore, those cities would cease to exist. It would be the worst single disaster to befall our planet in all of history, and this is only one relatively small fragment of the comet that has broken up and has fallen on Jupiter.

Another way of measuring the disaster it would cause on earth was found in the *Jerusalem Report* magazine which described an impact that could reach the power of "3.4 million times the most powerful nuclear explosion ever unleashed on earth, the 58-megaton hydrogen bomb the Soviets test-detonated in 1961."

Comet Falls on July 16, Eve of Tisha Be' Av

Here are some curious facts. July 16, 1994, was the eve of Tisha Be' Av, which historically is a day of tragedies for Israel and the Jewish people. Tisha Be' Av simply means the ninth day of the Hebrew month of Av. Both of Israel's ancient temples were destroyed on Tisha Be' Av. It is traditionally a day when religious Jews and many not-so-religious mourn for the temple and repent of sins with fasting and prayer. Tisha Be' Av means the ninth day of the month of Av on the Hebrew calendar.

Here is a list of historic times in which disaster fell on the Jews during Tisha Be' Av. This list was compiled for the July 28, 1994, edition of the *Jerusalem Report* magazine by Raphael Rosner, head of Beth Hatefutsoth, Tel Aviv's Diaspora Museum. (Note: Jewish authors use B.C.E. and C.E. instead of B.C. and A.D.).

> Circa 1200 B.C.E.: The children of Israel are condemned to 40 years of wandering in the Sinai wilderness.
>
> 586 B.C.E.: Babylonians sack and destroy Jerusalem and Solomon's Temple.
>
> 70 C.E.: Romans devastate the second temple.
>
> 1096: The First Crusade begins, destroying Jewish communities in Europe.
>
> 1290: The Jews are expelled from England.
>
> 1306: The Jews are expelled from France.
>
> 1492: The Jews are expelled from Spain.
>
> 1648: Thousands of Polish Jews are massa-

cred by Khmelnytsky's hordes.

1882: Pogroms sweep Russia.

1914: World War I breaks out.

1942: Nazis convene at Wannsee, Germany, and finalize their plans for the destruction of World Jewry.

An article written by Shlomo Riskin, in the *Jerusalem Post* dated July 16, 1994, describes Tisha Be' Av as a day of fasting. "During the fast itself we behave as full-fledged mourners. . . . We have to be totally in touch with our pain. . . . We experience again the agony of Jeremiah's lamentations, turn over our couches and chairs, and literally feel the earth weep underneath us. Our hearts break. We have become mourners. . . .

> Judaism teaches that death is the result of sin, not so much from a personal perspective as from a universal one. Adam, the first human being, sinned, and thus became mortal. Hence our Sages declare, "There is no death without transgression" (B.T. Torah. Shabbat 55a).
>
> And our vision of ultimate redemption and the concomitant perfection in its wake involves the prior recognition and repentance of the sin which caused the destruction, the sin which caused the exile. We dream of the resultant defeat of death, of a dimension in which 'death will be swallowed up forever. . . .' So the first fact of mourning is a separation of oneself from society's clamor and misleading paths. . . . Thus, the mourning requirements of separation from the world . . . to re-establish his priorities, to recognize sin, to repent. . . . After all, if sin-price, misplaced values, hedonistic goals — brought about destruction and exile, only repentance can bring about redemption. . . .

These are themes which find expression in the New Testament as well as in the Jewish writings. Shlomo Riskin concludes with an interesting comment:

> This may be what our sages meant when they taught that anyone who truly mourns the destruction of the temple on Tisha be' Av merits to see its rebuilding (p. 23).

These are a few notes from a longer article in the *Jerusalem Post.*

The Comet and the Planet Jupiter

A number of Jewish publications have expressed keen interest in the fact that the first of the 21-piece comet began to fall on Jupiter on the eve of Tisha be' Av.

Some have expressed that it is a "sign" of the coming of the Messiah. The Orthodox Hebrew magazine *L'Mishpaha,* devoted two pages to a scientific commentary on the incredible comet. They note that a comet blazed through the skies at the time of the destruction of Jerusalem and the Second Temple in the year 70.

Our Jupiter comet was discovered a year ago by American astronomers David Levy and Eugene and Carolyn Shoemaker, all Jewish persons. The *Jerusalem Report Magazine* commented: "Some refer to the coming crash as a 'gift,' a chance to see a disaster on an almost unimaginable scale, right here in our very own solar system." *Jerusalem Report* July 28, 1994, p. 20-21. (We received ours in the mail before July 16.)

Commenting on the comet-fall on Jupiter, Rabbi Mordechai Shienberger, who lives in the Old City of Jerusalem said, "There is a hand which orders everything. The Creator manages the earth."

Take note, friend, it could happen here. In fact that is what seems to be described in the Book of Revelation:

And when he had opened the seventh seal, there was silence in heaven about the space of half an hour.

And I saw the seven angels which stood before God; and to them were given seven trumpets.

And another angel came and stood at the altar, having a golden censer; and there was given unto him much incense, that he should offer it with the prayers of all saints upon the golden altar which was before the throne. And the smoke of the incense, which came with the prayers of the saints, ascended up before God out of the angel's hand. And the angel took the censer, and filled it with fire of the altar, and cast [it] into the earth: and there were voices, and thunderings, and lightnings, and an earthquake.

And the seven angels which had the seven trumpets prepared themselves to sound.

The first angel sounded, and there followed hail and fire mingled with blood, and they were cast upon the earth: and the third part of trees was burnt up, and all green grass was burnt up.

And the second angel sounded, and as it were a great mountain burning with fire was cast into the sea: and the third part of the sea became blood; And the third part of the creatures which were in the sea, and had life, died; and the third part of the ships were destroyed.

And the third angel sounded, and there fell a great star from heaven, burning as it were a lamp, and it fell upon the third part of the rivers, and upon the fountains of waters; And the name of the star is called Wormwood: and the third part of the waters became wormwood; and many men died of the waters, because they were made bitter.

And the fourth angel sounded, and the third part of the sun was smitten, and the third part of the moon, and the third part of the stars; so as the third part of them was darkened, and the day shone not for a third part of it, and the night likewise (Rev. 8:1-12).

For the many reasons described in the *Jerusalem Report* article it seems that Israel, in the Negev Desert, was the premier place to observe the comet-fall. The *Report* mentioned the words of Professor Brosch: " 'We're at the right place on the planet. We have the most modern observatory at this latitude,' says Tel Aviv University astronomer Noah Brosch, who will be stationed at the university's Wise Observatory in the Negev town of Mitzpeh Ramon tracking the comet and the aftereffects of its impact. . . ."

The Jerusalem Report takes note of the comments of various Jewish religious leaders, saying, "Some students of Jewish mystical texts have gone so far as to suggest that the coming of this month's comet might also signify the imminent return of the Messiah."

Jeremiah, a prophet of the Lord wrote: "O house of David, thus saith the Lord; Execute judgment in the morning, and deliver him that is spoiled out of hand of the oppressor, lest my fury go out like fire, and burn that none can quench it, because of the evil of your doings" (Jer. 21:12).

Behold, I am against thee, O destroying mountain, saith the Lord, which destroyest all the earth: and I will stretch out mine hand upon thee, and roll thee down from the rocks, and will make thee a burnt mountain" (Jer. 51:25).

23. Many More Signs

What we have presented in this chapter is only a small representation of the prophetic signs of our Lord's return. In previous books we have discussed many other signs relating to the economy, national destiny, Europe and the Revived Roman Empire, false Christs, UFO deception, the energy crisis, and many more. Now read on in the following chapters where we will explore together prophecies of the past, present, and future. Some chapters will issue a call to action, based on what we know of God's divine plan.

Endnotes
[1]David Allen Lewis, *Prophecy 2000* (Green Forest, AR: New Leaf Press, 1990).
[2]*New American*, November 11, 1996, p. 23-27.

Chapter 2

ARISE MY LOVE
AND COME AWAY

End-Time Call to the Bride

June, 1967 — the Six Day War was over. Israel had taken possession of East Jerusalem, the Old City, including the temple mountain and the ancient Western Wall. Excitement was high, a spirit of jubilation reigned throughout the land. It was an idyllic moment.

One day about 20 years later I was in a Jerusalem deli-restaurant with my wife, Ramona, and our friend Avigdor Rosenberg. Avigdor introduced me to Israel Eldad, an Israeli historian of renown. I exclaimed, "Israel Eldad, why I remember what you said after the capture of East Jerusalem in 1967!"

Surprised, he asked me, "And what is it that you remember?"

I replied, "I recall your saying 'From the time that King David conquered Jerusalem until Solomon built the temple, just one generation passed. So it will be with us!' " Mr. Eldad seemed amazed that I recalled this quote, so I told him that I had it copied down in the margin of my Bible.

Who Stands Behind the Wall?

I recall that Zerah Warhaftig, Israel's Minister of Religious Affairs, made a most remarkable statement. On June 27, 1967, he said, "The land of Israel is the Holy Land. In the center of Jerusalem is the Western Wall, and according to our sages, from that wall the divine presence has never stirred; as it is written in the Song of Songs, 'Behold, he standeth behind our wall.' "

Wondering about Zerah Warhaftig's reference to the Song of Solomon, I had looked the passage up in my Bible. There it was in the Song of Songs:

> The voice of my beloved! behold, he cometh leaping upon the mountains, skipping upon the hills. My beloved is like a roe or a young hart: behold, *he standeth behind our wall, he looketh forth at the windows,* shewing himself through the lattice. My beloved spake, and said unto me, Rise up, my love, my fair one, and come away. For, lo, the winter is past, the rain is over and gone; The flowers appear on the earth; the time of the singing of birds is come, and the voice of the turtle is heard in our land; The fig tree putteth forth her green figs, and the vines with the tender grape give a good smell. Arise, my love, my fair one, and come away" (Song of Sol. 2:8-13).

> I charge you, O ye daughters of Jerusalem, by the roes, and by the hinds of the field, that ye stir not up, nor awake my love, till he please (Song of Sol. 3:5).

The meaning of beautiful symbols here unfold to us. Meditate on the fig tree, winter being over, summer at hand; then the beloved calls to his bride to rise and come away.

One cannot help but think of Matthew 24 and to compare some interesting similarities. What does it mean? Are we in the last days? Does not the coming of our Lord for the Church ever draw nearer?

The Olivet Discourse and the Budding Fig Tree

> And he shall send his angels with a great sound of a trumpet, and they shall gather together his elect from the four winds, from one end of heaven to the other (Matt. 24:31).

Now, some say that this refers to the rapture of the Church, others say it is the gathering of all the living Tribulation saints at the end of that awful time of trouble and judgment. The latter view is strengthened if one sees that the "heaven" referred to is the first heaven, earth's atmosphere.

Actually there are three heavens referred to in the Bible. The first is the envelope of air around this earth, the firmament of God's power. "Praise ye the Lord. Praise God in his sanctuary: praise him in the firmament of his power" (Ps. 150:1). The second heaven is the physical universe, the stars, planets, moons, and asteroids. "The heavens declare the glory of God; and the firmament showeth his handywork" (Ps. 19:1). The third heaven is the very abode of God (2 Cor. 12:2). There is no seventh heaven, nor a ninth heaven. This is a non-biblical, occult concept.

Some Comparisons

"Now learn a parable of the fig tree" (Matt. 24:32). Compare with "The fig tree putteth forth her green figs" (Song of Sol. 2:13).

It is important to note that in every Bible passage which deals with figs or the fig tree in a symbolic manner, and where the identity of the symbol is given in the context, without exception it refers to Israel. Some examples are Jeremiah 29:17; Hosea 9:10; Joel 1:6-7; and Jeremiah 24:1,

5, 10. This symbolism was known to those hearing Jesus on Mount Olivet.

"When his branch is yet tender, and putteth forth leaves, ye know that summer is nigh" (Matt. 24:32). Compare with "The flowers appear on the earth; the time of the singing of birds is come, and the voice of the turtle is heard in our land; The fig tree putteth forth her green figs, and the vines with the tender grape give a good smell. Arise, my love, my fair one, and come away" (Song of Sol. 2:12-13). Hear Jesus calling out the Church, his bride. It is the rapture of the Church.

"So likewise ye, when ye shall see all these things, know that it is near, even at the doors" (Matt. 24:33). Compare with "My beloved spake, and said unto me, Rise up, my love, my fair one, and come away. For, lo, the winter is past, the rain is over and gone" (Song of Sol. 2:10-11).

Winter Passes, Who Is at the Doors?

Having seen the parallel between some verses in Matthew 24 and some verses in Song of Solomon 2, we note other great treasures in Matthew 24, the first part of Jesus' great sermon given on Mount Olivet.

> Verily I say unto you, This generation shall not pass, till all these things be fulfilled. Heaven and earth shall pass away, but my words shall not pass away. But of that day and hour knoweth no man, no, not the angels of heaven, but my Father only (Matt. 24:34-36).

The Generation Question

What is a generation? The New Testament Greek word *genea* can be translated two ways. It can mean a literal generation, but *genea* is also translated *nation* in Philippians 2:15;KJV. A related word *Genos* is translated *nation* in Mark 7:26 and Galations 1:14. Jesus begins with the parable of the fig tree. Perhaps He is saying: *This genea — Israel, the fig tree nation will not be destroyed. This shall all be fulfilled.*

We confront a second problem and that is, how long is a generation? The word is obviously not a technical term since one can find a 40-year generation in Exodus, a 70-year generation in Psalms, a 35-year generation in the Book of Job, and some find evidence for a 100-year generation. Some point out that if you follow the Jewish calendar we are in the year 5755. Hence we will not reach the year 6000 (2000 Gregorian) for 245 years. Most of us do not think this has a significant bearing on our topic.

The third problem is in determining when the final generation begins. Some point to 1880 when the first major return of the Jews to Palestine took place. Perhaps that is when the fig tree (Israel) began to put forth leaves. Or was it 1897 when Theodore Herzl convened the First Zionist congress in Basel, Switzerland? Many thought that 1917, with the Balfour Declaration favoring the Jewish return to the land, was the beginning point. Another year to watch was 1922, with the League of Nations giving Great Britain the mandate (rule) over Palestine. But the most popular date was May 14, 1948, when Israel became a nation. But the passage does not actually say when the fig tree becomes a nation.

Second only to 1948 in popularity is 1967 when Israel captured East Jerusalem including the Western Wall and the Temple Mount. That was thought to be the end of the times of the Gentiles. But, not so. Revelation 11:1-3 sees Jerusalem trodden one more time by the Gentiles, for the space of 42 months. The end of the times of the Gentiles is at the end of the seven years of trouble, when Jesus Christ comes back and smites the image of Gentile world power on its feet and grinds it to dust. (Refer to Dan. 2 and 7.)

It seems strange that so many have used this passage to try and set the date for the rapture of the Church. Jesus spoke of the impossibility of doing this. Until now every attempt at date-setting the coming of the Lord has proven to be false prophecy. As we approach the year 2000 there is a growing frenzy of date-setting in the churches and in the Christian media. It is not good, and only destroys people's confidence in the Word of God. No one can destroy prophecy nor lessen God's sovereignty, but all this dating of the rapture of the Church erodes some people's trust, not only in prophecy, but in the Bible in general. Did we not read a moment ago, "But of that day and hour knoweth no man, no, not the angels of heaven, but my Father only" (Matt. 24:36). Why do some rebel against such a plain statement?

Does the Passage Deal with the Rapture of the Church?

We can demonstrate that the anticipated event is the rapture of the Church, the bride of Christ, and not His second coming at the end of Daniel's 70th week. (See Dan. 9:24-27). Our basis for saying this is that no one can know the time of His coming to take His bride away. On the other hand, people on earth after the Rapture can figure out the exact day of Jesus' visible second coming to the Mount of Olives. Before we explain this point please note a parallel passage to Matthew 24:32-36, found in Mark's Gospel.

You Know Not When the Time Is

> Now learn a parable of the fig tree; When her branch is yet tender, and putteth forth leaves, ye know that summer is near: So ye in like manner, when ye shall see these things come to pass, know that it is nigh, even at the doors. Verily I say unto you, that this generation shall not pass, till all these things be done. Heaven and earth shall pass away: but my words shall not pass away. But of that day and that hour knoweth no man, no, not the angels which are in heaven, neither the Son, but the Father. Take ye heed, watch and pray: for YE KNOW NOT WHEN THE TIME IS. . . . what I say unto you I say unto all, Watch (Mark 13:28-37).

One tactic of date setters in getting around the Matthew 24 warning is to say, "Well, I may not know the exact day or hour, but I've narrowed it down to the year it will happen. Or I have determined it will happen during the Feast of Tabernacles, so Jesus will come on one of the days of that week. But Mark's statement in verse 32 answers that: *"Ye know not when the time is."* And, a year is time, a month is time, a week is time, a day is time, and an hour is time. And you know not when the time is. Date setting destroys the potential imminency of Jesus coming for the Church. Our Lord could come today.

The admonition to be watchful for Jesus' coming is for the Church from the beginning until now. It is good for our spiritual growth not to know the time. That way we live in hopeful anticipation each day but never with an escapist mentality. We are responsible for the quality of life and of our witness to others. We live productively in time with eternity's values in view. Your end is near. No one really lives very long on this earth. Your passage into the third heaven is near, always only a breath away, whether you go by way of resurrection or the Rapture! "Watch therefore: for ye know not what hour your Lord doth come" (Matt. 24:42). There is no need to set a date to get you ready if you truly believe that Jesus could come at once!

Legitimate Date Setting

Those who are on earth during the Tribulation can know the exact day Jesus will return to the Mount of Olives. It will be exactly 2,520 days after the signing of the covenant by some leaders of Israel and the Antichrist. Halfway through the Tribulation the Antichrist defiles the future temple of Israel and exactly 1,260 days after that Jesus will come, with the resurrected and raptured saints with him. Jesus will stand on the Mount of Olives, Armageddon is fought, Jesus declares the thousand year Kingdom and the Regnum Millennium begins. (See Zech. 14.) This is based on Daniel 9:24-27, the 70 weeks vision. For more information see, *The Coming Prince,* by Sir Robert Anderson.

Let us recap this information. By observing the covenant signing and the abomination in the temple, people saved after the rapture (Rev. 7) can exactly calculate the day of the Second Coming. Therefore, the Matthew 24:32-26 passage has to refer to the undatable rapture of the Church. The signing of the seven-year covenant marks the beginning of the seven-year tribulation. Exactly 1,260 days after the signing, Antichrist defiles the temple. And 1,260 days after that, Jesus stands, visibly, on the Mount of Olives. (See Dan. 9:24-27; Matt. 24:15-22; 2 Thess. 2:3-4; and Rev. 11:1-2.

> Therefore be ye also ready: for in such an hour as ye think not the Son of man cometh (Matt. 24:44).

Love Song of Christ and the Church

That the Church is the bride is shown by Paul's letter to the Church in 2 Corinthians 11:2: "For I am jealous over you with a godly jealousy; for I have espoused you to one husband, that I may present you as a chaste virgin to Christ."

The Song of Songs which is Solomon's is a love song. This poem is an allegory of the love between Christ, the bridegroom and His bride, the Church. "The fig tree putteth forth her green figs, and the vines with the tender grape give a good smell. Arise, my love, my fair one, and come away" (Song of Sol. 2:13). "Who is this that cometh up from the wilderness, leaning upon her beloved?" (Song of Sol. 8:5).

Oh, listen for His call. Ever watch for His coming. Some have grown weary as they are buffeted in the battle for the Kingdom. Hold steady, beloved friends, our Lord will surely return before long. Perhaps soon. Keep your eyes on the eastern skies as you strive to attain to the "prize of the high calling of God in Christ Jesus our Lord." God loves you more than you can ever know. Trust Him! "Watch ye therefore, and pray always, that ye may be accounted worthy to escape all these things that shall come to pass, and to stand before the Son of man" (Luke 21:36).

A Song of Songs

Daughters of Jerusalem, my lovely Shulamite
Come hide within my loving arms, for onward comes
the night.
Daughters of Jerusalem, you are my pure delight
Listen, I'm calling to you.

I'm waiting at the lattice door, open and let me in
For I am nourished with thy eyes, all glorious within.
Put on the strength of Zion, Our reign will soon begin
Oh listen I'm calling to you.

Daughters of Jerusalem, my bride, my lily queen
I'm drawn to you, run after me, the pastures now are
green.
Daughters of Jerusalem, it is the time to dream
Oh listen, I'm calling to you.

I see the chain of gold my love, upon thy neck so fair
And all the nations soon shall see thy beauty, oh so rare.
My kingdom I'll divide my love, with thee my love I'll
share
Listen, I'm calling to you.

Daughters of Jerusalem, my fairest in array
Come lay upon my bosom, where the one disciple lay
Daughters of Jerusalem, It is the close of day
Listen I'm calling to you.

I sent the Holy Ghost and fire to gather in to one
My virgin pure and undefiled, Father's will be done
You must run the race my love, until the race is done
Listen I'm calling to you

Calling to you, Oh listen I'm calling to you my love
Calling to you, Oh listen I'm calling to you.
— Author Unknown

Yes, Jesus, we are listening, and we welcome your call. "Even so, come Lord Jesus!" This world has become a terminally bad neighborhood to live in. But the day of the Bride and the Bridegroom is near at hand! "Even so, come Lord Jesus!"

We take note that "The winter is past. . . . The fig tree putteth forth her green figs," and we hear the call of our Lord, "Arise, my love, my fair one, and come away" (Song of Sol. 2:11-12).

The Bride of Christ — the Church or the New Jerusalem?

We have received a number of inquiries relating to the identity of the bride of Christ in the New Testament. The most widely held view is that the Church of the firstborn, consisting of all born-again persons, is the bride of Christ. There are a number of alternate points of view. Here is an examination of a concept currently in vogue in some circles — that the New Jerusalem is the Bride.

Some believe that the Holy City, the New Jerusalem, is the bride of Christ. Those who hold to this view are not entirely without scriptural foundation for their views. However, we believe that a careful examination of the entire biblical context bears out that the Church is the Bride. First of all, let's look at the evidence in the Book of Revelation that is marshaled for the view that the city is the Bride.

The first of the passages offered is Revelation 21:2 "And I John saw the holy city, new Jerusalem, coming down from God out of heaven, prepared as a bride adorned for her husband."

In the next chapter of the Apocalypse we find the second reference for the Bride-City concept: "And there came unto me one of the seven angels which had the seven vials full of the seven last plagues, and talked with me, saying, Come hither, I will shew thee the bride, the Lamb's wife" (Rev. 21:9).

Examples of How the Symbol of the Bride Is Used in the Bible

The prophets of Israel frequently used the bride symbol in their writings. Israel is referred to as the bride of Jehovah. Isaiah wrote, "For as a young man marrieth a virgin, so shall thy sons marry thee: and as the bridegroom rejoiceth over the bride, so shall thy God rejoice over thee" (Isa. 62:5).

Jeremiah, the weeping prophet of Israel, lamented: "For thus saith the Lord of hosts, the God of Israel; Behold, I will cause to cease out of this place in your eyes, and in your days, the voice of mirth, and the voice of gladness, the voice of the bridegroom, and the voice of the bride" (Jer. 16:9; also see Jer. 25:10; 33:11).

Joel was speaking of the people, not a city, when he wrote, "Gather the people, sanctify the congregation, assemble the elders, gather the children, and those that suck the breasts: let the bridegroom go forth of his chamber, and the bride out of her closet" (Joel 2:16).

What did the Gospel writer John have in mind when he wrote, "He that hath the bride is the bridegroom: but the friend of the bridegroom, which standeth and heareth him, rejoiceth greatly because of the bridegroom's voice: this my joy therefore is fulfilled" (John 3:29).

The Feminine Nature of the Church

The apostle Paul confirms the feminine nature of the Church in 2 Corinthians 11:2. He writes, "For I am jealous over you with godly jealousy: for I have espoused you to one husband, that I may present you as a chaste virgin to Christ."

One of the strongest passages is found in Ephesians:

> For the husband is the head of the wife, even as Christ is the head of the church: and he is the saviour of the body. Therefore as the church is subject unto Christ, so let the wives be to their own husbands in every thing.
>
> Husbands, love your wives, even as Christ

also loved the church, and gave himself for it; That he might sanctify and cleanse it with the washing of water by the word, That he might present it to himself a glorious church, not having spot, or wrinkle, or any such thing; but that it should be holy and without blemish. So ought men to love their wives as their own bodies. He that loveth his wife loveth himself. For no man ever yet hated his own flesh; but nourisheth and cherisheth it, even as the Lord the church: For we are members of his body, of his flesh, and of his bones. For this cause shall a man leave his father and mother, and shall be joined unto his wife, and they two shall be one flesh. This is a great mystery: but I speak concerning Christ and the church (Eph. 5:23-32).

Jerusalem Went Out to Meet Jesus — Who or What Went Out?

When the gospel states that Jerusalem went out to meet Jesus, what is portrayed? Do you get a picture of the buildings of the city getting up and going out to the Saviour? Or do you see the people of the city rising up and going out to meet Him?

Then went out to him Jerusalem, and all Judaea, and all the region round about Jordan (Matt. 3:5).

Similarly the same thing is stated in Mark 1:5: "And there went out unto him all the land of Judaea, and they of Jerusalem, and were all baptized of him in the river of Jordan, confessing their sins."

Let me offer a simple, homely illustration. I live in Springfield, Missouri. Our town is affectionately known as the "Queen City of the Ozarks."

In describing our city of about 140,000 souls I could

point out that we are a college town. Here are located Southwestern Missouri State University, Central Bible College, Drury College, Baptist Bible College, Phillips Junior College, Evangel College, the Assemblies of God Theological Seminary and a fine nursing school. This is the headquarters city of the Bible Baptist Fellowship and of the Assemblies of God. We are a city filled with evangelical and other churches.

We have more than our share of industries, restaurants, places of entertainment, and the Bass Pro Store is the number one tourist attraction in our state.

But, have I shown you the REAL Springfield, Missouri? Does the city consist of mortar, brick, wood, and stone? Are buildings what make the city? No, it is the people that make the real Springfield. The church buildings, colleges, homes, factories, and places of business are simply a manifestation of the people who are here. Take away the people and there is no real Springfield left — just empty buildings.

Further Considerations in the Book of Revelation

Since the Book of Revelation is the source for the only proof texts given to demonstrate that the Bride is the city, it is necessary to put the question into the entire context of the Revelation.

In the passage recorded in Revelation 18:23 the writer is speaking to the cursed city of Babylon: "And the light of a candle shall shine no more at all in thee; and the voice of the bridegroom and of the bride shall be heard no more at all in thee: for thy merchants were the great men of the earth; for by thy sorceries were all nations deceived."

John shares the sobering command of the Lord in verse four of the same 18th chapter: "And I heard another voice from heaven, saying, Come out of her, my people, that ye be not partakers of her sins, and that ye receive not of her plagues" (Rev. 18:4).

Revelation 21 describes the glory of the city that the

redeemed will inhabit in eternity. It is called the bride of Christ because the bride lives there. There would be no bride without the presence of the redeemed. We will use only selected verses. Each will be clearly identified. I suggest that you look up and read the entire context in chapters 21 and 22 of the Revelation.

And I John saw the holy city, new Jerusalem, coming down from God out of heaven, prepared as a bride adorned for her husband. And I heard a great voice out of heaven saying, Behold, the tabernacle of God is with men, and he will dwell with them, and they shall be his people, and God himself shall be with them, and be their God. And God shall wipe away all tears from their eyes; and there shall be no more death, neither sorrow, nor crying, neither shall there be any more pain: for the former things are passed away (Rev. 21:2-4).

And there came unto me one of the seven angels which had the seven vials full of the seven last plagues, and talked with me, saying, Come hither, I will shew thee the bride, the Lamb's wife. And he carried me away in the spirit to a great and high mountain, and shewed me that great city, the holy Jerusalem, descending out of heaven from God (Rev. 21:9-10).

And had a wall great and high, and had twelve gates, and at the gates twelve angels, and names written thereon, which are the names of the twelve tribes of the children of Israel (Rev. 21:12).

And the wall of the city had twelve foundations, and in them the names of the twelve apostles of the Lamb (Rev. 21:14).

And the twelve gates were twelve pearls: every several gate was of one pearl: and the street of the city was pure gold, as it were transparent glass.

And I saw no temple therein: for the Lord God Almighty and the Lamb are the temple of it. [This verse demonstrates that the city appears on the New Earth following the Millennium. There will be a temple in Jerusalem during the Millennium.] And the city had no need of the sun, neither of the moon, to shine in it: for the glory of God did lighten it, and the Lamb is the light thereof. And the nations of them which are saved shall walk in the light of it: and the kings of the earth do bring their glory and honour into it. And the gates of it shall not be shut at all by day: for there shall be no night there. And they shall bring the glory and honour of the nations into it (Rev. 21:21-26).

And he shewed me a pure river of water of life, clear as crystal, proceeding out of the throne of God and of the Lamb. In the midst of the street of it, and on either side of the river, was there the tree of life, which bare twelve manner of fruits, and yielded her fruit every month: and the leaves of the tree were for the healing of the nations. And there shall be no more curse: but the throne of God and of the Lamb shall be in it; and his servants shall serve him: And they shall see his face; and his name shall be in their foreheads. And there shall be no night there; and they need no candle, neither light of the sun; for the Lord God giveth them light: and they shall reign for ever and ever (Rev. 22:1-5).

The Bride Participates in Giving the Invitation to Salvation

And the Spirit and the bride say, Come. And let him that heareth say, Come. And let him that is athirst come. And whosoever will, let him take the water of life freely (Rev. 22:17).

It is not an inanimate city which issues the invitation, it is the redeemed who are to live in the city, the bride of Christ that is mandated to give forth the invitation to eternal life. It was His human followers to whom Jesus gave the command: "Go ye therefore into the highways, and as many as ye shall find, bid to the marriage" (Matt. 22:9). "Go ye therefore, and teach all nations, baptizing them in the name of the Father, and of the Son, and of the Holy Ghost" (Matt. 28:19). "And he said unto them, Go ye into all the world, and preach the gospel to every creature" (Mark 16:15).

There are other questions relating to the Bride, the Church, and the further inquiry as to whether the Church is actually feminine or whether it is to be identified with the masculine "restrainer" of the Antichrist as found in 2 Thessalonians 2. Briefly, the Church is feminine in the love relationship that exists between Christ and the believers. The Church is masculine, as a warrior, in its relationship to our ancient enemy, Satan, the devil. In this regard Paul writes many things in the Epistles regarding the believer as a soldier in the army of God. See my book *Smashing the Gates of Hell in the Last Days*,[1] for further information on how the Church is being used by the Holy Spirit to restrain evil.

Endnotes

[1]David Allen Lewis, *Smashing the Gates of Hell in the Last Days* (Green Forest, AR: New Leaf Press, 1987).

Chapter 3

CREATION AND THE END TIMES

Thou art worthy, O Lord, to receive glory and honour and power: for thou hast created all things, and for thy pleasure they are and were created (Rev. 4:11).

This is it! We are living in the final era of earth's history. Soon will come the visible, manifest kingdom of God. This thousand year time period, called the Millennium, is the inauguration of eternity at which time the Creator will make a new earth and new heavens.

And he laid hold on the dragon, that old serpent, which is the Devil, and Satan, and bound him a thousand years (Rev. 20:2; also see Rev. 20:3-7).

And I saw a new heaven and a new earth: for the first heaven and the first earth were passed away; and there was no more sea (Rev. 21:1).[1]

The Millennium will not be brought about through human effort. As my college professor and mentor Dr. Stanley Horton often says, "The Kingdom comes on the heels of earth's greatest tribulation and the outpouring of the judgment of God on this rebellious world. Jesus Christ will establish the thousand-year Kingdom at the time of His second coming."[2]

As Marshall Fishwick pointed out in his book *Faust Revisited,* the devil is real, not just an evil force or principle, but a real person. He is the originator of rebellion and is characterized by his lies and deceptions.

> Ye are of your father the devil, and the lusts of your father ye will do. He was a murderer from the beginning, and abode not in the truth, because there is no truth in him. When he speaketh a lie, he speaketh of his own: for he is a liar, and the father of it (John 8:44).

He will attack God and his people at every possible point. His anger will know no bounds.

> Therefore rejoice, ye heavens, and ye that dwell in them. Woe to the inhabiters of the earth and of the sea! for the devil is come down unto you, having great wrath, because he knoweth that he hath but a short time (Rev. 12:12).

In the battle for the souls of humanity, the deceiver is always active, prowling, "seeking whom he may devour" (1 Pet. 5:8).

Battle For The Species

A major front in the great end-time warfare is the battle zone between creationism and evolution. It is a subject of major concern to Christians. Without the Genesis record of the creation of the first man Adam, and our mother, Eve, and their fall from grace, there is no salvation, in fact no need for salvation.

> Wherefore, as by one man sin entered into the world, and death by sin; and so death passed upon all men, for that all have sinned (Rom. 5:12).

In 1859 the battle was enjoined in earnest. The line in the sand was drawn by a scientist named Charles Darwin. His book *The Origin of the Species* descended upon a waiting world. All 1,250 copies of the book sold out on the day of publication, much to the surprise of both Darwin and the publisher.

Later, Bertrand Russell, no friend of Christianity, said that the world was waiting for Charles Darwin. This atheist correctly analyzed that unregenerate humanity longed for a theory with scientific respectability that would allow them to throw off the yoke of God's dominion. Russell said, "Evolution is unproven and unprovable. I believe it because the only alternative is a miraculous special creation which is patently impossible."[3] Take heed to these sobering words from Psalm 14:1, "The fool hath said in his heart, There is no God. They are corrupt, they have done abominable works, there is none that doeth good." So important is this message of Psalm 14, it is repeated in Psalm 53:1.

Worship The Creator

God chose to introduce himself on page one of His Book, the Bible, as the Creator. The first doctrine expounded is creationism. Every Bible college and seminary should offer courses.

On the last pages of the Bible, God is seen as the creator of new heavens and a new earth. Paradise is restored. Crime, violence, death, and pain are no more to be found. At one point in the Apocalypse we see mighty angels flying through the heavens preaching the everlasting Gospel to a lost, tormented world. And what message do they declare in the tribulation crisis hour? *Worship the Creator.*

> And I saw another angel fly in the midst of

heaven, having the everlasting gospel to preach
unto them that dwell on the earth, and to every
nation, and kindred, and tongue, and people, Saying with a loud voice, Fear God, and give glory to
him; for the hour of his judgment is come: and
worship him that made heaven, and earth, and the
sea, and the fountains of waters (Rev. 14:6-7).

The great Apostle John, noted for his love for Christ,
introduces Jesus in his Gospel as the Creator of all things,
then as the Saviour of all who will believe on and receive
Him.

In the beginning was the Word, and the Word
was with God, and the Word was God. The same
was in the beginning with God. **All things were
made by him; and without him was not any
thing made. that was made.** In him was life; and
the life was the light of men. And the light shineth
in darkness; and the darkness comprehended it
not. There was a man sent from God, whose name
was John. The same came for a witness, to bear
witness of the Light, that all men through him
might believe. He was not that Light, but was sent
to bear witness of that Light. That was the true
Light, which lighteth every man that cometh into
the world. He was in the world, and **the world was
made by him,** and the world knew him not. He
came unto his own, and his own received him not.
But as many as received him, to them gave he
power to become the sons of God, even to them
that believe on his name (John 1:1-12;emphasis
added).

In the Epistle to the Church at Rome, the apostle Paul
affirms that it is through the creation that God makes himself
known to mankind.

For therein is the righteousness of God revealed from faith to faith: as it is written, The just shall live by faith (Rom. 1:17-25).

The heavens declare the glory of God; and the firmament sheweth his handywork. Day unto day uttereth speech, and night unto night sheweth knowledge (Ps. 19:1-2).

King Solomon in the years of his wisdom observed, "To know wisdom and instruction; to perceive the words of understanding. . . . A wise man will hear, and will increase learning; and a man of understanding shall attain unto wise counsels. . . . The fear of the Lord is the beginning of knowledge: but fools despise wisdom and instruction (Prov. 1:2-7).

Powerful Evidence

Many years ago I had an ongoing conversation with an atheist. This dialogue went on for three and a half years. One of our favorite topics of discussion was the matter of creation versus evolution. I often pointed out that one of my strongest arguments was that the universe shows design. Design demands a designer.

One day Larry thought he had the answer. He said, "David, I can now prove you wrong. The universe does not show design. Everything in nature is rough hewn. Look at the forests, the jagged shoreline, the waves of the sea. There are no straight lines nor symmetry in nature. If you can show me where straight lines and symmetry occur in nature, where the hand of intelligent beings have not laid a hand, I will admit that you are right. The only place where symmetry occurs is where man's intelligent design has been superimposed on the raw materials of earth man."

Then I knew for sure that Larry had handed me a powerful idea for creationism. I replied, "Larry, consider the feldspar crystal! Wonder at the perfect design of the geometric pattern in each six-pointed and six-segmented snowflake. Gaze through a microscope at the rod bacillus. And best of all ponder the basic building blocks of the universe, the atom." Larry was shattered. At one point he was on his knees in prayer. I have lost contact with him but have hope for his salvation.

I have a watch given to me by an Arab friend in Israel. It has two time clock faces, and a map of the world on the face of it. Suppose I told you, "I like this watch, but do you know that Arab Christian who gave it to me tried to tell me that he knew where it was *made*." Suppose I were to tell you "I do not believe in watchmakers, after all I have never actually seen one. I think this Gulf War commemorative watch is the product of natural evolution." You would rightly think I was being very foolish. Anyone can see the watch is designed, and design demands a designer.

Come into the planetarium with me. In this wondrous museum we see a working model of our solar system, with the sun at the center and around it revolve the nine planets and their various moons. I know some very clever person designed and made this working, moving model. If the model demands the existence of a designer, *then what about the real solar system the model is designed from?* The Psalmist was right, "The fool says there is no God."

God is not as the foolish sinners, rebuked by Paul in Romans, supposed. They abandoned worship of the Creator and mistakenly began to worship nature. There are millions of New Agers today who believe that the planet earth is a living goddess named Gaia. They believe that the earth is a conscious being. We are gods and goddesses too, as we become one with Gaia/earth. This is the fruit of a hundred years of evolution being taught as a fact in our educational system.

The Bible teaches us to respect and care for the creation, but we must never worship the earth. God is in Heaven in His divine personal concentrated presence. Also by His omnipresence He is always present in every place, in every state of relativity and reality at all times. In short, God is everywhere all the time. *But He is the Creator, not part of the creation.*

Jesus taught us, "When ye pray, say, Our Father which art in heaven, Hallowed be thy name. Thy kingdom come. Thy will be done, as in heaven, so in earth" (Matt. 6:9 and Luke 11:2). Praying in this fashion honors the difference between the Creator and the creation.

Dr. Richard Benedict Goldschmidt[4] was a well-known and respected German scientist. He conducted experiments for years with gypsy moths, selected because they are found all over the world and because of their brief reproduction cycle. He interbred scores of types of gypsy moths, hoping to produce something other than gypsy moths. He changed their environment with heat and cold, with diet, with chemicals, and even radiation. After many years his sad conclusion was that he never succeeded in producing anything other than gypsy moths. There were color, size, and pattern differences, but they were still gypsy moths. His forlorn conclusion was that as far as gypsy moths were concerned, evolution simply did not work. Dr. Goldschmidt could have saved a lot of hard work and disappointment simply by reading the Book of Genesis.

Does Change Take Place?

Creationists do not deny that change does take place. After all, the varied races of humanity all came from one man and one woman, Adam and Eve. You can breed dogs for generations and possibly produce a new kind of dog, recognized and certified by the American Kennel Association and the scientific community. But breeding dogs always produces dogs, *never* cats or pigeons or turtles.

Genesis tells us that God created the original kinds of living things:

> And God said, Let the earth bring forth the
> living creature after his kind, cattle, and creeping

thing, and beast of the earth after his kind: and it was so (Gen. 1:24; also see: Gen. 1:25, 6:20, 7:14).

It is easy to accept a common ancestry of all canines, bovines, felines, and humans, etc., and it is easy to demonstrate that cows never produce pigs or horses or geese. Evolutionists theorize that there are "missing" links that bridge the gaps between species. Missing indeed! They never will be found, for they never existed.

Study the vast field of literature known as *scientific creationism* and you will find more than adequate answers to every aspect of the theory of evolution.

Let it never be said of the Church, "My people are destroyed for lack of knowledge: because thou hast rejected knowledge, I will also reject thee, that thou shalt be no priest to me: seeing thou hast forgotten the law of thy God, I will also forget thy children" (Hos. 4:6).

The Mars Rock Question

The big question on the front cover of the May 1996 *Reader's Digest* was, "Are We Alone In The Universe?"

In the book *UFO: End-Time Delusion*[5] you will find an important answer to the question of why it is important to the humanistic world and its secular society to prove the Bible wrong, that evolution is the answer, that God is only the "force" underlying the Universe.

The Mars Rock was supposed to have been formed 15 billion years ago, and then blasted loose from the surface of Mars by an asteroid, finally ending up on earth 16,000 years ago. Inside the rock are microscopic formations that may have been living things, proving that there was life on Mars, long ago, and implying that this certainly disproves the Genesis account of creation.

Where does the newly announced Mars Rock, discovered in Antarctica in 1986, fit into the picture? NASA chief Dan Golden seemed ecstatic as he said, "We're now on the doorstep to the heavens. What a time to be alive!" Noted astronomer Carl Sagan said, "These findings raise the possibility of a universe burgeoning with life."[6] Several talk show hosts, news people, and sundry other media-ites boldly announced that this would pose a real problem for fundamentalist Christians who insisted on taking the Genesis account of creation literally.

Wrong — no potato-sized rock poses any threat to the Rock of Ages, Almighty Creator of the Universe. Neither the finders nor the examiners of the little stone have any firm answers as to its nature or meaning, or even if it did drift into earth from Mars. I certainly do not have a technical answer to the questions posed by the Mars rock — yet. Be patient, in due season we will know all that can be known about it, and it will not contradict the Bible. God's world(s) never contradict God's Word.

On the day of the big Mars rock announcement, Edna Devore, spokesperson for the SETI Institute, spoke of both government and private investments in the Search for Extra Terrestrial Intelligence. She revealed that in a 10-year period of time, the U.S. government spent $58 million of your tax dollars developing technology to make the search, primarily using radio telescopes to listen for messages from other planets. Edna Devore said, "In the event that we find evidence we have a protocol, an *internationally* agreed upon protocol, to go out and announce immediately, for people everywhere, that an intelligent signal has been picked up (CNN special report). Italics added here and following for emphasis.

Ruffin Prevost of an organization called Para-Scope [sic] was asked by a talk show hostess, "What do we do, Ruffin? What do you think will happen? Are we going to be meeting good guys — when they do land here? . . . I can't imagine them coming all that way just to blow us up."

Ruffin referred to the recent Hollywood movie, *Independence Day*, saying, "I think the movie did present a pretty accurate depiction of what might happen if aliens landed, whether they were benevolent or bad guys." Prevost can be located on the Internet World Wide Web at WWW.parascope.com. SETI Inst. can be located at WWW.SETI-inst.edu. SETI offers curriculum for grades 3-9.

Premature Death Notice!

While some media people were heralding the death knell of biblical creationism, most of the scientists suggest a more cautious approach, and admitted that the nature of the rock could be interpreted in several different ways.

David McCay from the Johnson Space Center admitted, "There are alternative explanations for each of the lines of evidence that we see."

Everet Gibson said, "The sample we have before us is 4.5 billion years old. . . . [Mars] was *probably* warmer and wetter. Water was more abundant . . . as time evolved *we feel that* the solution *may have* resulted in the formation of these carbonate globules which we see within the fractures in this meteorite. . . . What it exactly is we do not know."

This interesting comment was made: "By this means we have been able to look and see the first organic molecules that *we believe* come from Mars."

Evolution, then, turns out to be a manmade religion based on faith in chaos rather than God.

Well, I Guess...

Wess Huntress, a NASA scientist, made a long rambling commentary, especially notable for the following phrases and admissions.

> The features that you see *may* be any number of things, for example they *could be* parts of that dried-up clay or they could be micro-fossils from Antarctica or micro-fossils from Mars. It is our interpretation, the one we *favor,* is that these are in fact micro-fossil forms from Mars.
> But keep in mind, *that is an interpretation —*

we have no independent data that these are fossils
. . . as we look in other areas of the carbonate, we
see these forms which are elongated . . . are these
strange crystals, *are they dried up mud?* We
believe these are micro-fossils from Mars . . .
whether this is a micro-fossil or whether this is a
dried-up mud crack we can't really say . . . again
we don't know what these are. . . . We have a
number of forms which it is very tempting for us
to interpret as Martian micro-fossils, but we have
no confirming evidence and you will hear more
about the pitfalls of identifying such things based
on appearance alone. . . ."

William Schopf, professor at UCLA, sounded a note of
caution, "There are meteorites called carbonaceous condrites
that contain large amounts of organic matter that is of non-
biological origin, so we want to know, is that organic matter
demonstrably biological. And second, in regard to fossil-like
objects, we'd like to know that they are assuredly fossils and
not mineralic *pseudo fossils, or what we used to call foolers,
things that fool you* and you'd prefer they didn't. . . . Let me
emphasize that it is subjective, it is my opinion. . . ."

David McCay sagely added, "I think you have seen that
this is a result that is going to be very controversial. . . ."

David Golden called for an accelerated Mars program,
manned missions to Mars. "I believe it will be a worldwide
mission and this is why I spoke to the *World Space Community* and I invited them . . . we are going to work together on
the International Space Station."

Dr. Richard Zare raised a radical question, "Who is to
say that we are not all Martians? That Mars was the place
that life first started. . . . Or how do we know that what we
are seeing on Mars didn't first come from the earth through
another asteroid impact that brought it to Mars? . . . We have
lots to learn, *provided it's life.*"

The NASA briefing on CNN continued for two hours.

Space Bubba

Lionell Johns in the White House Office of Science and Technology spoke on reaction to space aliens. "It would be some years before our technical abilities and scientific understanding would permit us to *get together with those folks* [space aliens!] Those folks indeed! "Hey, Roger, meet good ole Bubba, he's from Alpha Proximar, and guess what, he likes apple pie, and grits, and we're goin' coon huntin' on Saturday."

Canadian Landing Pad

In the quiet town of Saint Paul, Alberta, Canada, there is a most remarkable sight. It is a municipally sponsored landing pad for visiting UFOs (none yet). We spoke to the director of the facility and information center, named in honor of the late Dr. J. Alan Hynek. I have often quoted Hynek in regard to his idea that UFOs were from a paranormal (spiritual) realm. Hynek was a famous UFO researcher, author, and astronomer. He was the top civilian consultant for the U.S. Air Force *Project Blue Book*, which delved into the UFO mystery.

Much of the findings and conclusions have never been released to the public. I reference Hynek because, coming from the world of science, he arrived at the same conclusion that some other Christian scholars and I have come to from our research, which is biblically based. That conclusion is that the UFOs are supernatural in nature, but have the ability to materialize physical objects and appearances. This subject is extensively supported in my book *UFO: End-Time Delusion.* We demonstrate that supernatural entities known as demons are behind much of the UFO appearances, and all the attendant tragedies in the lives of alleged "contactees" such as Wesley Strieber, Barney and Betty Hill, and tens of thousands of others.[7]

Predictions

In 1955 I began making predictions about evolution,

UFOs, and the powers of Satan which will give credibility to the end-time pan-delusion now sweeping the world. This deception was to be accomplished in the following ways:

1. Reinterpret the origin of man, the earth, the physical universe, and the nature of God.

2. Philosophical deception by "scientists" like Charles Darwin, who had no science degree to his credit. The only college degree Darwin had was from a theological seminary. In Darwin we see the fruits of religious apostasy, run amok.

3. Invasion of the entire educational system to popularize these agnostic ideas.

4. Using scientific jargon to give the religion of evolution a cloak of respectability.

5. Deride, denounce, and denigrate those who believe the Bible account of literal creation, as we find it on page one of the Bible, and as the basic foundation of the entire Bible.

6. Popularize evolution, UFOs, and alien extraterrestrials in the movies, entertainment, and documentaries on television, and in print media.

7. Promote programs such as NASA's SETI (Search for Extraterrestrial Intelligence), funded by millions of your tax dollars and by private foundations.

8. Create public support for the Mars Space Mission.

9. Fake evidence for evolution, as in the infamous Piltdown man hoax and numerous other cases.

10. Put a faked scientific veneer on a mis-leading interpretation of the past (à la von Däniken — *Chariots of the Gods*). Or, should we say, "The chariots of the frauds?"

11. Claims that ET aliens were here before and masterminded the building of the pyramids,

the stone faces on the Easter Islands, Stonehenge on the Salisbury Plains of England, and the lines in the Nazca Plains in Peru. Mr. von Däniken told my daughter Sandy and I that the aliens will be back and that we had better accept them, since we could never defeat them.

12. Use the New Age movement to brainwash the public with these ideas.

Politicians and international leaders are seriously talking about how we should respond if aliens show up and offer to help us solve all our problems. Highly secret government agencies exist to make preparation for the first public meetings with the aliens.

I urge you to seriously consider my claims that evolution, UFOs, the New Age, secular humanism, Wicca, Satanism, and "scientism" are all in league together, and must be taken seriously if the Church is to be maximally effective.

In the face of every secular challenge we must be prepared to give answers. Whoever said it was easy to be a Christian? We are at war. But there is joy in the midst of battle. There is assurance of victory, even now, if we want it, work for it, and are willing to dig out answers to contemporary questions.

But sanctify the Lord God in your hearts: and
be ready always to give an answer to every man
that asketh you a reason of the hope that is in you
with meekness and fear (1 Pet. 3:15).

Since the creation vs. evolution struggle is an integral part of the end-times prophetic scenario, we are adding a variety of creation books to our mail order list. These books range from children's books to those suitable for average adult readers. Later we will add more technical works on scientific creationism. You may request our catalogue.

Write to David Allen Lewis, P.O. Box 11115, Springfield, MO 65810 (USA).

Endnotes:

[1] Also see Isaiah 65:17 and 66:22; and 2 Peter 3:13.

[2] Comment at a meeting of the Springfield Regional Eschatology Club, 1995.

[3] Cited by Hal Lindsey on TBN TV, Praise The Lord Program, 6/8/96.

[4] Born 1878, died 1958. Goldschmidt's fields of research included genetics and zoology. *Encyclopedia Britanica* (Micropedia) does not mention his disappointment in failing to produce something other than gypsy moths, only saying that his findings were controversial.

[5] David Allen Lewis and Robert Shreckhise, *UFO: End-Time Delusion* (Green Forest, AR: New Leaf Press, 1991).

[6] U.S. *News and World Report*, August 19, 1996, p. 45.

[7] Lewis and Shreckhise, *UFO: End-Time Delusion*.

Chapter 4

THE IMAGE OF THE BEAST

Beyond Cloning: Will Man Create Man in the Image of Man?

In 1956, as a 22-year-old evangelist, I pondered the question, "Can science create life?" I had read in the Bible how it would happen in the end of days. I was scorned for my thinking and proclamation. It was too far ahead of the times.

I also predicted that scientists would produce a living human-like "thing." Of course, I was told that it was impossible, and that if I did not stop making such radical statements I would lose all credibility. And yet some thoughtful pastors and lay people listened and believed.

In 1969 I met Dr. Raymond G. White at Greenville, Texas. He gave me a copy of a top secret U.S. Defense Department document (declassified) which strengthened my position.

In 1978 I read a book by David Rorvik which said that a human male had already been cloned.

I started writing a book on these and other revolutionary concepts in the light of Bible prophecy. The book was almost finished. I was waiting for the authentic cloning of a mammal to complete this chapter.

In 1997 Dr. Ian Wilmut cloned a sheep, an adult mammal. With the birth of Dolly, a cloned sheep, I knew my book was done.

We are living in amazing days. Prophecy marches on! Christ is coming!

Scientist Reports First Cloning Ever of Adult Mammal

The following is from the *New York Times*.

In a feat that may be the one bit of genetic engineering that has been anticipated and dreaded more than any other, researchers in Britain are reporting that they have cloned an adult mammal for the first time.

The group, headed by Dr. Ian Wilmut, a 52-year-old embryologist at the Roslin Institute in Edinburgh, has created a lamb using DNA from an adult sheep. Their achievement shocked leading researchers who had said it could not be done.

In theory, researchers said, the same techniques could be used to take a cell from an adult human and use the DNA to create a genetically identical human — a time-delayed twin. That prospect raises the thorniest of ethical and philosophical questions.

Dr. Wilmut said he was interested in the technique primarily as a tool in animal husbandry, but other scientists said it had opened doors to the unsettling prospect that humans could be cloned as well.

"It's unbelievable," said Dr. Lee Silver, a biology professor at Princeton University who said the announcement had come just in time for him to revise his forthcoming book so the first chapter will no longer state that such cloning is impossible.

"It basically means that there are no limits," Dr. Silver said. "It means all of science fiction is true. They said it could never be done and now here it is, done before the year 2000."

Although researchers have created genetically identical animals by dividing embryos very early in their development, Dr. Silver said no one had cloned an animal from an adult until now.

But others said that it was hard to imagine enforcing a ban on cloning people when cloning got more efficient. "I could see it going on surreptitiously," said Lori Andrews, a professor at Chicago-Kent College of law who specializes in reproductive issues. "I can imagine new crimes," she said.

People might be cloned without their knowledge or consent. After all, all that would be needed would be some cells. If there is a market for a sperm bank selling semen from Nobel laureates, how much better would it be to bear a child that would actually be a clone of a great thinker or, perhaps, a great beauty or great athlete?

"The genie is out of the bottle," said Dr. Ronald Munson, a medical ethicist at the University of Missouri in St. Louis. "This technology is not, in principle, policeable."

Dr. Munson called the future possibilities incredible. For example, could researchers devise ways to add just the DNA of an adult cell, without fusing two living cells? If so, might it be possible to clone the dead?

"I had an idea for a story once," Dr. Munson said, in which a scientist obtains a spot of blood from the cross [or shroud] on which Jesus was crucified. He then uses it to clone a man who is Jesus Christ — or perhaps cannot be."[1]

Revelation 13 introduces us to the Revived Roman Empire, the beast system, and the beast himself — the Antichrist. In verse 11 we find that there is a second beast. The second beast is the false prophet, cohort of the Antichrist, and head of the final apostate world religion. The false prophet introduces the world to a duplicate image of the Antichrist, and through demonic psychic talent and the powers of modern science it is actually brought to life.

False Prophet and His Powers

The false prophet, the second beast of Revelation 13, will be a unique and wondrous person who has great psychic powers. He will work miracles for the purpose of deception. In Revelation 13:11-15 we read:

> And I beheld another beast coming up out of the earth; and he had two horns like a lamb, and he spake as a dragon. And he exerciseth all the power of the first beast before him, and causeth the earth and them which dwell therein to worship the first beast, whose deadly wound was healed. And he doeth great wonders, so that he maketh fire come down from heaven on the earth in the sight of men, And deceiveth them that dwell on the earth by the means of those miracles which he had power to do in the sight of the beast; saying to them that dwell on the earth, that they should make an image to the beast, which had the wound by a sword, and did live. And he had power to give *life* unto the image of the beast, that the image of the beast should both speak, and cause that as many as would not worship the image of the beast should be killed [emphasis added].

What could the writer mean when he says that the false prophet has power to give life to the image of the beast? Is it possible that it could mean exactly what the text says? We think so.

Let me refer to the Greek definition of "life" as given in *Strong's Concordance. Strong's* is a reliable work and commonly known throughout the Christian world. We refer to it here because of its availability to everyone. *Strong's* Greek definition for the word life, *pneuma* (pnyoo'-mah) is literal, not figurative. It is also translated "Spirit" in 111 passages and is translated "human (spirit)" in 49 other passages. The following is an expansion of *Strong's* from the Greek Lexicon in the OnLine Bible computer program:

1. A movement of air, a gentle blast of the wind, hence the wind itself, breath of the nostrils or mouth.

2. The spirit, i.e. the vital principal by which the body is animated, the rational spirit, the power by which the human being feels, thinks, decides.

Compare this with the words of Genesis 2:7: "And the Lord God formed man of the dust of the ground, and breathed into his nostrils the breath of life; and man became a living soul."

Whatever else may be said about the image, it is not an inanimate object. It lives, it acts, it speaks and communicates. It forces humanity to submission and obedience to its commands and *it is alive.*

We live in the days of the end-time biological revolution. We must ask, will man create man in the image of man? Will an image truly be alive? Will it have a soul? Will it be human? Will it be energized by a demon?

We admit that the 15th verse is so strange that it could evoke a reaction of incredulity, casting doubt in the reader's mind as to the literal nature of the passage.

One might be tempted to exclaim, "It cannot mean what it says, there is no way this prophecy could be literal." I think that we can offer evidence that the passage means precisely what it says. First, we will look at some scientific reports and projections showing what the goals of some scientists are.

A Secret Report

Dr. Raymond G. White attended services I was conducting in a local church in Greenville, Texas, in 1975. I was introduced to him and told that he had served as the human factors engineer on Air Force 1, the presidential command emergency aircraft. The message of the evening was on the subject of how the Antichrist would not only demand but receive almost universal worship during the Tribulation. Dr. White invited me to his home for further conversation.

He showed me a declassified U.S. military top secret scientific report, and I was given a copy. Although declassified, it had never officially been released to the press or the public. Many years have gone by, and though I have referred to it in speaking and preaching, I have never put my thoughts about this report on paper until now. This information has never been published by us except in cassette lecture form.

The report consists of many 8.5 x 11 photocopied pages. The copy he gave me was made from what is known as an "autograph," which was given to Dr. White by the Committee. White was one of 92 leading scientists who worked on and produced the report.

The report contains the projections of these scientists as to what our present technology will lead to in the next 25, 50, 75, and 100 years. The report deals with eight areas, including social concerns, military technology, politics, environment, the biological revolution, etc. At the top of page one the report is labeled, "Technological Forecast. Dr. Herbert S. Bennett; Communications/ADP Laboratory; United States Army Electronics Command." The eight levels of concern dealt with in the report were "Suggested by

Harvey Brooks at the conference on 'Technology, Transfer and Innovation' held 16-17 May 1966 in Washington, DC."

The paper reads like an account of science running amok. Dr. White wanted me to especially notice the projection that within the next hundred years scientists would produce a living, breathing human-like creature that could not be detected from a normal person by external examination. Almost all of the 92 project scientists agreed with this premise. I had come to this same conclusion many years earlier. My thoughts were solely based on certain prophecies in the Bible. Wanting to elicit response from Dr. White, I responded, "Why that sounds unbelievable!"

White replied, "Well, last night I heard you teach something that most people would find hard to believe, and that is your idea that a political figure, the Antichrist, will persuade humanity to bow and worship him." Then he mused, "I just wonder if there might not be some connection between our two seemingly impossible ideas." Our conversation and pondering continued many hours into the night.

Humanity Worships the Antichrist

Indeed, the coming Antichrist will demand, and receive worship. How will this malevolent political leader accomplish this? Just imagine if the president of the USA or the prime minister of Canada or the queen of England were to announce, "I am God." Do you think there would be a massive, favorable response? Not likely, I assure you! At least not at the present.

By what means, then, will the Antichrist achieve his goal to be worshiped? See how strongly, how clearly, this is revealed as being accomplished in the following passages from the Bible:

> And all that dwell upon the earth shall worship him, whose names are not written in the book of life of the Lamb slain from the foundation of the world (Rev. 13:8).

The apostle Paul sheds light on our subject, "That man of sin shall be revealed, the son of perdition; Who opposeth and exalteth himself above all that is called God, or that is worshipped; so that he as God sitteth in the temple of God, shewing himself that he is God" (2 Thess. 2:3-4).

These Scriptures show the Antichrist taking action to abolish all religions and exalt himself as God. He is not only against Christianity, but also vents his wrath against all religions except those that accept his supremacist humanism. "And all that dwell upon the earth shall worship him."

The Apocalypse reveals the hatred of the Antichrist for all religions when it depicts him as destroying the harlot synchretical religious world system of the last days. "And the ten horns which thou sawest upon the beast, these shall hate the whore, and shall make her desolate and naked, and shall eat her flesh, and burn her with fire" (Rev. 17:16).

This will synchronize nicely with current philosophies that proclaim the deity of man, a concept which is at the very core of the New Age movement. It will also dovetail with the awe with which modern science is reverenced by masses of people today. The arrogance of humanity knows no bounds. Jesus warned of false Christs and false prophets, and later the apostles Paul and Peter wrote warnings regarding false prophets, all of which lead humanity to consider the divinity of mankind.

It will be but a short step to the moment when the Antichrist proclaims, "As the recognized political ruler over divine humanity, I proclaim my own supreme deity. I demand that you bow to worship me. When you do so you not only recognize my divinity, but also your own deity. Man is god. There is no other. God did not make man in His image, rather man fashioned a god in the image of man.

Our final step into liberation from the dark religious superstitions of the past will be when man makes man in the image of man. The "god out there" will be dethroned. The god within us will be enthroned.

The deception is complete. The whole world bows to the man of sin. The beast has come forth from his lair and the whole world wonders after him.

The Biological Revolution Is Here

The heading of a *Look* magazine article (circa 1970s) proclaimed "In the Next 25 Years Man Will Master the Secret of Creation."

Le Pointe, a French magazine, graphically portrays an artificial "man," showing how many body parts can already be replaced, thanks to the genius of modern science.

God Takes a Dim View...

The prophet Habakkuk pondered the anger of God directed toward those who try to make something alive out of inanimate matter such as metal, a wooden log, or stone:

> What profiteth the graven image that the maker thereof hath graven it; the molten image, and a teacher of lies, that the maker of his work trusteth therein, to make dumb idols? Woe unto him that saith to the wood, Awake; to the dumb stone, Arise, it shall teach! Behold, it is laid over with gold and silver, and there is no breath [He, "ruwach," meaning "spirit"] at all in the midst of it. But the Lord is in his holy temple: let all the earth keep silence before him (Hab. 2:18-20).

The word breath is "ruwach" in Hebrew, and is variously translated "breath, spirit, wind, mind."

An Act of God

In the *Look* magazine article mentioned earlier, senior editor J. Robert Moskin wrote, "In the next 25 years it is likely that man *will create life in a test tube.* He will transform dead chemicals into living material that can grow and reproduce itself. *He will perform an act of God.* That is the great scientific revolution of the era immediately ahead of us. It overshadows even the more publicized race into space. They will give us the power to manipulate the development of living things, including man himself." (Emphasis added.)

The newspaper article was datelined UPI, Buffalo, NY. "An English researcher says he has artificially created the first living and reproducing cell. Dr. James F. Danielli, director of the Center for Theoretical Biology at the State University of New York at Buffalo, made the announcement Wednesday night. . . . In a letter inviting scientific colleagues to a December 7 dinner, he announced the artificial cell creation."

Let me explain that these quotations come from the 1960s and into the 1980s when I was researching the subject. The original documents are preserved on 35 mm slides. Never did I think at that time of putting this in print. The only reason the documents are preserved in my files at all is because of the way I construct and present lectures accompanied by 35mm slides.

Let me walk through part of my slide program with you. On the screen before me is a page from the science section of *Time* magazine. This cover story is headlined "Shaping Life in the Lab." The article speaks in glowing terms of "dazzling things to come — a new alchemy that may one day turn the basest of creatures into genetic wonders."

Rorvik

David Rorvik's book *In His Image — the Cloning of a Man* swept the scientific community and created a furor of controversy.[2] Rorvik, a science writer, claims to have managed a project in which a wealthy U.S. businessman paid a hospital and doctors in a South American country to clone a child from a cell of his body. An ova was donated by a surrogate mother. The nucleus was removed from the ova, and a blood cell from the male donor was implanted in the ova. The ova was then placed back in the womb of the surrogate mother who was thus impregnated, and nine months later she gave birth to the baby boy, a clone or duplicate of his father.

According to Rorvik there now exists a young man who is a carbon copy of his father, having gotten all his genetic makeup from a cell from his father's body. That person is now about 20 years old.

Rorvik's claims created an uproar in the scientific community, but Dr. Landrum Shettles, a famous geneticist who may still live in Randolph, Vermont, says that Rorvik is entirely credible. Time will tell. One thing is sure: We are in the age of the biological revolution.

Hello, Dr. Frankenstein

Here is a *Time Magazine* cover story, "Life in the Laboratory." Add to this a cover story in *Newsweek* with the bold headline, "The Gene Doctors . . . Preparing Synthetic DNA," and you begin to get a glimpse of really weird science in operation.

Time magazine, August 6, 1990, has an article "In Search of Artificial Life," by Philip Elmer Dewitt who writes:

> Some scientists believe that things inside their computers are actually alive. What's really scary is that it may be true. . . .
>
> Can something that "lives" inside a computer actually be alive? That is the bizarre question at the heart of artificial-life research, a fast-growing scientific field that seeks to illuminate the nature of life by recreating lifelike behavior in non-living systems. . . . The most notorious computer life forms are the electronic viruses that have been injected, inadvertently or maliciously, into computer networks.

It seems to me that we would have to redefine life to accept this idea. Dewitt continues:

Are these things alive? That depends on how the term is defined. Surprisingly, there is no clear definition of "life." Most of the criteria put forward in the past are anthropocentric. Life on earth is carbon-based and built around the nucleic acids RNA and DNA, but that may be a historical accident. Most living things metabolize and multiply, but not all. Viruses have no metabolisms of their own; mules cannot reproduce. Many living things grow, but so do clouds and garbage dumps. It is the same with life in general.

Dewitt quoted Christopher Langton, a researcher at New Mexico's Los Alamos National Laboratory who gets credit for coining the term "artifical life."

Contends Langton: "Artificial life will be genuine life. It will simply be made of different stuff." This is the leap of faith made by a growing number of scientists, many of whom are associated with the Santa Fe Institute, a research facility that is the center of the artificial-life movement. "They feel like they are taking the first step into taboo territory," says Steven Levy, a New York City-based author who is writing a book on artificial life. "It's almost a religion."

Dewitt raises other sobering questions:

In the process, the researchers are asking questions that touch on some of biology's most enduring mysteries: How does nature create order from chaos? How did life emerge from non-life? What does it mean to be alive?

Of course, this is an evolutionary philosophy which I most heartily reject in its extreme uniformitarian view. In short, this author is a Genesis, page 1, creationist.

We have reviewed some of my original research,

which is preserved in our slide film document banks. It is clear that a significant number of scientists believe that life will be artificially created, the cloning of a human will be possible, and that various other ways of producing a human-like *thing* are potential.

The Big Question

Claims have been made and many questions have been asked. It is time now for a bigger question, and that is "How far will God allow man to go in his arrogant quest for self divinity?" Will man be capable of producing man in man's own image? The answer will surprise you. The Bible is not completely silent on this subject. It has a prophetic Word concerning the biological revolution of the end times.

Exploration of our 35 mm documentary storage bank continues with more evidence. Consider these clippings and headlines extracted from our film documents.

AP news feature line drawing: Caption, "According to scientists, if and when the genetic age arrives, there may be no need for sex in reproduction."

Clipping: "Leading Research Scientist Predicts . . . Human Beings Will Be Created in Laboratories Within 100 Years." This clipping quotes Dr. Danielli saying, "The important thing will be to modify man so that if we need a life form that has strong immunity to illness or one that is much smarter than humans today we will be able to create it. . . . What we want to create is something of a super-brain to cope with these tremendous challenges in the future." Dr. Danielli heads a research team financed by NASA.[3]

Weekly World News, a tabloid dated July 5, 1983, projects a sensational headline: "Scientists Create A Human Being! Doctors play God in secret laboratory and spawn a genetic nightmare." We doubt that this was true in 1983. But what is going on in hidden research laboratories today and what does tomorrow hold? The fact is that most scientific research is secret, and the general public only learns of its results after its accomplishment. This same article declares

"Human Beings Will Be Created In Laboratories Within 100 Years."

Can the screaming tabloid headlines really be true? While to most of us it doesn't seem likely, we must admit that we live in strange and changing times!

Again we are forced to ask, what limits has God placed on mankind? Will He intervene to prevent monstrosities, reminiscent of the fictional works of the legendary Dr. Frankenstein?

On the Internet

With the cloning of "Dolly" serious scientists, philosophers and theologians are forced to take a long, hard look at what is now in store for the human race.

The following e-mail file just arrived here at the research center.

"LARCHMONT, N.Y., March 4 /PRNewswire/ — Leading bioethicists, genetic researchers and legislators will be coming together at the symposium, Mammalian Cloning: The Implications for Science and Society on June 26 & 27, 1997 to address the serious issues raised by the recent advances in the field of genetic engineering. While the conference will examine the potential benefits and commercial applications of this technology such as new drug development, livestock productivity enhancement, and the protection of endangered species to name a few; its primary focus will be to provide a forum where scientific, research and ethical issues can be addressed in a systematic approach and new guidelines for continuing research can be recommended.

"The recent announcements of the successful cloning of a sheep in Scotland and the *cloning of monkeys in Oregon* have made it abundantly clear that there could be some dangerous gaps and risk-filled gray areas in the ethical standards applied to animal engineering and biomedical research necessary to advance therapeutic approaches to human disease. These advances have shown that human cloning may no longer be in the realm of fantasy nor in the far distant future; and the White House has responded by making this a top priority scientific issue. It is clear that there should be no further postponement of the establishment of ethical guidelines which incorporate the seemingly separate paradigms underlying both animal engineering biomedical research.

"Co-Sponsors of the conference include: Research! America, The Hastings Center, and The Center for Bioethics, University of Pennsylvania.

"The conference will be co-chaired by: French Anderson, MD, Director of Gene Therapy Laboratories, University of Southern California School of Medicine; Craig Ventor, PhD, President and Chair, The Institute for Genomic Research; Arthur Caplan, PhD, Director, Center for Bioethics, University of Pennsylvania Health System; and Alex Capron, LL.B., Co-Director, Pacific Center for Health Policy and Ethics.

"Speakers include Dr. Ian Wilmut, (Roslin Institute, Scotland); Neal First, PhD (Department of Reproductive Biology and Animal Biotechnology, University of Wisconsin); Leroy Walters, PhD (Kennedy Institute of Ethics, Georgetown University); Erik Parents, PhD (Hastings Center); Fr. Kevin Fitzgerald, PhD (Department of Medial Humanities, Loyola University); Lee Silver, PhD (Department of Molecular Biology, Princeton University); Dr. Robert Nelson (Institute of Religion, Texas Medical Center).

Additional Speakers will be announced.
SOURCE BioConferences International, Inc.
CO: BioConferences International, Inc.
ST: New York, District of Columbia
03/04/97 14:46 EST http://www.prnewswire.com

Another Voice in the Wilderness — 1966

The projections of Richard R. Landers almost seem tame, although most people thought them outlandish when published in 1966. The book *Man's Place in the Dybosphere* claims that "Living, breathing, self- reproducing machines are no longer just the products of imaginative science fiction. They actually exist. The machine-dominated world of the dybosphere is here."[4]

The Babel File — Genesis 11

Let's go back to Genesis. When seeking biblical solutions to hard questions it is always profitable to go back to the book of beginnings. Here is God's evaluation of what man can do. In Genesis 6 we find the account of mankind's rebellion in the building of the Tower of Babel.

> And the Lord said, Behold the people is one, and they have all one language; and this they begin to do: and now nothing will be restrained from them, which they have imagined to do (Gen. 11:6).

At Disney World's Epcot Center, I read this prominently displayed inscription: "If We Can Dream It We Can Do It."

According to Genesis 11:6, whatever man conceives in his mind he will do, unless there is direct intervention from God as was the case at the Tower of Babel.

What are scientists "imagining to do"? The late Dr. Isaac Asimov, a brilliant biochemist, formerly a teacher in one of our Ivy League colleges, and prolific author of books ranging from philosophy and science fiction to science textbooks said, "Men will not only create life but will make human beings superior to ourselves and thereby leap over millions of years of evolution. Homo Sapiens will become Homo Superior."[5]

The April 1968 issue of *Christian Life* magazine boldly carried an article titled "Made-to-Order Men." Written by two professors at Wheaton College, Dr. Ray Brand and Dr. Russell Mixter tackle the concept of genetic engineering, sperm banks, test tube babies, etc.

A Canadian issue of *Time* magazine from the 1970s ran a cover story headlined, "The New Genetics: Man Into Superman." We hear an echo of Asimov's prediction in *Time's* words, "Not only manmade man is possible but manmade superman too." Something beyond cloning!

Cloned Sheep Stirs Debate on Its Use on Humans

Gustav Niebuhr wrote the following for the *New York Times.*

The cloning of an adult mammal offers a striking example of how technology can outpace the moral and social thinking that would guide it, setting off a debate among ethicists, psychologists and theologians over how this new science might change the world.

The dawn of the era of cloning is "a little like splitting the atom," said Dr. Glenn Bucher, president of the Graduate Theological Union in Berkeley, Calif., "with enormous prospects for evil and enormous prospects for good."

Cloning seemed utterly remote until last Saturday, when an embryologist in Edinburgh, Dr. Ian Wilmut, stunned scientists and nonscientists alike by announcing that he had created a lamb from the DNA of a ewe.

Talk inevitably leaped ahead to the idea of cloning humans, a possibility that raises a host of moral, psychological and legal questions, not to mention highly likely opposition from some powerful religious authorities like the Vatican.

He said he was concerned that people would see cloning as a way to replicate themselves, to "replace" a dying child or to create someone who could be a compatible organ donor.

Rabbi Richard Address, director of the committee on bioethics of the Union of American

Hebrew Congregations, which represents 1,000 Reform synagogues, distinguished the idea of cloning humans from the development of technology to eliminate genetic diseases.

Although the intention of eliminating diseases is healing, Address said, the development of human clones seems to be closer to designing people "to our specifications," an enterprise that he likened to trying to be God.

Rabbi Moshe Tendler, a professor Jewish medical ethics at Yeshiva University in New York, said, "The real problem is whenever man has shown mastery over man, it has always meant the enslavement of man."[6]

Antichrist Dreams

A *Life* magazine article titled "The New Man" asks some serious questions: "Will man direct his own evolution?" and *"Which men will we assign to play God?"* (Emphasis added.)

Gina Kolata wrote in the *New York Times*,

When a scientist whose goal is to turn animals into drug factories announced on Saturday in Britain that his team had cloned a sheep, the last practical barrier in reproductive technology was breached, experts say, and with a speed that few if any scientists anticipated.

"For starters, quipped Dr. Ursula Goodenough, a cell biologist at Washington University in St. Louis, with cloning, "there'd be no need for men."

"But on a more serious note, Dr. Stanley Hauerwas, a divinity professor at Duke University, said that those who wanted to clone "are going to sell it with wonderful benefits" for medicine and animal husbandry. But he said he saw *"a kind of drive behind this for us to be our own creators."*[7]

The coming Antichrist will exploit a heady atmosphere of humanistic dreams. Man is God! This is, indeed, the unifying theme of the New Age movement, now embraced by over 1 billion human beings.

A *Life* magazine cover article, "Control of Life," confirms the idea that many scientists believe that we have entered the era of the "Profound and Astonishing Biological Revolution."

The November 5, 1986, edition of the *Sacramento Bee* printed an article, "Milestone in Animal Cloning — Danish scientist produces many calf embryos by separating cells." Datelined College Station, Texas, it states, "The first successful method to clone large numbers of animals has been devised by scientists manipulating tiny calf embryos." Then comes the startling statement, "There is no technical reason similar cloning could not be done in humans." Some of the experiments done by Steen Wiladsen in Denmark, the USA, and Canada seem to be revolutionary! "While Wiladsen did not originate embryo-transfer experiments, he has been a pioneer in making artificial twins, and in making *chimeric animals, such as the geen, an animal made of goat and sheep tissue."*

This gives rise to a horrifying vision of a mad world partly populated by manmade monsters that are part animal and part human.

The New Theology of Scientism

The new theology of the new world religion is simply put: Man is his own God. You do not need a redeemer, you only need a powerful meditative technique to get you in touch with your own inner deity. With the new advances of science we realize that man controls his own destiny. Was the old God the Creator? Well, now man has taken over the process of creation, and whatever the old God could do, now man can do by himself, without outside help or interference.

We have not brought these quotes and clippings to your attention to prove what has or is being done. Rather, it is to demonstrate what man believes he can do.

My Startling Prediction

I am not basing my prediction nor conclusions on the brief, tentative, highly selective, and questionable evidence presented thus far. No, my prediction is based solely on the solid foundation of God's Word, the Bible.

I predict that science will not only make life, but will produce an artificial, living, moving, thinking, talking, breathing, human-like *thing*. It will be the image of the beast, and it will be alive. It speaks, it takes action, and according to the Bible it is alive. I think that this speaks of a science *beyond cloning. The image of the beast will likely not be a clone, but a laboratory construction of some sort.*

Many Years Ago

When I was a boy a well-known evangelist was preaching in my home church in Britton, South Dakota. He taught each night on the Book of Revelation. When he came to the passage in Revelation 13 regarding the image he said, "I suppose they will have a big statue of the Antichrist and there will be a loudspeaker in it. The voice of the Antichrist will come out of the statue and people will think it is alive!"

As a young lad, with no disrespect to the evangelist, I said to my mother, "No old loudspeaker would make me think a statue was alive. I think I would walk up to the statue and kick it in the shins to see if it would say 'ouch.' " Then I wondered in my heart and mind, *What does the Bible verse about the image of the beast really mean?*

This question nagged in my mind for years. From the age of 11 I have been reading and studying the Book of Revelation. Then one day in 1954, while I was holding evangelistic services in St. Ignace, Michigan, with pastors Harley and Betty Hansel, I was pondering Revelation 13. I prayed, "God, what does this mean?" The Holy Spirit whispered deep in my heart, "When you believe what it says, you will understand what it means." Then I believed that the passage was not a figure of speech, it was literal.

False Prophet

> And deceiveth them that dwell on the earth by the means of those miracles which he had power to do in the sight of the beast; saying to them that dwell on the earth, that they should make an image to the beast, which had the wound by a sword, and did live. And he had *power to give life* unto the image of the beast, that the image of the beast should both *speak, and cause* that as many as would not worship the image of the beast should be killed (Rev. 13:14-15; emphasis added).

The image lives, speaks, and acts (causes). How might the production of a living human-like *thing* aid the Antichrist in persuading people to worship him?

The New World Religion

The new world religion could best be described as psychic humanism. We are already seeing the wedding of science and metaphysics. The New Age movement, with over 20,000 cults and Eastern world religions counted in its ranks (over one billion followers) is well suited to provide a framework of the New World Order — New World Religion.

One day the Antichrist will make a great speech to a vast audience, comprised of those present and those viewing on worldwide television. Just listen to his arrogant words, "All men are divine. Man is the only god! When you bow and worship me you are bowing to the deity of man. Everything those old religions ascribed to God is now the province of man. Now, man is god the creator.

"We have proven the deity of man. There is no god but

man! You have probably heard rumors of our greatest scientific project, the creation of a living, artificial, yet real, human person. Today you will see that it is no rumor, but a reality. We have conquered the deepest mysteries of creation. Life's profound puzzle, the very secret of life itself has yielded to our science. We are now ready to demonstrate the final proof of man's divine nature.

"You all know of the attempt on my life and how by the combined talents of science and the psychic energy of the prophet, I was brought back from death and regained life. Nations have always feared the assassination of their leaders. Now we can put all of that fear behind us, for in addition to restoring my personal life and health, science and holistic metaphysics have joined together to make a duplicate of myself. Behold!"

The Image Revealed

Then the velvet curtains part and out walks the very image of the beast. The Antichrist cries out, "Behold the genius of man! Observe! Here is the final proof of man's deity! Man has created man in the image of man! Who can deny the deity of man? Anyone who denies the divine nature of man is a traitor to the human race and is dangerous to the well-being of society. They must be put to death! Now I ask you, who is god?"

A murmur begins in the assembled audience. Well-placed servants of Apollyon begin the chant, "Man is God!" The murmur grows like a rumbling wave of sound, it crescendos to a veritable roar. "MAN IS GOD! HUMANITY IS GOD! SCIENCE IS GOD! I AM GOD! APOLLYON IS GOD! The chant rises and swells: MAN IS GOD! MAN IS GOD!"

Does it seem impossible? Turn back the pages of history. Not very long ago a man of consummate evil, a notable antichrist, Adolph Hitler, mesmerized a continent and almost conquered the world. Adolph Hitler caused the death of not only six million Jews, but also directly caused the death of over 50 million other human beings who died on the funeral pyre of World War II, offered up to the demon god Moloch as human sacrifices. And World War II was but a dress rehearsal for a global conflict that ends in the fiercest of battles — Armageddon. You see, another who is worse and more dangerous than Hitler will soon stand on the stage of the end-time drama.

Two Beasts of Revelation 13

The Antichrist and the False Prophet come to a lost world with a promise of peace, exalting and encouraging the arrogance of a race bemused with thoughts of personal deity. They curse all true believers on earth. They damn the Jews. They speak great swelling words against the God of heaven (Dan. 11:36) and send out three evil spirit emissaries to kindle the blaze of Armageddon, stoking again the fire of Moloch's hellish altar of death.

Song of Lost Hope

Songwriter Larry Norman penned the following words revealing the despair that will mantle a rebellious human race in the time of the great global trauma:

> In the midst of a war
> He offered us peace.
> He came like a lover
> From out of the east.
>
> With the face of an angel
> And the heart of a beast,
> And his intentions were
> Six Sixty Six.
>
> He walked up to the temple
> With gold in his hand,
> And he bought off the priests
> And propositioned the land.

And the world was his harlot
And laid in the sand
While the band played
Six Sixty Six.

We served at his table
And slept on the floor.
Then he starved us and beat us
And nailed us to the door.

Well, I'm ready to die,
I can't take any more.
And I'm sick of his lies and his tricks.
He told us he loved us
But that was a lie.
There was blood in his pockets
And death in his eyes.

Well my number is up
And I'm ready to die,
If the band will play
SIX-SIXTY-SIX.

Human Wisdom and Knowledge Cannot Save You

For the Christian believer there is a bright future ahead. For the one who rejects Christ only darkness, wars, and gloom. Let us seriously consider the words of the great Hebrew prophet Isaiah:

For thou hast trusted in thy wickedness: thou hast said, None seeth me. Thy wisdom and thy knowledge, it hath perverted thee; and thou hast said in thine heart, I am, and none else beside me. Therefore shall evil come upon thee; thou shalt not know from whence it riseth: and mischief shall fall upon thee; thou shalt not be able to put it off: and desolation shall come upon thee suddenly, which thou shalt not know (Isa. 47:10-11).

W.E. Vine, in his book titled *Isaiah: Prophecies, Promises, Warnings* wrote:

> The 47th chapter declares the doom of Babylon. . . . All this Babylon would bring upon herself through her treatment of God's people. . . . This has been the case with all the potentates who have been permitted to occupy the land of Palestine and hold His people in captivity, and the same thing will obtain in regard to the Antichrist in the future. Verses 8-10 depict further the character of the guilty city, her voluptuousness, her self-exaltation, as well as her self-edification in adopting the title "I AM," which alone belongs to God, her false sense of security, her sorceress and enchantments (astrology had its origin in Babylonia), her seared conscience in declaring that no eye saw her wickedness, and so virtually denying the existence and omnipresence of God. Possessed of natural wisdom and knowledge, she had used these to pervert her ways.[8]

Barnes Commentary: "I am and none else besides me." The language of pride. She regarded herself as the principal city of the world, and all others as unworthy to be named in comparison with her (comp. Note on 45:6). Language remarkably similar to this occurs in Martial's description of Rome (xii.8): *"Terrarum dea gentiumque, Roma, Cui par est nihil, et nihil secundum* — Rome, goddess of the earth and of nations, to whom nothing is equal, nothing second." This is from Albert Barnes *Notes On The Old Testament, Isaiah Vol. II.*[9]

Here are some interesting "translations" for comparison:

> Your "wisdom" and "knowledge" have caused you to turn away from me and claim that

you yourself are Jehovah. . . . That is why disaster shall overtake you suddenly — so suddenly that you won't know where it comes from — And there will be no atonement then to cleanse away your sins (Isa. 47:10-12;LB). [The Living Bible is a paraphrase, not a translation. It offers interesting commentary on some texts.]

You have trusted in your wickedness and have said, "No one sees me." Your wisdom and knowledge mislead you when you say to yourself, I am, and there is none besides me. Disaster will come upon you, and you will not know how to conjure it away. A calamity will fall upon you that you cannot ward off with a ransom; a catastrophe you cannot foresee will suddenly come upon you. Keep on, then, with your magic spells and with your many sorceries, which you have labored at since childhood. Perhaps you will succeed, perhaps you will cause terror (Isa. 47:10-12;NIV).

And you felt secure in your wickedness and said, "No one sees me," Your wisdom and your knowledge, they have deluded you: For you have said in your heart, "*I am,* and there is no one besides me." But evil will come on you which you will not know how to charm away; And disaster will fall on you for which you cannot atone, and destruction about which you do not know will come on you suddenly (Isa. 47:10-11;ASV).

For you trusted in sin, saying, "No one will see me." *Your science and learning,* themselves will overthrow you — though you said in your heart, "I shall last, if none else!" (Isa. 47:10; *The Holy Bible in Modern English* by Ferrar Fenton).

Some Will Be Amazed

Do not be surprised at the increase of knowledge in the field of biological sciences, nor by strange announcements about the cloning or creation of living creatures in the laboratory. Finally, in the Tribulation, an artificially created, living, breathing, thinking, human-like *thing* will be produced. It will not be an android, it will be a living human-like *thing*. I think that it will be demoniacally energized. It will have a soul, like an animal (Num. 31:28), but it will not have a spirit, nor will it have eternal life. Be sure of this, it is not a computer nor a television set, nor the Internet. Some will be in the presence of this being. Some will see him on television. Many could interact with him/it in the realm of virtual reality. It will look, feel, speak, and act like a human being, but it is not a human being in that it has no spirit. In using the word *create* in connection with human activity we are using the term in the secondary sense, not the primary Genesis 1:1 sense where God calls forth and creates out of nothing.

> And he had POWER TO GIVE LIFE unto the image of the beast (Rev. 13:15).

Life's Questions

There are some questions science cannot answer. What is your life? What is the purpose of your existence? Does life have meaning? Where are we going? For answers to these profound questions we must turn to God and His Holy Word, the Bible. The previous chapter on creation and evolution in the end times demonstrates the importance of this debate as we enter the final end-time realm of spiritual warfare.

Endnotes

[1]*New York Times*, February 23, 1997, by Gina Kolata.
[1]David Rorvik, *In His Image — the Cloning of a Man* (Philadelphia, PA: J.B. Lippincott Company, 1978).

[2]"Brain Grafts . . . the First Experiments," *Science*, March 1986.

[3]Richard R. Landers, *Man's Place in the Dybosphere* (Englewood Cliffs, NJ: Prentice Hall, 1966).

[4]*True* magazine interview, February 1966.

[5]W.E. Vine, *Isaiah: Prophecies, Promises, Warnings* (Grand Rapids. MI: Zondervan, 1971), p. 136-137.

[6]*New York Times*, March 1, 1997.

[7]*New York Times*, February 24, 1997, by Gina Kolata.

[8]Albert Barnes, *Notes on the Old Testament, Isaiah Vol. II.*[9] (Grand Rapids, MI: Baker Book House, 1950, p. 179).

Chapter 5

SIGN OF THE FIG TREE

From childhood I have known that the major sign of prophecy is the sign of the fig tree, the nation of Israel.

I accepted Christ as my Saviour in 1942 at the age of ten years. Mother and I went to hear a new preacher in town who was holding services in a little basement mission below Velta Carter's clothing store. We lived in the small rural town of Britton, South Dakota. Rev. Grant Wacker rented the space from the IOOF, the International Order of Odd Fellows.

Word went around our village that "the peculiar people are holding meetings in the Odd Fellows hall." I guess that was high humor for a town in which every vaudeville show that came through featured, at some point in the program, a rumpled-looking drunk who staggered around the stage amusing us with his witticisms. One line inevitably was spoken to an overly made-up lady, who bragged, "How do you like my new perfume, Jake? It's Evening in Paris." Jake responded, " Haw, haw, haw, Evening in Paris, eh? Just take a smell of this," as he waved a bottle of booze about. "This here smell is Saturday night in Britton." It always brought the house down.

Entertainment was sparse in our town, consisting mostly of the movie theater, which charged ten cents for admission, and changed the film showing every week or so. That is why we went to the new Assembly of God Pentecostal mission. Mother and I went out of curiosity, hoping to be entertained. Some ladies had told mom about the strange services and urged us to go, for a good time. We went with the poorest of motives, but God in His grace met us there and our lives were transformed.

Pastor Grant A. Wacker told me that I was his first convert. Actually mother and I went to the altar for salvation in the same service. Dad did not join the fold for another 20 years, then got saved at the age of 62 in the Assembly of God Church in Aberdeen, South Dakota.

When I was 11 years old, in 1943, God used a German evangelist, Hans Bretschneider, to introduce me to Israel. He preached and taught us about end-time prophecy, the Book of Revelation, and about Israel, which did not exist at that time. We did not know about the holocaust underway in Germany, and when Bretschneider told us what he knew about what was happening, it seemed remote and unrelated to life in Britton, South Dakota. Remember, I had never heard about Jews previous to this. There was no one in Britton who identified himself as a Jew.

Bretschneider introduced us to Abraham, Moses, and the Jewish Messiah, Jesus. He did not talk about them as a fossil people, with only a past and no future. He spoke of them as a living people with a wonderful future in the plan of God. He said that the Jews would return to Palestine and establish a new nation. That branded him as a lunatic in the eyes of non-believing outsiders. Even the Christian church people had a hard time swallowing such a novel notion. It would never happen. The *Reader's Digest* published an article, at about that same time, written by editor Frederick Painton, which stated that there never could be another Jewish nation in Palestine. Old-line denominational churches had bought into the heresy of replacement theology.

Just who did this upstart German think he was anyway, always quoting the Bible and talking about the sign of the fig tree, claiming that it was Israel, about to be reborn? He quoted the words of Jesus:

> And he spake to them a parable; Behold the fig tree, and all the trees; When they now shoot forth, ye see and know of your own selves that summer is now nigh at hand. So likewise ye, when ye see these things come to pass, know ye that the kingdom of God is nigh at hand. Verily I say unto you, This generation shall not pass away, till all be fulfilled. Heaven and earth shall pass away: but my words shall not pass away (Luke 21:29-33).

"Behold the fig tree [Israel] and all the trees [rest of the nations]." "All the trees" refers to all the nations which God has always watched, warned, and judged or blessed in accord as to how the nations treated Israel and the Jewish people. This is revealed in the Abrahamic Covenant. God will bless those who bless Israel and will curse those who curse Israel. The wrath of God is revealed at the end of the "times of the Gentiles," when Jesus comes back to fight against all the nations of the world, all of whom have sent armies to destroy Israel. Read Zechariah chapters 12-14. For a complete study of the subject of Israel, please read my book *Can Israel Survive in a Hostile World?*[1]

Through the anointed preaching of the evangelist, a fire was born in my soul for a people whom I knew not and a nation that then was not. It was not until I was in my teens that I met a person whom I knew was Jewish. Arlo Levi was a classmate and friend in Central High School in Aberdeen, South Dakota. One day I was visiting in Arlo's home, and suggested that we go to some event that was coming up. Arlo said, "I can't go, David, that is on the day of Yom Kippur."

I looked at him in amazement, exclaiming, "Arlo, are you Jewish?"

He said, "Dave, where did you think I got the name of Levi?"

Years later I shared this personal anecdote with Prime Minister Menachem Begin, who was greatly amused by it. Mrs. Lewis and I met with Mr. Begin on 15 occasions. He was always interested in sharing Bible truths regarding Israel's future destiny. I heard him tell a senior aide, Mr. Yeheil Kadeshai, that we brought inspiration and comfort to him.

Many years went by. God called me to be a Christian ambassador to the nation of Israel. In 1975 we formed the organization *Christians United For Israel,* following a prayer demonstration I led in front of the White House during the Gerald Ford administration. We displayed a large banner proclaiming our group of about one hundred clergy persons to be *Christians United for the biblical right of Israel to her land.* As our rally ended we were invited to meet President Gerald Ford's top advisor on Mideastern affairs, Mr. Robert Oakley, to come to the old Executive Office Building, where our delegation conferred with him for over an hour. We gave Oakley a letter for President Ford. Later we received a telegram from Senator "Scoop" Jackson, telling us that the letter was hand delivered to Ford.

Later, in 1978, I was one of five founders of the *National Christian Leadership Conference for Israel.* During the Reagan administration I also led this group in a similar demonstration in Lafayette Park, across from the White House in Washington, D.C. Dr. Isaac Rottenberg rented a sound truck with huge columns of speakers. I think we rattled the windows on Pennsylvania Avenue. Once again our delegation was invited to a conference. Our meeting that time was with Morton Blackwell, who was an advisor to President Ronald Reagan. On December 30, 1996, Christians United For Israel was a signatory to a full page in the *Jerusalem Post*, proclaiming support for Israel in the controversial "Jerusalem controversy."

This has been a long journey of spiritual insight, adventure, and blessing. Someday I may write a book about it. And it all began when a German evangelist reached out and touched the life of a little boy in a humble mission church in Britton, South Dakota, which lies about 10 miles south of Kidder and 40 miles from Sisseton.

The following several chapters deal with the nation of Israel — Sign of the Fig Tree.

Endnotes
[1]David Allen Lewis, *Can Israel Survive in a Hostile World?* (Green Forest, AR: New Leaf Press, 1993).

Chapter 6

JERUSALEM OUTSIDE THE WALLS

Sir Moses Montefiore and the Mishkenot Sha'ananim

The Lord doth build up Jerusalem: He gathereth together the outcasts of Israel (Psalm 147:2).

The story of Jerusalem is one of the most wonderful in the world, besides being of unparalleled importance to the human race. — Mrs. Oliphant [1]

Fulfilled prophecies of Holy Scripture demonstrate the remarkable accuracy of the Bible and attest to its divine inspiration. Of all the books ever written the Bible is unique for its prophetic content. There is nothing that can compare to its record of unerring accuracy. Whatever it predicts either has been or will be fulfilled.

One of the most important names in modern Jewish history is that of Sir Moses Montefiore, a British Jew of the last century. He is also important in the fulfillment of a major prophecy about the Holy City. God truly uses human instrumentality in fulfilling His Prophetic Word, and Montefiore was an instrument in the hand of the Lord to bring to pass a prophecy given by Zechariah 600 years before Christ lived on earth.

That prophecy has been fulfilled only in recent history. This short prophecy went unnoticed by all except the most meticulous of commentators and scholars, until recent times. Here is the prediction of Zechariah, who foresaw a time when the little walled town of Jerusalem would become a mighty metropolis!

How could Zechariah have known that his little Jerusalem would one day be a great metropolis? From the prophet's day, until the mid-19th century, Jerusalem was never more than a small walled town.

The Prophecy

Run, speak to this young man, saying, Jerusalem shall be inhabited as towns without walls for the multitude of men and cattle therein (Zech. 2:4).

The entire context of Zechariah reveals this prophecy taking place in the time period just before the Messiah's return. The prophecy is spoken for a time when Israel would be regathered in the land. The Book of Zechariah looks to the time period preceding the coming of Messiah, and foretells that coming in some detail. To completely appreciate the prophecy of Zechariah 2:4 read the whole Book of Zechariah. To merely note that the prophecy is for the day of Israel's restoration read:

So the angel that communed with me said unto me, Cry thou, saying, Thus saith the Lord of hosts; I am jealous for Jerusalem and for Zion with a great jealousy (Zech. 1:14).

Therefore thus saith the Lord; I am returned to Jerusalem with mercies: my house shall be built in it, saith the Lord of hosts, and a line shall be stretched forth upon Jerusalem. Cry yet, saying, Thus saith the Lord of hosts; My cities through prosperity shall yet be spread abroad; and the Lord shall yet comfort Zion, and shall yet choose Jerusalem (Zech. 1: 16-17).

Montefiore

Sir Moses Montefiore, a successful broker noted for his good deeds and charity, was elected sheriff of London in 1837. About the same time he was knighted by Queen Victoria. He was the first Jew to be knighted in Britain in modern times. Sir Moses was noted for his charity and good deeds in many nations.

The Jewish community in England had elected Montefiore in 1835 to be the president of its "board of deputies" which represented the welfare of not only Jews in England but also throughout the world.

Due to his success in business he was able to retire at the age of 40 and from then on pursued his passion in life, showing charity to the less fortunate. He traveled the world over, meeting with heads of states and others to promote the welfare and protection of various Jewish communities in the Diaspora.

Sir Moses in the Holy Land

Montefiore made the first of seven pilgrimages to Turkish-ruled Palestine in 1827. He found the beloved Holy City of Jerusalem in a state of disrepair and squalor. At the beginning of the 19th century, Jerusalem was surrounded by stone walls, with a population of only a few thousand Jews. (Widely varying records of the time indicate a Jewish population in Jerusalem of between 4,000 and 10,000.)

Most lived in wretched poverty. Jerusalem's tawny walls ambled around a two and one-half mile perimeter. Indeed, Jerusalem could well be described as a small town in a rural setting. Sir Moses was deeply distressed at the sad state of affairs and determined to do something about it. He determined to build fine quality homes outside the city walls. The people could then move out of the Old City and enjoy a higher standard of living.

This is how Jerusalem looked in 1860. There was nothing outside the walls. This is from a lithograph in a book by Tweedie, printed in 1860.

What he did there in the mid-19th century began the fulfillment of a prophecy uttered by Zechariah in 520 B.C.

Building Jerusalem Outside the Walled City

In 1856 construction began on the first homes in what would become the Yemen Moshe neighborhood. The very first buildings were called the Mishkenot Sha'ananim, meaning "serene dwellings."

These were the first dwellings to be built outside the walled city. In addition to using his own resources, Montefiore received money from the Judah Touro family of New Orleans, Louisiana. Touro had established the "North American Relief Society for Indigent Jews of Jerusalem, Palestine," and from this fund donated fifty thousand dollars for the project, "to ameliorate the condition of our unfortunate brethren in the Holy Land." It is doubtful if either Montefiore or Touro realized they were being instrumental in fulfilling a great biblical prophecy. But truly God uses human instrumentality to fulfill His sovereign will.

Teddy Kolleck, former mayor of Jerusalem commented, "It was the first Jewish neighborhood in Jerusalem, built outside the Old City walls." It would have been hard for anyone living before modern times to envision the sleepy little town of Jerusalem as a great, modern city. But 2,500 years ago the prophet had said, "Jerusalem shall be inhabited as towns without walls for the multitude of men and cattle therein" (Zech. 2:4).

Luxurious Living Refused

Montefiore offered the lovely dwellings at a reasonable cost to those living in the crowded Old City. He thought they would be happy to improve their living conditions, but he was wrong. They were afraid to be outside the walls at night! The area was infested with roving robber bands and brigands who searched constantly for victims. No one wanted to chance being outside the walls of Jerusalem at night!

At one point, Montefiore offered the apartments for no rent at all. A few people moved a bit of furniture and personal belongings into the new housing, but would only spend the daytime hours there. At night they returned to the safety of the walls. How could Zechariah's words come to pass?

Finally, Growth Outside Old Jerusalem

Finally, 132 years ago, Zechariah's prediction was on a course of fulfillment.

Montefiore's people hired a security force to police the area. People were then happy to move into the beautiful Mishkenot Sha'ananim. Other neighborhoods were developed outside the Old City. The Maheneh Yisrael and the Nahalat Shiv'ah areas were built in 1869. The Me'a She'arim, today a notable area inhabited by the Orthodox believers, and the Even Yisrael were constructed in 1873. The Beit Ya'akov and Mishkenot Yisrael were erected in 1979. The city outside the walls grew in well-defined neighborhoods, and today Jerusalem is composed of Zechariah's "towns without walls." What Montefiore built here was the beginning of today's Jerusalem of over 500,000 residents. It was the beginning of the fulfillment of Zechariah 2:4: "Jerusalem shall be inhabited as towns without walls for the multitude of men and cattle therein."

The city outside the walls continued to grow in distinct and well-identified neighborhoods. Modern Jerusalem today is composed of Zechariah's "towns without walls."

1967, Another Milestone

When Israel's war of independence was fought in 1948, the Mishkenot ended up being right on the border between Jordan and occupied East Jerusalem and the new state of Israel. A bleak "no man's land," it was a dangerous area and had fallen into a state of damage and disrepair. In June 1967 the Six Day War broke out. Jordan attacked Israel, and in turn the Jews took back the Old City. The Yemen Moshe became a very desirable place to live.

The Mishkenot Today

For some time the Mishkenot had fallen into disrepair. In the late 1960s, Mayor Teddy Kolleck wanted to do something special with the Mishkenot Sha'ananim because of its historical importance. After all, this was the beginning of modern Jerusalem outside the walls. A renovation was undertaken, and now many of the luxurious apartments are used to house visiting artists and writers as guests of Jerusalem. Here in the "serene dwellings" they can draw upon the inspiration of the Holy Land for their creative works. Housing in the Yemen Moshe, all around the Mishkenot, is highly desired and extremely expensive.

The Mishkenot, a long, low-slung, red-roofed complex, is the most notable section of the Yemen Moshe. It is easily spotted by the picturesque windmill that towers over the southern end of it. The windmill was part of Montefiore's plan to provide a living for the people who would move out of the Old City into the Yemen Moshe. The grinding of grain was to provide a small industry for workers. The scheme never worked, however. There is just not enough wind in Jerusalem to make it practical.

Inside the windmill you will find a small museum with pictures of the Montefiore family and some of their memorabilia on display. You will see a replica of Montefiore's horse-drawn carriage nearby. In the neighborhood, you will find a delightful five-star Kosher French restaurant, named after the Mishkenot Sha'ananim.

Endnotes

[1] Oliphant, Mrs. (sic), *Jerusalem-The Holy City, Its History and Hope* (London: Macmillan, 1893), From the introduction.

Chapter 7

MARK TWAIN IN PALESTINE

Excerpts From *Innocents Abroad* by Mark Twain

When the Jews began to return to the land in the 1800s, they found a barren wasteland. Many who traveled in the area wrote of their experiences and observations. Perhaps the most famous of these was Mark Twain (Samuel Langhorne Clemens) who wrote a two volume set of books about his world tour, titled *Innocents Abroad.*[1]

Here are some of Mark Twain's remarkable observations. Today the land is transformed and Twain would be amazed to see how the desert is blossoming like a rose (Isa. 35:1). Only the paragraph headings, in capital letters, have been added. Observers of history are the only people who can understand the present. We note that the only time the land of Palestine-Israel prospered has been when the Jews were there and in control. Twain only saw the desolation. He did not think anything desirable would ever again exist there. How wrong he was. Not only is much of the land reclaimed, covered with forests, flowers, and fruit trees, but it appears to be one of the most desired and hotly contested pieces of real estate in the world.

Innocents Abroad was first published in 1869. We are quoting from the 1899 reprinted edition.

Innocents Abroad — Chapter 45
LIVING CONDITIONS

The little children were in a pitiable condition — they all had sore eyes, and wereafflicted in various other ways. They say that hardly a native child in all the East is free of sore eyes, and that thousands of them go blind in one eye or both every year. I think this must be so, for I see many blind people every day, and I do not remember seeing any children that hadn't sore eyes. And would you suppose that an American mother could sit for an hour, with her child in her arms, and let a hundred flies roost upon its eyes all that time undisturbed? I see that every day. It makes my flesh creep.

Yesterday we met a woman riding on a little jackass, and she had a little child in her arms; honestly, I thought the child had goggles on as we approached, and I wondered how its mother could afford so much style. But when we drew near, we saw that the goggles were nothing but a camp meeting of flies assembled around each of the child's eyes, and at the same time there was a detachment prospecting its nose. The flies were happy, the child was contented, so the mother did not interfere.

Innocents Abroad — Chapter 46
TWAIN REFERS TO BIBLE PROPHECIES

To this region one of the prophecies is applied: "I will bring the land into desolation; and your enemies which dwell therein shall be astonished at it. And I will scatter you among the heathen, and I will draw out a sword after you; and your land shall be desolate and your cities waste" (Lev. 26:33).

No man can stand here by deserted Ain Mellahah and say the prophecy had not been fulfilled.

It is seven in the morning, and as we are in the country, the grass ought to be sparkling with dew, the flowers enriching the air with their fragrance, and the birds singing in the trees. But alas, there is no dew here, nor flowers, nor birds, nor trees. There is a plain and unshaded lake, and beyond them some barren mountains. The tents are tumbling, the Arabs are quarreling like dogs and cats, as usual, the campground is strewn with packages and bundles, the labor of packing them upon the backs of the mules is progressing with great activity, the horses are saddled, the umbrellas are out, and in ten minutes we shall mount and the long procession will move again. The white city of the Mellahah, resurrected for a moment out of the dead centuries, will have disappeared again and left no sign.

Innocents Abroad — Chapter 47
PALESTINE IN RUINS

Gray lizards, those heirs of ruin, of sepulchers and desolation, glided in and out among the rocks or lay still and sunned themselves. Where prosperity has reigned, and fallen; where glory has flamed, and gone out; where beauty has dwelt, and passed away; where gladness was, and sorrow is; where the pomp of life has been, and silence and death brood in its high places — there this reptile makes his home and mocks at human vanity.

Innocents Abroad — Chapter 48
FEW TREES — NO TIMBER

Magdala is not a beautiful place. It is thoroughly Syrian, and that is to say that it is thoroughly ugly and cramped, squalid, uncomfortable, and filthy — just the style of cities that have adorned the country since Adam's time, as all writers have labored hard to prove and have succeeded. The streets of Magdala are anywhere from three to six feet wide and reeking with uncleanliness. The houses are from five to seven feet high and all built upon one arbitrary plan — the ungraceful form of a dry-goods box. The sides are daubed with a smooth white plaster and tastefully frescoed aloft and aglow with disks of camel dung placed there to dry. . . . There is no timber of any consequence in Palestine. . . .

The celebrated Sea of Galilee is not so large a sea as Lake Tahoe by a good deal — it is just about two-thirds as large. And when we come to speak of beauty, this sea is no more to be compared to Tahoe than a meridian of longitude is to a rainbow. The dim waters of this pool cannot suggest the limpid brilliancy of Tahoe; these low, shaven, yellow hillocks of rocks and sand, so devoid of perspective, cannot suggest the grand peaks that compass Tahoe like a wall, and whose ribbed and chasmed fronts are clad with stately pines that seem to grow small and smaller as they climb, till one might fancy them reduced to weeds and shrubs far upward, where they join the everlasting snow. Silence and solitude brood over Tahoe; and silence and solitude brood also over this lake of Gennesaret. But the solitude of the one is as cheerful and fascinating as the solitude of the other is dismal and repellent.

Land of Solitude

It is solitude, for birds and squirrels on the shore and fishes in the water are all the creatures that are near to make it otherwise, but it is not the sort of solitude to make one dreary. Come to Galilee for that. If these unpeopled deserts, these rusty mounds of barrenness, that never, never, never do shake the glare from their harsh outlines, and fade and faint into vague perspective; that melancholy ruin of Capernaum; this stupid village of Tiberias, slumbering under its six funereal plumes of palms; yonder desolate declivity where the swine of the miracle ran down into the sea, and doubtless thought it was better to swallow a devil or two and get drowned into the bargain than have to live longer in such a place; this cloudless, blistering sky; this solemn, sail-less, tintless lake, reposing within its rim of yellow hills and low, steep banks, and looking just as expressionless and unpoetical (when we leave its sublime history out of the question) as any metropolitan reservoir in Christendom — if these things are not food for "Rock Me to Sleep, Mother," none exist, I think.

Innocents Abroad — Chapter 51
A DREARY LAND

Arriving at the furthest verge of the plain, we rode a little way up a hill and found ourselves at Endor, famous for its witch. Her descendants are there yet. They were the wildest horde of half-naked savages we have found thus far. They swarmed out of mud beehives; out of hovels of the dry-goods box pattern; out of gaping caves under shelving rocks; out of crevices in the earth. In five minutes the dead solitude of silence of the place were no more, and a begging, screeching, shouting mob were struggling about the horses' feet and blocking the way. "Baksheesh! Baksheesh! Baksheesh! Howajji, Baksheesh!" It was Magdala over again, only here the glare from the infidel eyes was fierce and full of hate. The population numbers two hundred and fifty, and more than half the citizens live in caves in the rock. Dirt, degradation, and savagery are Endor's specialty.

Innocents Abroad — Chapter 52
RUINS AND WORTHLESS SOIL

After a while we came to the shapeless mass of ruins which still bears the name of Beth-el. It was here that Jacob lay down and had that superb vision of angels flitting up and down a ladder that reached from the clouds to earth, and caught glimpses of their blessed home through the open gates of heaven.

The pilgrims took what was left of the hallowed ruin, and we pressed on toward the goal of our crusade, renowned Jerusalem.

The further we went, the hotter the sun got, and the more rocky and bare, repulsive and dreary the landscape became. There could not have been more fragments of stone strewn broadcast over this part of the world if every ten square feet of the land had been occupied by a separate and distinct stonecutter's establishment for an age. There was hardly a tree or shrub anywhere. Even the olive and cactus, those fast friends of a worthless soil, had almost deserted the country. No landscape exists that is more tiresome to the eye than that which bounds the approaches to Jerusalem. The only difference between the roads and the surrounding country, perhaps, is that there are rather more rocks in the roads than in the surrounding country.

Innocents Abroad — Chapter 56
The entire chapter

TWAIN'S FINAL OBSERVATIONS
The Curse

We visited all the holy places about Jerusalem which we had left unvisited when we journeyed to the Jordan, and then, about three o'clock one afternoon, we fell into procession and marched out at the stately Damascus Gate, and the walls of Jerusalem shut us out forever. We paused on the summit of a distant hill and took a final look and made a final farewell to the venerable city which had been such a good home to us.

For about four hours we traveled downhill constantly. We followed a narrow bridle path which traversed the beds of the mountain gorges, and when we could we got out of the way of the long trains of laden camels and asses, and when we could not we suffered the misery of being mashed up against perpendicular walls of rock and having our legs bruised by the passing freight. Jack was caught two or three times, and Dan Moult as often. One horse had a heavy fall on the slippery rocks, and the others had narrow escapes. However, this was as good a road as we had found in

Palestine, and possibly even the best, and so there was not much grumbling.

Sometimes in the glens we came upon luxuriant orchards of figs, apricots, pomegranates, and such things, but oftener the scenery was rugged, mountainous, verdureless, and forbidding. Here and there towers were perched high up on acclivities which seemed almost inaccessible. This fashion is as old as Palestine itself and was adopted in ancient times for security against enemies.

We crossed the brook which furnished David the stone that killed Goliath, and no doubt we looked upon the very ground whereon that noted battle was fought. We passed by a picturesque old Gothic ruin whose stone pavements had rung to the armed heels of many a valorous Crusader, and we rode through a piece of country which we were told once knew Samson as a citizen.

We stayed all night with the good monks at the convent in Ramleh, and in the morning got up and galloped the horses a good part of the distance from there to Jaffa, or Joppa, for the plain was as level as a floor and free from stones, and besides, this was our last march in Holy Land. These two or three hours finished, we and the tired horses would have rest and sleep as long as we wanted it. This was the plain of which Joshua spoke when he said, "Sun, stand thou still on Gibeon, and thou moon in the valley of Ajalon" (Josh. 10:12). As we drew near to Jaffa the boys spurred up the horses and indulged in the excitement of an actual race — an experience we had hardly had since we raced on donkeys in the Azores Islands.

We came finally to the noble grove of orange trees in which the Oriental city of Jaffa lies buried; we passed through the walls, and rode again down narrow streets and among swarms of animated rags, and saw other sights and had other experiences we had long been familiar with. We dismounted for the last time, and out in the offing, riding at anchor, we saw the ship! I put an exclamation point there because we felt one when we saw the vessel. The long pilgrimage was ended, and somehow we seemed to feel glad of it. [For a description of Jaffa, see *Universal Gazetteer*.] Simon the Tanner formerly lived here. We went to his house. All the pilgrims visit Simon the Tanner's house. Peter saw the vision of the beasts let down in a sheet when he lay upon the roof of Simon the Tanner's house. It was from Jaffa that Jonah sailed when he was told to go and prophesy against Nineveh, and no doubt it was not far from the town that the whale threw him up when he discovered that he had no ticket. Jonah was disobedient, and of a faultfinding, complaining disposition, and deserves to be lightly spoken of almost. The timbers used in the construction of Solomon's Temple were floated to Jaffa in rafts, and the narrow opening in the reef through which they passed to the shore is not an inch wider or a shade less dangerous to navigate than it was then. Such is the sleepy nature of the population of the only good seaport Palestine has now and always had. Jaffa has a history and a stirring one. It will not be discovered anywhere in this book. If the reader will call at the circulating library and mention my name, he will be furnished with books which will afford him the fullest information concerning Jaffa.

So ends the pilgrimage. We ought to be glad that we did not make it for the purpose of feasting our eyes upon fascinating aspects of nature, for we should have been disappointed — at least at this season of the year. A writer in Life in the Holy Land observes:

Monotonous and uninviting as much of the Holy Land will appear to persons accustomed to the almost constant verdure of flowers, ample streams, and varied surface of our own country, we must remember that its aspect to the Israelites after the weary march of 40 years through the desert must have been very different.

Which all of us will freely grant. But it truly is "monotonous and uninviting," and there is no sufficient reason for describing it as being otherwise.

Of all the lands there are for dismal scenery, I think Palestine must be the prince. The hills are barren, they are dull of color, they are unpicturesque in shape. The valleys are unsightly deserts fringed with a feeble vegetation that has an expression about it of being sorrowful and despondent. The Dead Sea and the Sea of Galilee sleep in the midst of a vast stretch of hill and plain wherein the eye rests upon no pleasant tint, no striking object, no soft picture dreaming in a purple haze or mottled with the shadows of the clouds. Every outline is harsh, every feature is distinct, there is no perspective — distance works no enchantment here. It is a hopeless dreary, heartbroken land.

Small shreds and patches of it must be very beautiful in the full flush of spring, however, and all the more beautiful by contrast with the far-reaching desolation that surrounds them on every side. I would like much to see the fringes of the Jordan in springtime, and Shechem, Esdraelon, Ajalon, and the borders of Galilee — but even then these spots would seem mere toy gardens set at wide intervals in the waste of a limitless desolation.

A Land in Sackcloth

Palestine sits in sackcloth and ashes. Over it broods the spell of a curse that has withered its fields and fettered its energies. Where Sodom and Gomorrah reared their domes and towers, that solemn sea now floods the plain, in whose bitter waters no living thing exists — over whose waveless surface the blistering air hangs motionless and dead — about whose borders nothing grows but weeds, and scattering tufts of cane, and that treacherous fruit and promises refreshment to parching lips, but turns to ashes at the touch. Nazareth is forlorn; about that ford of Jordan where the hosts of Israel entered the Promised Land with songs of rejoicing, one finds only a squalid camp of fantastic Bedouins of the desert; Jericho the accursed lies a moldering ruin today, even as Joshua's miracle left it more than three thousand years ago; Bethlehem and Bethany, in their poverty and their humiliation, have nothing about them now to remind one that they once knew the high honor of the Saviour's presence; the hallowed spot where the shepherds watched their flocks by night, and where the angels sang, "Peace on earth, good will to men," is untenanted by any living creature and unblessed by any feature that is pleasant to the eye. Renowned Jerusalem itself, the stateliest name in history, has lost all its ancient grandeur and is become a pauper village; the riches of Solomon are no longer there to compel the admiration of visiting Oriental queens; the wonderful temple which was the pride and the glory of Israel is gone, and the Ottoman crescent is lifted above the spot where, on that most memorable day in the annals of the world, they reared the Holy Cross. The noted Sea of Galilee, where Roman fleets once rode at anchor and the disciples of the Saviour sailed in their ships, was long ago deserted by the devotees of wars and commerce, and its borders are a silent wilderness; Capernaum is a shapeless ruin; Magdala is the home of beggared Arabs; Bethsaida and Chorazin have vanished from the earth, and the "desert places" round about them, where thousands of men once listened to the Saviour's voice and ate the miraculous bread, sleep in the hush of a solitude that is inhabited only by birds of prey and skulking foxes.

Palestine is desolate and unlovely. And why should it be otherwise? Can the *curse* of the Deity beautify a land? Palestine is no more of this workday world. It is sacred to poetry and tradition — it is dreamland.

Chapter 8

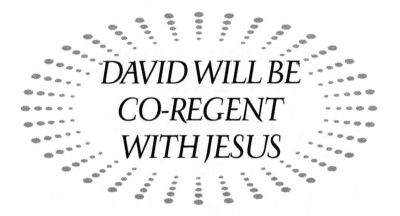

DAVID WILL BE CO-REGENT WITH JESUS

Co-Regents in the Millennium

In our book *Prophecy 2000* we stated that both the Church and National Israel will play a role in the coming Messianic Kingdom. The millennial kingdom will be personally governed by Jesus Christ and His resurrected ancestor, King David, who will act as co-regent with Christ.

Several readers wrote asking for the biblical basis of this concept. One pastor wrote: "I have never heard of such an idea and when I questioned the proprietor of the bookstore, an ordained Church of God minister, if he knew anything about it, he recommended that I write to David Lewis and make my inquiry directly."

Here is my answer: Actually all believers will rule and reign with Christ in the Millennium, but David is afforded special honors. I take the following references to David literally:

> And I will set up one shepherd over them,
> and he shall feed them, even my servant David; he
> shall feed them, and he shall be their shepherd
> (Ezek. 34:23).

The "I" of "I will set up one shepherd . . ." is the Lord
Jesus. The shepherd prince is David, as shown in the next
verse:

> And I the Lord will be their God, and my
> servant *David a prince among them*; I the Lord
> have spoken it (Ezek. 34:24).

> And they shall dwell in the land that I have
> given unto Jacob my servant, wherein your fa-
> thers have dwelt; and they shall dwell therein,
> even they, and their children, and their children's
> children for ever: and *my servant David shall be
> their prince for ever* (Ezek. 37:25).

In Ezekiel 44:3 Christ is referred to as the prince — but
not as Prince David. "It is for the prince; the prince, he shall
sit in it to eat bread before the Lord; he shall enter by the way
of the porch of that gate, and shall go out by the way of the
same." This passage evidently refers to Jesus. Some of the
"prince" passages could mean Christ or David. But in those
where David is named it means David.

Commentators are divided in opinion as to whether the
prince in Ezekiel 45 refers to Jesus or David. My view is that
since Messiah Jesus owns all the world, He does not need an
allotted portion. Therefore the passage most surely refers to
David who will be given a portion in the land.

> And a portion shall be for the prince on the
> one side and on the other side of the oblation of the
> holy portion, and of the possession of the city,
> before the oblation of the holy portion, and before
> the possession of the city, from the west side
> westward, and from the east side eastward: and

the length shall be over against one of the portions, from the west border unto the east border (Ezek. 45:7).

Other similar passages refer to David the prince who rules over Israel. "All the people of the land shall give this oblation for the prince in Israel" (Ezek. 45:16).

Even though the sacrifices of the Millennium are commemorative and memorial in nature, not redemptive or propitiatory, it seems unlikely that Jesus himself would make sacrifices. The prince here is therefore David. Notice the prince prepares a sin offering for himself, which Jesus would not do. "And upon that day shall the prince prepare for himself and for all the people of the land a bullock for a sin offering" (Ezek. 45:22).

The making of animal sacrifices in a millennial temple are memorials, as the New Covenant ordinance of communion is a memorial. "After the same manner also he took the cup, when he had supped, saying, This cup is the new testament in my blood: this do ye, as oft as ye drink it, in remembrance of me. For as often as ye eat this bread, and drink this cup, ye do shew the Lord's death till he come" (1 Cor. 11:25-26).

The same holds true for the following references:

> And the prince shall enter by the way of the porch of that gate without, and shall stand by the post of the gate, and the priests shall prepare his burnt offering and his peace offerings, and he shall worship at the threshold of the gate: then he shall go forth; but the gate shall not be shut until the evening (Ezek. 46:2). (Refers to David.)

> And the burnt offering that the prince shall offer unto the Lord in the sabbath day shall be six lambs without blemish, and a ram without blemish (Ezek. 46:4). (Refers to David.)

Now when the prince shall prepare a voluntary burnt offering or peace offerings voluntarily unto the Lord, one shall then open him the gate that looketh toward the east, and he shall prepare his burnt offering and his peace offerings, as he did on the sabbath day: then he shall go forth; and after his going forth one shall shut the gate (Ezek. 46:12). (Refers to David.)

Thus saith the Lord God; If the prince give a gift unto any of his sons, the inheritance thereof shall be his sons'; it shall be their possession by inheritance (Ezek. 46:16). (Refers to David.)

But if he give a gift of his inheritance to one of his servants, then it shall be his to the year of liberty; after it shall return to the prince: but his inheritance shall be his sons' for them (Ezek. 46:17). (Refers to David.)

Moreover the prince shall not take of the people's inheritance by oppression, to thrust them out of their possession; but he shall give his sons inheritance out of his own possession: that my people be not scattered every man from his possession (Ezek. 46:18). (Refers to David.)

And the residue shall be for the prince, on the one side and on the other of the holy oblation, and of the possession of the city, over against the five and twenty thousand of the oblation toward the east border, and westward over against the five and twenty thousand toward the west border, over against the portions for the prince: and it shall be the holy oblation; and the sanctuary of the house shall be in the midst thereof (Ezek. 48:21). (Refers to David.)

Moreover from the possession of the Levites, and from the possession of the city, being in the midst of that which is the prince's, between the border of Judah and the border of Benjamin, shall be for the prince (Ezek. 48:22). (Refers to David.)

Hosea refers to the re-gathering of the children of Israel, in the last days, and speaks of David being king — although David has long been dead when Hosea writes. Hence this is David after the resurrection, reigning with Christ in the Millennium:

Afterward shall the children of Israel return, and seek the Lord their God, and David their king; and shall fear the Lord and his goodness in the latter days (Hos. 3:5).

Chapter 9

U.S. EMBASSY SHOULD MOVE TO JERUSALEM

Why, of all nations, is Israel treated most frequently by a double standard of judgment? From what seething pit of anti-Semitism do the crooked dealings of the Gentile nations come forth?

The capital of Israel is Jerusalem. Embassies of foreign nations belong in the capital city of the host nation. Yet, since 1948 the United States has its embassy in Tel Aviv. What madness is this? I know of no nation in the world, only Israel, that is treated in this insulting and slanderous manner.

Let's make this real plain and simple. Someday the country of Cuba and the USA might decide to make peace, normalize relations, exchange ambassadors, and open embassies in the respective nations. Havana is the capital of Cuba. That is where we would build our embassy and position our ambassador.

Suppose the president of Cuba said, "I will not recognize Washington, D.C. as the capital of the United States of America. You took that land from the Indians and we

Cubans think that Washington should be an international-
ized city. We propose to put our Cuban embassy in Portland,
Oregon." We would send such an insolent Cuban ambassador packing back to Havana, and wash our hands of the
whole thing. There would be no diplomatic relations between the U.S. and Cuba.

Jerusalem has never, in all of history, been the capital
of any nation other than Israel, the Jewish people.

Israel has proven to be a true friend of the USA, our
only reliable ally in the Mideast. Israel has the only true
democracy in the Mideast. Israel, more than any other
nation, has voted for the interests of the USA in the United
Nations. I ask you, why have we treated our true friend in
such a way as this? Now is the time to implement the
decision of both the House and the Senate to move the U.S.
embassy to Jerusalem

In March 1995, 93 percent of the U.S. senate signed a
letter sent by New York Senators Alfonse D'Amato (R) and
Pat Moynihan (D) to Secretary of State Warren Christopher,
stating their belief that the U.S. embassy, currently located
in Tel Aviv, should be moved to Jerusalem within the time
frame of the peace process, or by 1999.

In April, Sen. Jon Kyl (R-AZ) announced his proposal
for new legislation which would provide funding for the
U.S. embassy in Israel, only if the administration announced
by October that the embassy will relocate to Jerusalem and
if the U.S. recognizes Jerusalem as the capital of Israel.

In the following month, Senate majority leader and
leading Republican presidential contender Bob Dole (R-
KS) introduced the bill in the Senate, where it passed with
flying colors. The bill allocated $105 million for site surveys
and land acquisition.

A similar bill was offered in the House by Speaker
Newt Gingrich, and it passed. Now we ask why the construction is delayed. It will shock you to learn that some American Jews are resisting the embassy project, fearful that it will

anger the PLO. Many American-Jewish leaders are simply afraid to speak out for fear of being accused of having dual loyalties. I can understand their frustration and fears. That is why it is so important for you and I as Christians with no political agenda, to speak out to our congressmen and senators to hasten the building of the U.S. embassy on the recently acquired land in Jerusalem. Christians must boldly declare themselves on this vital issue and send a message to the enemies of Israel who are still, in spite of all the smoke and mirrors rhetoric, bent on the destruction of all Israel. No one can accuse us of having dual loyalties.

Pandering?

While some saw Mr. Dole's action as little more than pandering to the Jewish and evangelical Christian vote before his run for the presidency, it was a hard charge to press against the (then) 53-year-old Mr. Kyl. He is a Presbyterian who had just begun his first six-year term in the Senate from a state which has some 72,000 Jews, about 1.8 percent of the population.

During his four terms in the House of Representatives, Mr. Kyl earned a reputation in pro-Israel circles as one of Congress' leading advocates of the U.S.-Israel program to develop the Arrow missile. A former member of the House Armed Services Committee, he was an ardent opponent of the Clinton administration's plans to make high-quality satellite technology available to Arab states.

For Mr. Kyl, moving the embassy is long overdue. "It's easy for politicians who support Israel to say the embassy belongs in Jerusalem. But I have seen so many politicians focus on words, not action. Next year is the 3,000th anniversary of the city since King David moved the capital from Hebron. I thought: *This is the time.*"

Silly Argument

He does not think much of the Clinton administration's argument that moving the embassy runs counter to America's policy of not recognizing Israel's sovereignty over the city, and could endanger the Israeli-Palestinian peace process.

"The argument has been raised that now is not the time because it would upset the delicate negotiations. There has hardly been a time, except during a time of war, when Israel has not been involved in delicate negotiations. It seemed to us that while there might be some temporary disruption, it will actually be helpful in the long run," he said.

He maintained that the Palestinians "probably need some realism injected into this, because obviously they have people whom they're trying to please who are hard-liners they can never please."

Helpful Move

"Ironically, it's somewhat beneficial to them to finally get this out on the table so that they can go back and say: 'Look, there are certain things that we're just not going to be able to get, so stop holding out,' " he said, adding that since Israel has stated its intention to retain sovereignty over all of Jerusalem, "it is not honest for the U.S. to hold out the hope to the Palestinians that they're going to be able to prevent Israel from maintaining control over the city."

Although he has visited Israel three times, he has no immediate plans to return. However, he said, he intends to be in Jerusalem when "the first spade of dirt is turned" for the new embassy.

While the State Department, Clinton administration, and the Rabin government were less than enthusiastic about the Jerusalem bill, many observers see the legislation as little more than the fulfillment of one of President Clinton's campaign promises. During the 1992 campaign, he promised to move the embassy from Tel Aviv to Jerusalem and to recognize Jerusalem as the state's capital. Mr. President, now that you have been elected to a second term in office, isn't it time for action? We ask that you pursue the building of the USA Embassy in Jerusalem with all possible haste.

Merge

Now that the legislation has been passed, the U.S. embassy in Tel Aviv will probably be merged with the U.S. consulate in Jerusalem. The consulate in Jerusalem has a notorious reputation among American Jews in Israel, who say it operates mainly to help Arabs and is not very responsive to the needs of Jews living in Jerusalem. American parents living in Israel who want to register their children as Americans have frequently reported that the Jerusalem consulate will not print Israel on any documents.

Not surprisingly, Arab Americans did not greet the news of Mr. Kyl's proposed legislation happily. In the Saudi daily paper, Asharq al-Awsat, Dr. James Zogby, president of the Washington-based Arab American Institute praised the Clinton administration for "remaining quite firm in its determination to adhere to the terms of the peace process."

Dr. Zogby also had kind words for U.S. Ambassador to Israel Martin Indyk, who at his Senate confirmation hearings, delivered a strongly worded rebuke to those who support moving the embassy. "It is the President's feeling — the administration's feeling — that we should do nothing to undermine or pre-empt those negotiations, that we should wait and let the parties sort out this very sensitive issue before doing anything," he said.

Fairer

Those who support the move say it would be fairer to all parties not to allow the Arabs to harbor any hope that Israel will grant them sovereignty over any part of Jerusalem. Also, moving the embassy to Jerusalem is popular not only in Congress, but throughout the country. "The majority of Americans in every poll support a united Jerusalem as the capital of Israel and placement of our embassy there," said Richard Hellman, president of the Christians' Israel Public Action Campaign.

The Christian Israel Public Affairs Committee (CIPAC)

headed up by Richard Hellman in Washington, D.C. was strongly supportive of Mr. Kyl's legislation, and urged all concerned Americans to call their senators and ask them to co-sponsor the bill to move the Embassy to Jerusalem. The response to CIPAC's call to action was heeded by many Christians, and we believe this had a strong affect on our legislators.

Split Jewish Community

Even Dr. Zogby recognized he would have an uphill fight with everyone but Jewish Americans, who he saw as split on the effort. Fortunately, the bill in favor of Israel was passed. Now is the time to demand action on this matter.

"Those who want to force the issue are quite pleased that their efforts have so far won the support of the Senate. Even the 1996 Republican presidential candidate, Bob Dole signed the letter — a fact which has raised genuine concerns among Moslem and Arab-American Republicans who were supporting his campaign," Zogby wrote.

Dr. Zogby had placed his hopes on the administration's ability to derail Congress. "One might recall that President Reagan faced the same pressure and he, too, resisted despite having promised to support such an embassy move during the 1980 campaign against President Carter," he wrote.

Vatican Interference

Mr. Dole's legislation came on the heels of a press report issued by the Vatican, calling for the diminution or cessation of plans by the State of Israel and world Jewry to celebrate the 3,000th anniversary of Jerusalem as a city.

Responding, Rabbi Fabian Schonfeld, chairman of the Rabbinical Council of America's Interfaith Committee, expressed the RCA's "great alarm" at the report.

"The only time during the past 2,000 years that the religious prerogatives of every faith community within the confines of Jerusalem have been respected, has been since the Israeli forces liberated the Old City in 1967. It is only under Israeli rule that members of all other religions have enjoyed full access to their shrines. This fact has been true even of the Temple Mount, the holiest and most revered location in all Judaism. Nevertheless, Israel sustains access to an Islamic mosque," he said.

In a prepared statement, the RCA called on the Israeli government and people "not to be deterred from implementing all celebratory plans" and called upon world Jewry "and people of good faith to commemorate this momentous event - the 3,000th anniversary of Jerusalem with the proper religious, educational, and celebratory events signifying a united and unified Jerusalem, the eternal capital of the Jewish people, during the upcoming year." (*The Jewish Voice,* June 1995).

Beyond all political considerations, I propose that the USA should recognize the uniqueness of Jerusalem by carrying out the plan to build a new U.S. embassy in Jerusalem.

Jerusalem — a Special City

Jerusalem is the only city in the whole world that God ever designated as His own city, a Holy City. Not Rome, not New York, nor Chicago, Paris, Geneva, Brussels — only Jerusalem is the Holy City, God's special bit of real estate.

The following references are a partial concordance of the words holy city.

> And the rulers of the people dwelt at Jerusalem: the rest of the people also cast lots, to bring one of ten to dwell in Jerusalem the holy city, and nine parts to dwell in other cities (Neh. 11:1).

> All the Levites in the holy city were two hundred fourscore and four (Neh. 11:18).

> For they call themselves of the holy city, and stay themselves upon the God of Israel; the Lord of hosts is his name (Isa. 48:2).

Awake, awake; put on thy strength, O Zion; put on thy beautiful garments, O Jerusalem, the holy city: for henceforth there shall no more come into thee the uncircumcised and the unclean (Isa. 52:1).

The sons also of them that afflicted thee shall come bending unto thee; and all they that despised thee shall bow themselves down at the soles of thy feet; and they shall call thee, The city of the Lord, The Zion of the Holy One of Israel (Isa. 60:14).

Seventy weeks are determined upon thy people and upon thy holy city, to finish the transgression, and to make an end of sins, and to make reconciliation for iniquity, and to bring in everlasting righteousness, and to seal up the vision and prophecy, and to anoint the most Holy (Dan. 9:24).

Thus saith the Lord; I am returned unto Zion, and will dwell in the midst of Jerusalem: and Jerusalem shall be called a city of truth; and the mountain of the Lord of hosts the holy mountain (Zech. 8:3).

Then the devil taketh him up into the holy city, and setteth him on a pinnacle of the temple (Matt. 4:5).

And came out of the graves after his resurrection, and went into the holy city, and appeared unto many (Matt. 27:53).

But the court which is without the temple leave out, and measure it not; for it is given unto the Gentiles: and the holy city shall they tread under foot forty and two months (Rev. 11:2).

And I John saw the holy city, new Jerusalem, coming down from God out of heaven, prepared as a bride adorned for her husband (Rev. 21:2).

And he carried me away in the spirit to a great and high mountain, and shewed me that great city, the holy Jerusalem, descending out of heaven from God (Rev. 21:10).

And if any man shall take away from the words of the book of this prophecy, God shall take away his part out of the book of life, and out of the holy city, and from the things which are written in this book (Rev. 22:19).

Chapter 10

RABIN
ASSASSINATED

In the twilight, in the evening, in the black
and dark night (Prov. 7:9).

Night had fallen over the Holy Land. Tel Aviv was
alive with the sound of music and hopes for peace were in the
air. Not known to join frequently in public singing, the
Prime Minister surprised those around him by unfolding the
song sheet and lifting his voice singing "Shir ha-shalom —
The Song of Peace." The words swelled and crescendoed
from the lips of the assembled crowd. Yitzhak Rabin was
overjoyed with the enthusiastic throng of over 100,000
Israelis who had shown up for the peace rally. But now the
song sheet, which he folded and put in his shirt pocket, is
covered with his blood.

Yigal Amir, a fiery young zealot, a political extremist,
lurked near the path Rabin would walk to his automobile.
Amir, posing as a driver for the prime minister's entourage,
walked directly behind the leader of Israel. He pulled a gun
and fired into Mr. Rabin's body two times. One of the leaden

slugs dealt a fatal wound. The police said Amir came out of the crowd in Tel Aviv's Kings of Israel Square and fired three shots with a Beretta pistol. Rabin, hit in the back and stomach, died 90 minutes later. The third bullet wounded a bodyguard. Steven Wulf, who wrote in *Time*: "The hollow-point bullets smashed into Rabin, who had always refused to wear a bulletproof vest. One ruptured his spleen; the other severed major arteries in his chest and shattered his spinal cord, drenching the leaflet in his pocket, the "Song of Peace," in blood."

Whether or not he made the right decisions in the peace process, we must decry this foul deed of hate and violence. All people of good will and conscience must strongly renounce and resist this type of behavior.

Israel is a democracy. Never had this small nation experienced the murder of one of its leaders at the hand of a fellow Jew. Likud leaders were quick to denounce this new Jewish terrorism. Benjamin Netanyahu, leader of the conservative party made it clear that Amir's behavior was unacceptable. He declared that while strong disagreement exists between Labor and Likud, issues should be settled by ballots, not bullets. Israel has always taken pride in its democracy which, while often verbally violent, allows peaceful transition of power.

Yigal Amir, Assassin

TEL AVIV, Israel (Nov. 6) Reuters — "A Jewish yeshiva student Yigal Amir confessed in a Tel Aviv court Monday to killing Israeli Prime Minister Yitzhak Rabin, saying: "I acted alone but maybe with God." Police said his brother Hagai Amir was an accomplice who prepared at least one of the dumdum bullets that smashed into Rabin at a peace rally in Tel Aviv Saturday.

Amir said he shot the Israeli leader because he was handing over land to Palestinians. He called Rabin a groveler who was "not my prime minister."

Police told a magistrate they were investigating if the 25-year-old law student belonged to an illegal group, the shadowy extremist organization known as Eyal.

"I did not commit the act to stop the peace process because there is no such concept as the peace process, it is a process of war," Amir said, using his court appearance to air views.

The court ordered Amir held for 15 days while police prepared possible charges, including premeditated murder, the attempted murder of Rabin's bodyguard, and participation in an illegal organization. At a later hearing in Tel Aviv, a magistrate ordered the killer's brother, also arrested Saturday, held for seven days. "He [Hagai Amir] took a bullet, drilled a hole in it and turned it into a lethal bullet which causes far more damage than a regular one," a police officer told the court in a transcript carried by Israel's domestic news agency Itim. A dumdum bullet has a cut in its point that causes it to expand on impact. Police said one of the bullets the brother prepared was taken from Rabin's body.

Hagai Amir "was a willing accomplice in this assassination, even if he only failed to prevent the crime," the officer said. "On the day of the incident they both sat and watched television and Hagai saw him (Yigal) leave. We believe he knew where he was going and didn't try to stop him."

The Itim report quoted the assassin's brother as telling the judge: "I added an iron pellet to the tip of the bullet. This created a hollowness which enabled the bullet to be more accurate, and nothing else."

The man who admitted to Israel's first assassination of a prime minister sat calmly during his court appearance, hands clasped and flanked by two policemen." — Reuters.

Dignitaries, heads of state, diplomats, and friends came from all over the world to Mount Herzl in Jerusalem. They came to attend the funeral of Prime Minister Yitzhak Rabin, to pay their respects, to speak words of condolence to his surviving wife and children. Perhaps the most poignant words of eulogy were spoken by Rabin's granddaughter.

Rabin's Granddaughter

The lovely Noa Ben-Artzi Philosof, brought tears to the eyes of many with her eulogy of her slain grandfather, given at his funeral on Mount Herzl in Jerusalem.

Forgive me if I do not want to talk about peace. I want to talk about my grandfather. You always awake from a nightmare but since yesterday I only awake into a nightmare — the nightmare of life without you and that is impossible to fathom.

The television does not stop broadcasting your pictures and you are so alive and real that I can almost touch you, but only just, because I can't anymore.

Grandfather, you were the pillar of fire in front of the camp and now we are just a camp left alone in the dark and we are so cold and sad.

I know they are speaking in terms of a national disaster. But how can you try to console an entire nation or let it share in your private pain when grandmother cannot stop crying and we are mute, feeling the vast emptiness now that you are gone?

Few really knew you. They can say many

things about you but I feel they do not know at all the enormous extent of the pain and tragedy.

And yes, this is a holocaust — at least for us, the family and friends — because we are left without a pillar of fire.

Grandfather, you were and still are our hero. I wanted you to know that in everything I've done in life, I saw you before my eyes.

Your esteem and love were with us in every step we took and along every road we walked. We live in the light of your values, always.

You never abandoned us and now you have been abandoned. And now here you are, my eternal hero, cold and alone and I can do nothing to save you. You are so wonderful.

Great men have already eulogized you but no one has felt, like I have, the caress of your warm and soft hands, or your warm embrace which was reserved for us alone and your half-smile which always told me so much. That same smile, is no longer and froze with you.

I harbor no feelings of revenge because the pain and my loss are so great — too great. The earth crumbled under our feet and somehow we are trying to sit in the empty space that is left — but with little success.

I cannot finish but apparently a strange hand, a miserable hand has already finished for me.

Given no choice, I part with you, my hero, and ask you to rest in peace and think of us and miss us because here down below we love you so much.

Angels in heaven who are with you now, I ask you to protect him, and protect him well because you are deserving of this protection.

We love you, grandfather, forever.

Rabin's View on Terrorism

"If you ask me what is the obstacle to the implementation [of the peace plan], it is terror. Arafat stopped the terrorism by the P.L.O. No Israeli has been killed by them since the end of 1992. Terror is carried out mainly by the Hamas and the Islamic Jihad with the clear purpose of undermining the peace process. We face a unique kind of terrorism — the suicidal terror mission. There is no deterrent to a person who goes with high explosives in his car or in his bag and explodes himself. We find remnants of his body. Sometimes you can't identify him. Is the peace process reversible? It might be. But only if terror will succeed."

Little did anyone know or even think that Rabin would be struck down by a terrorist. Not an Arab, but a fellow Jew.

A Wider Conspiracy Theory

There is a conspiracy of her prophets in the midst thereof, like a roaring lion ravening the prey; they have devoured souls; they have taken the treasure and precious things; they have made her many widows in the midst thereof (Ezek. 22:25).

Yigal Amir is a member of Eyal, a little-known Jewish underground militant group. This accused assassin is now in custody in an Israeli prison. Daily we are learning more about his clandestine band. Other than in their discussion groups, they seem to have been involved in no overt terrorist activities prior to the killing of Prime Minister Yitzhak Rabin. Eyal appears, at the moment, to have only 12 members, who are described as Jewish religious extremists.

"They have secret meetings and maybe they hold (arms) training sessions, but they have never been linked to any serious terrorist activity," said Ehud Sprinzak, a professor at Hebrew University who has specialized in studies of Jewish militants. Eyal "was formed at the end of 1991 or beginning of 1992 by students at Tel Aviv University," according to Sprinzak.

Sprinzak said Eyal may have "offshoots" at Bar Ilan — a religious university near Tel Aviv where Rabin's accused killer Yigal Amir and Eyal head Avishai Raviv studied. He said, "They wanted to prove to the Kahanists it was possible to be more extreme, but except for a lot of rhetoric, they weren't," Sprinzak said.

According to Sprinzak, Avishai Raviv, the head of Eyal, in custody on suspicion of conspiring to kill Rabin, "wasn't needed because Amir seems like a serious guy, capable of planning and carrying out the killing by himself." Sprinzak expressed doubt that Raviv was involved in a conspiracy. "But I wouldn't be surprised if they talked and talked and talked and finally somebody decided to do it," he said. Others strongly disagree with the Sprinzak theory. Some very odd aspects to this "conspiracy" surfaced in the *Jerusalem Report Magazine.*

Rabin Cursed by Kabbalist Black Magic

Saturday, November 4, 1995. A day that will go down in history. It was early afternoon in Missouri. My predated November 16 issue of *The Jerusalem Report* magazine had just arrived in the mail. I sat in my bedroom chair. CNN was on the television, muted. I glanced up occasionally to see what was on. I started to read an article In the *Jerusalem Report* titled, "Invoking the Spirits." What is this?" I mused. I could hardly believe my eyes as I read;

> *Yitzhak Rabin does not have long to live.* The angels have their orders. Suffering and death await the prime minister, or so say the kabbalists who have cursed him with the pulsa denura — Aramaic for "lashes of fire" — for his "heretical" policies. "He's inciting against Judaism," says the Jerusalem rabbi, who clad in tefillin, read out the most terrifying of curses in the tradition of Jewish

mysticism — opposite Rabin's residence on the eve of Yom Kippur.

"And on him, Yitzhak, son of Rosa, known as Rabin," the Aramaic text stated, "we have permission . . . to demand from the angels of destruction that they take a sword to this wicked man . . . to kill him . . . for handing over the land of Israel to our enemies, the sons of Ishmael.

The rabbi, who won't have his name published but identifies himself as a member of the right-wing Kach movement, says the curse generally works within 30 days. That put the expiry date — for Rabin or the curse — in early November.

For Jewish mystics of both North African and East European descent, curses taken from the tradition of "practical kabbalah" are heavy weaponry — not to be used every day, but certainly available in wars, religious struggles, and even political battles. Not only the ultra-Orthodox but many traditional-leaning Israelis regard them with the utmost seriousness.

Invoking the pulsa denura is a perilous undertaking, for if the ceremony is not performed in a strictly prescribed fashion, it can strike the conjurers themselves.

Before Rabin, the last person so cursed was Saddam Hussein. One day during the 1991 Gulf War, as Scuds rained down on Israel, a minyan of fasting kabbalists gathered at the tomb of the prophet Samuel just outside Jerusalem. There they entered a dark cave, where one of the holy men placed a copper tray on a rock and lit the 24 black candles he'd placed on it. As the mystics circled the candles, they chanted the curse seven times, calling on the angels not merely to visit death upon "Saddam the son of Sabha," but to ensure that his wife was given to another man.

That done, small lead balls and pieces of earthenware were thrown on the candles and the shofar was sounded. "The black candles," explains *Yediot Aharonot* journalist Amos Nevo, who documented the ceremony, "symbolize the person being cursed. When they're put out, it's as if the person's soul is being extinguished." Lead, he says, is for the ammunition in the war against the cursed one, earthenware symbolizes death, and the shofar opens the skies so the curse will be heard.

With Saddam still in power, there would appear to have been a technical hitch. "Don't worry, his end will be bitter," says Moshe Nimni, aide to Rabbi Yitzhak Kadouri, the oldest and most prominent of the North African mystics in Israel, who was one of the curse-casters. Besides, he says, Saddam is plagued by an international boycott, and his daughters and their husbands have deserted him.

For Rabin and Saddam, the experience of Gershon Agron, Jerusalem mayor in the fifties, should be sobering. When Agron initiated the first pool in the capital where men and women could swim together, he was cursed by rabbis of the extreme ultra-Orthodox Edah Haredit, says sect spokesman, Yehudah Meshi-Zahav. Within a year. he was dead — smitten by hepatitis.

Or there's the case of archaeologist Yigal Shiloh, who excavated the City of David outside Jerusalem's Old City walls. After bones were found there, says Meshi-Zahav, rabbis cursed the site. A year later, in 1987, Shiloh died of cancer.

In the smoke-filled rooms of politics, imprecations are also important weaponry. When Poalei

162 • Signs of His Coming

Agudat Yisrael broke ultra-Orthodox ranks and took the then-unthinkable step of joining the government in 1960, curses flew. Soon after, party head Benjamin Minz, was dead of a coronary." By Peter Hirschberg with reporting by Yuval Lion. *The Jerusalem Report.* November 16, 1995, Page 17.

Kabbalah is thought by many to be a benign method of interpreting the Scriptures through numerics. This is a naive view. Kabbalah is occultism. Here we see the most evil possible face it could wear. The uttering of curses on others is similar to voodoo and witchcraft. It should be made clear that only a small minority of Kabbalists engage in this extremism, however. Only a small part of Jewish Orthodoxy is kabbalistic. Regardless of what one thinks of curses, the fact that they are uttered by religious leaders can give a feeling of legitimacy to a potential assassin. One of the Ten Commandments is, "Thou shalt not kill [Heb. murder]," neither with swords, clubs, nor curses.

History Repeats

An ancient prophet recorded, "And the Lord said unto me, A conspiracy is found among the men of Judah, and among the inhabitants of Jerusalem (Jer. 11:9).

And they were more than forty which had made this conspiracy (Acts 23:13).

Ill Winds Blowing for Bible Believers and Conservatives

Fallout from the news of Prime Minister Rabin's murder does not augur well for serious Bible-rooted religious people. It's the old problem of "getting tarred with the same brush." A "religious" fanatic performs some violent, outrageous act and lo, the secular media begins condemning those with a "Bible mentality," that has "no relationship to reality." After the tragic death of Prime Minister Rabin you could hardly watch TV news or talk shows without hearing the anti-Bible rhetoric.

I should not have been, but I was amazed at what I heard from various commentators on television, blaming those with a biblical mindset for creating the climate that would lead to the assassination of a prime minister. Here are just a few of the outrageous statements I heard.

Thomas L. Friedman writes a column on foreign affairs for the *Wall Street Journal*. He has written a book *Beirut to Jerusalem.*

When interviewed on CNN he was asked if he thought that Rabin's killer, Yigal Amir, had acted alone or if he had associates. He replied, "I have no doubt that he is a lone assassin, or he and his brother are the two assassins, *but I don't think that is, really the point to keep in mind.* While their methods were outside the pale of any Israeli political party. . . . Amir's objective in assassinating the Prime Minister, was a political end to destroy the peace process. *And that is a political objective that is at the core of Israel's right wing Likud party and the other parties associated with it.* He acted alone, but the political objective he was trying to achieve was widely shared." (Emphasis mine throughout).

Host: "Former Secretary of State James Baker was on our morning news just last hour and he said that this verbal violence, and he even called it verbal terrorism, needs to be cooled down. He said that there probably will be some changes in security as well as the political discourse. Do you see that happening?"

Freedman "Well I certainly think the political discourse has to be toned down. . . .

Host: "Interior Minister Barak says he wants a crack down on extremists. Is that a possibility?"

Freedman: "I think it's a possibility, but again I think it's an illusion just to say that this guy is an extremist [and if] we crack down on them, the problem is over. The fact is you have a large segment of the Israeli political spectrum that shares the objectives that this man shared, which is to kill the peace process."

Host: "And so do you think this is not going to be the unifying, the assassination of the prime minister, [is] not going to unify the Israeli people?"

Freedman: "No, I don't think it's going to be unifying, I think it's going to be dividing. I think it should be dividing and that really was what King Hussein said in his eulogy to Yitzhak Rabin. He said, 'This is the time now for people who believe in peace who believe in the peace process to stand up and be counted.' Yitzhak Rabin was killed not because he was trying to unify the country, but because he was taking sides, the side in favor of the peace process."

Host: "And even so, though, do you think that Netanyahu, the Likud leader, and some of the other folks who disagree with that peace process will distance themselves from some of this rhetoric?"

Freedman: "Oh, they'll distance themselves from the act. They'll distance themselves from the most extreme rhetoric, but they will not distance themselves from the goal of killing the peace process." (CNN 11-6-95.)

Several guests commented on the Larry King Live TV program on CNN, November 6, 1995:

Abba Eban: "In this case it is not a problem of individual security in the technical sense. This comes off in a context of vigilance [sic] and hatred of fundamentalist thinking about Jewish history and about *biblical memories which are entirely outside the scope of the context of reality,* which have inflamed certain people and therefore there is an ideological background which is lacking in the case [of] other people."

King: " Michael, where does the anger come from?"

Michael Bar-Zohar: "From a very fanatical conviction that these leaders are going to give back part of the land of

Israel which for those people is holy, so they are traitors and by all kind of certain Rabbis decisions, they deserve to die in order to keep the land of Israel they now have."

King: "As the accused said, *'God told him to do it, right?'*"

Michael Bar-Zohar: "He tried twice to do it before."

James Baker: "There are people . . . as he just pointed out, that are saying, 'This is what you should do, because he is going to give away the land.'"

King: *"And the Bible says to do it."*

James Baker: *"So it's that kind of verbal violence that has to end and we've got to get back to a civil discourse."*

King: "And how do you stop it?"

Michael Bar-Zohar: "I think you are *outlawed*, even in a democracy. I think there is a clear and present danger, in fact in our times and with regard to heads of state. And I think it is *outlawed*."

James Baker: "It is outlawed."

Other Points of View

Benjamin Netanyahu brought a balanced and insightful comment when he was interviewed on television November 7, 1995. "I think everybody agrees that there weren't any of these manifestations inside my movement [Likud Party]. But the important thing is that such rhetoric whether it comes from the right or from the left extremes of the political spectrum, where ever it comes from it should be, of course, put down."

Bryant Gumble: "Are you prepared to view this murder as an isolated act then of an extremist or is *Jewish fundamentalism* a real and ongoing danger to the security of Israel and its leaders?"

B. Netanyahu: "Look, there [are] obviously some pockets, they're quite small as we can see, in fact very small. But you don't need much. You need one crazed individual. . . . But I think we should do our best to try to locate these people, wherever they fester, and take preventive action. I believe that is true, by the way, internationally.

Mr. Gumble also questioned Attorney Alan Dershowitz: "[It] will end up being only an indictment against one individual because the Israelis have to understand the enormous distinction between moral responsibility on the one hand by some of the extremists and the *rabbis and the fundamentalists who called for this horrible crime and technical legal responsibility* and they should be clear to make that distinction."

Israeli Conservatives Respond

The *Jerusalem Insider* faxed the following statements to us today:

The following are three statements made by Likud leaders in the aftermath of the tragic murder of Israel's Prime Minister, Yitzhak Rabin:

> 1. Benjamin Netanyahu, Likud Chairman: "This is one of the most horrific tragedies in the history of the State of Israel and the history of the Jewish people."
>
> "I am shocked to the depths of my soul by the murder of Yitzhak Rabin, one of the great warriors in the establishment of the State of Israel, the Commander of the Six-Day War and one of the important leaders of the State. This is an hour of deep mourning, shock and despair."
>
> "We must banish from our society all those who violate the most basic principle of humanity, of the Jewish people and of democracy . This is also an hour of challenge for all of us, and I pray that we will maintain our reserve and unity in the face of one of the most grievous disasters to strike us since the establishment of the State." (Israel TV Channel One 11.4.95)
>
> "A major disaster has befallen upon the people of Israel. Mr. Rabin, a human-being, a

warrior and one of Israel's most significant and important leaders, has contributed immensely to the people of Israel.

"The people of Israel have forsaken the dreadful phenomenon of political murder 2,000 years ago. This phenomenon was rejected due to a deep conviction that an internal strife was more dangerous than any external threat. I would like to state categorically: There will not be a recurrence of internal strife in Israel."

"Democratic governments change by the ballot and not by the bullet. Therefore, the Likud will recommend that President Weizman entrusts cabinet formulation to the candidate of the Labor Party to the post of the prime minister. Likud will not oppose the cabinet introduced to the Knesset by Labor."

"At this hour, it is incumbent upon us, and especially upon public servants, to display restraint and composure, in order to preserve the unity of the people at this critical time." (Israel Press Conference 11.5.95)

2. Former Prime Minister Yitzhak Shamir: "My reaction is characterized by deep mourning and astonishment. . . . One is required to calm down and to avoid internal strife. . . . The leaders of the country must act responsibly, and to avoid rhetoric which could trigger more disasters."

3. Uzzie Landau, M.K. and chairman of Likud's Policy Committee: "This is a most painful and troublesome moment for the late Prime Minister Rabin's family as well as for the people of Israel and the democratic institutions of the state.

One should condemn the murder and the

murderer, and do the utmost to prevent further deterioration. It is incumbent upon everyone to display composure and restraint, in order to advance the cause of internal unity in face of the tough domestic and external challenges ahead. Political debates should be conducted keenly, pointedly and responsibly. Moreover, all attempts to use the murder of Prime Minister Rabin as an instrument to incite against a prominent segment of the population, should be denounced in order to avoid further divisiveness.

The murderer is not a member of any significant or known political camp. He constitutes a pariah and a detestable phenomenon, which has been systematically, clearly, loudly, publicly and privately condemned by Likud's leadership and grassroots.

The Road to Peace

There is acrimonious debate going on in Israel over which path to peace the nation should follow in order, hopefully, to bring an end to intermittent wars and continuous terrorism. Rabin, head of the liberal Labor Party showed himself ready to make concessions to the neighbors of Israel. Land for peace! Mr. Rabin was not the first to travel the land for peace road. Land for peace was tried before, with fair results, and a peace treaty with Egypt that is still holding together.

Menechem Begin's Role

The process was actually started by a member of the Likud rightist party during the administration of Prime Minister Menechem Begin who invited Anwar Sadat, president of Egypt, to come to Israel and begin peace talks.

In one of many private conversations, Mr. Begin said to me, "David, my neighbors will be surprised at the concessions we will make if real peace can be achieved." Begin bargained away the Sinai Peninsula with the airfields built by Israel, the Gedi and Mitla Passes, and the Abu Rudis oil fields, discovered and developed by Israel. Sadat, honorably, signed a genuine peace treaty which, until now, has brought lasting peace between the two nations.

After the signing of a full peace treaty between Israel and Egypt, Moslem extremists in Egypt assassinated President Anwar Sadat, and the world mourned his passing.

The Oslo Plan

It is said that the Oslo convention was suggested by Johann Joergen Holst, foreign minister of Norway, whom some credit with being the architect of the peace plan between the PLO and Israel.

Other insiders claim that actually it was the wife of Joergen Holst who laid out the plan to him. At any rate he shared it with Yossi Beilin and Shimon Peres, foreign minister of Israel. Peres then presented the plan, already in motion, to a reluctant Yitzhak Rabin. It was hard for the old soldier, Rabin, to shake hands with his implacable enemy, Yassir Arafat, but they did make the famous handshake on September 13, 1993, on the White House lawn in Washington D.C.

The world media revealed the astounding information that secret negotiations had been conducted in Norway for over a year, led by the late Johann Joergen Holst, the Norwegian foreign minister. Holst presided over 14 secret meetings involving representatives of the Palestine Liberation Organization (PLO) and of Israel.

Peace Is Desirable

Peace is not evil. It is good. Good treaties, honored by the parties thereto are not bad, they are good. It is better to have peace than war. But these are dangerous times for Israel, and for all of us. We walk a tightrope over chasms of unimaginable depth.

The Day of the Handshake

On September 13, 1993, at about 11 a.m. Eastern time, Israel's Prime Minister, PLO leader Yassir Arafat, Israeli Foreign Minister Shimon Peres, along with U.S. President Bill Clinton and Secretary of State Warren Christopher, walked onto the White House lawn for the signing of one of the most incredible documents of our time — a peace accord between the PLO and Israel. It was the day of the incredible handshake.

It Was Expected

We fully expected the peace accord or something like it. We predicted it. In August 1993 we printed an article which referred to secret negotiations. We have prayed for the peace of Jerusalem, so if peace is achieved, thank God for it. We may think that Israel's leaders have taken unnecessary risks, but what is done is done, and even if Israel has made mistakes, we stand by her for our Lord's sake.

Oh brave New World Order! Have you brought us hope for mankind's survival, or do sinister agendas lurk in the shadows of international politics and pressure?

What manipulative tactics did you use on Mr. Rabin? What threats fell on his ears? What geo-political blackmail and arm twisting was exercised? Look at the distress in Mr. Rabin's face. What anguish has driven him as he comes to meet and shake hands, reluctantly, with his old enemy? All of this we observed in September 1993, but later that all changed. Rabin had entered into a strange partnership with Arafat. If it works, if it continues, if Arafat can bring his own terrorists under control, if the PLO covenant can be revised, then it is good.

Peace Treaties with Enemies

We must remember, peace treaties are not made with your friends. Peace treaties are made with your enemies. Without enemies there is no need for peace treaties! Some conservative Israelis have taken offense at this concept, but it is true nevertheless. As we examine various points of view, it is important to realize that the Bible is not a deck of tarot cards. We know what the final outcome will be, but there is a lot of foggy bottomland to be traversed until Messiah comes. We simply do not know what is coming in this process, nor exactly where we are on the prophetic timetable. So while we see the peace process as being flawed, yet we hope, yet we pray for the peace of Jerusalem, and all her neighbors roundabout. We must all do the best we can to stay the ravages of anarchy and war as God gives us wisdom and strength.

We all want peace, but this is a wicked, greedy, and deceitful world that has shown negligible success in keeping peace through the long history of humankind. For all the efforts of sane and hopeful leaders we still live in a world steeped in war and violence. Jesus did not gloat when He said, "There shall be wars and rumors of wars." Rather He was weeping over the inability of rebellious humanity to solve its deepest problems.

A Meeting in Ramallah

I participated in a meeting some years ago, which was conducted in the Arab town of Ramallah, Israel. The meeting was set up at my request and involved an Israeli government official, Mr. Yitzhak Achia, myself, and several leaders of the Palestinian District Leagues (now defunct). There was anger around the conference table. Accusations were hurled. Finally, a sense of calm and reason prevailed. At the end of the day, all agreed that while there were many problems to work out, it was time to stop the killing and violence, and create a framework of communication in which Palestinians and Jews strive to find solutions to the problems of the area.

Follow Peace

Peace is good. God is the author of peace. William Tecumseh Sherman, a great Civil War general declared,

"War is hell." These words were part of his graduation address at Michigan Military Academy, June 19, 1879. "War is at best barbarism. . . . Its glory is all moonshine. It is only those who have neither fired a shot nor heard the shrieks and groans of the wounded, who cry aloud for blood, more vengeance, more desolation. War is hell." We are to "Follow peace with all men" (Heb. 12:14).

What good can come of the peace effort? Out of his deep pit of anguish the sufferer Job asked, "Who can bring a clean thing out of an unclean? not one" (Job 14:4). Wrong, Job. God can bring good out of evil, purity out of impurity. That is the theme of redemption. God can take a broken, ruined life and bring forth a new creation. "Therefore if any man be in Christ, he is a new creature: old things are passed away; behold, all things are become new" (2 Cor. 5:17).

One day, God will take this ruined planet and renew it. The thousand-year reign of Messiah is but the inauguration of an eternity of perfection.

God brings good out of evil. Satan brings evil out of good. "By peace shall he destroy." Therefore it behooves us to "Be sober, be vigilant; because your adversary the devil, as a roaring lion, walketh about, seeking whom he may devour" (1 Pet. 5:8).

Evil is ever alert, unceasingly probing, continually watching, looking for an opening. We are not ignorant of the devil's devices.

We join the search for peace, but remember that "Hate is strong and mocks the song of peace on earth, good will to men." We are wary. We live in hope, but observe with caution.

When Messiah Reigns

Wars and violence will not completely cease until Messiah reigns from Jerusalem. Perhaps we can look forward to advancing peace in the Middle East and a time of relative peace in many parts of the earth. But the tide will turn for, "When they shall say, Peace and safety; then sudden destruction cometh upon them, as travail upon a woman with child; and they shall not escape" (1 Thess. 5:3).

> We looked for peace, but no good came; and for a time of health, and behold trouble! (Jer. 8:15).

Israel's Guaranteed Survival

Only Israel, of all nations, is guaranteed survival. Only Israel resists the Antichrist. While the entire Gentile world bows to the Beast, Israel stands alone and bravely counter-attacks his awesome forces. Judah takes up arms against the armies of hell. "And Judah also shall fight [Heb. *make war*] at Jerusalem" (Zech. 14:14). Great leadership arises in Judah! Israel declares of the Beast: "He shall tread in our palaces, then shall we raise against him seven shepherds, and eight principle men" (Mic. 5:5).

Listen devil, look out for the two mighty prophets, the seven shepherds, and the eight principle men. They are on your trail, oh you loser of all time and eternity. Your evil intention will not prevail.

For now we are commanded to pursue peace. "Let us therefore follow after the things which make for peace, and things wherewith one may edify another" (Rom. 14:19).

Prophetic Perspective

What does the peace effort mean in the light of Bible prophecy? When each of the World Wars ended it was said by some, this treaty being signed is the beginning of the Tribulation of seven years, and one of the signers or sponsors of the treaty must be the Antichrist.

The peace accord of September 13, 1993, is not the Antichrist covenant. The peace treaty with Jordan is not that covenant with hell. We are not in the Tribulation. What we see taking shape may be the framework that will develop into that agreement with hell (Isa. 28:18), but it is not in focus yet. One thing we have learned in recent years is that prophecy and world events can move at lightning speed. See the Berlin wall falling down! Observe the upheaval in the USSR and Eastern Europe. Watch how the European Community advances toward the formation of new Rome.

Let us always be alert to the signs of the times. We must also live our lives as responsible Christian citizens, ready to lend a hand in improving conditions here and now. We are aware that we are "polishing brass on a sinking ship," but this old ship has been slowly sinking since the fall of Adam and Eve, 6000 years ago. Thank God that not all believers forsook the daily tasks of improving the quality of life here and now, even as we look for the coming of our Lord and anticipate the day when He will set it all in order. Real Bible prophecy never promotes irresponsibility.

North American Comparison

If the USA had been under terrorist attack from our northern neighbor, Canada, and our southern neighbor, Mexico for the past 47 years we would be urging our leaders to make some kind of a treaty to end the slaughter. Any peace treaty, anywhere in the world that works, and is honored by the participants in the treaty is a good thing, even if it only works for a time.

Jesus advised, "Agree with thine adversary quickly, whiles thou art in the way with him" (Matt. 5:25). Moses wisely said, "When thou comest nigh unto a city to fight against it, then proclaim peace unto it" (Deut. 20:10). Making peace is better than going to war. In the Proverbs we read, "When a man's ways please the Lord, he maketh *even his enemies* to be at peace with him" (Prov. 16:7).

We pray for the peace of Jerusalem (Ps. 122:6) — and peace for all her neighbors.

Chapter 11

ANTI-SEMITISM IN THE CHURCH

Anti-Semitism is a spiritual force. It is satanic. It is in opposition to and an affront to God. It has no place in the Church. To battle anti-Semitism is to engage in spiritual warfare. What follows is an example of the blatant anti-Semitism now running rampant in some churches.

The following was sent to David Allen Lewis, from Jerusalem, by Gemma Blech.

Dear Dr. Lewis,

On November 26th 1996 I received a personal letter from a Christian friend in Seattle. In the letter she told me of a meeting called by the "Church Council of Seattle," with the conference title "Dividing Jerusalem." I was so affected by this letter, that I am writing it out and sending it near and far. I have no e-mail address for my friend and I have not asked her permission [to give out her phone number], so any reaction will, for the moment have to come back to me. I hope any who read this will be rescued from any apathy or complacency from which they might be suffering. The quote which follows is exact:

> I thought I would share an interesting experience I had two weeks ago. The Church Council of Greater Seattle printed an article in the paper about their upcoming conference. The focus of this conference was to be "Dividing Jerusalem," of which they claimed, "to which no religion or nation could lay exclusive claim." They also claimed that most Christians would agree with them. Well! I was quite furious about much of what I read in the article. They covered the "tunnel incident," totally ignoring the fact that it had been widely exposed as a farce.
>
> I decided to attend this conference, armed with three handouts of my own. One was a Scripture brochure I had put together called *God, Israel, and the Jews — What Does Scripture Say?* The second was a copy of the STILL UN-CHANGED PLO covenant. The third was a letter published in the *Washington Times*, written and signed by Arab Christians concerning the terrible persecution of Christians in Islamic countries. The reaction was immediate. I was called a "B(obscenity)," a "F(obscenity) Zionist Whore" among other things. They tried to throw me out five times — they even tried talking the security guard into throwing me out. I refused to leave, although I remained polite to everyone.
>
> One man was so upset by my literature, he stood up with the microphone and said: "The Jews are evil. They are corrupt. They have all the money and control our government. We should dismantle every Jewish organization in Seattle." I told him, "That was the most incredible display of

anti-Semitism I have ever heard." He said, "Thank you" and called me several unrepeatable things.

Nobody spoke up to distance themselves from his blatant anti-Semitism! One lady called my Scripture brochure "obscene." Another woman tried to encourage people not to accept my hand-outs. She said, "Oh, your Scripture brochure only quotes the Old Testament." (As if it is no longer valid!) "No," I said, "haven't you ever read Romans chapter 11?" She wasn't familiar with it. Another woman said: "The PLO Covenant doesn't matter. Don't you see? WE will bring peace to Jerusalem!" I said: "How can you say the PLO death call for Israel doesn't matter? Secondly, GOD will bring peace to Jerusalem."

After two and a half hours of non-stop resistance, the whole room was complaining loudly and disrupting their own meeting. Finally I left. I am sure none of this surprises you. You've seen it all. I've appealed to two reporters and two well-known Seattle radio hosts as well as a Christian radio station to give some time to exposing this blatant 'Christian' anti-Semitism under the banner of the Council of Churches. I am waiting to hear back.

I think we should all take note of this woman's courage, tenacity, and love for the truth!

Gemma Blech Bar
Kochba 95/8
French Hill Jerusalem 97892
Phone 011-972-2-582-7273
Fax 011-972-2-532-4934
Email: gblech@netmedia.net.il

Chapter 12

JEWISH ANTI-SEMITISM

Israeli Entertainer Despises Homeland

As God calls Israel back home, other forces try to stop the flow of immigration. Even so, the return of Jews from Russia, Ethiopia, and other nations is seen by many Christians and Jews as a distinct fulfillment of scores of biblical promises. The media often calls attention to the few Russian Jews who return to the C.I.S., but they largely ignore the thousands who still come each month to the Promised Land.

It has been said that not only most Gentiles are anti-Semitic, but even Jews can be anti-Semitic. A self-hating, heritage-rejecting, wannabe assimilated Jew can be particularly venomous and destructive. Just read the statements of Aviv Geffen, considered by many to be Israel's leading pop star. Well-known for his unorthodox views, the musician dropped another bombshell recently when he advised his fans to leave the country.

"I recommend to the youth to leave the country. There is no democracy here. I am one of the only people who speaks out. That's my job," Geffen said in an interview with *Ma 'a riv's* youth magazine after its readers chose Geffen as "Personality of the Year" in a poll.

"It's time to pack bags and escape from Israel. I am being serious," Geffen added. "I am ashamed of this government and the prime minister, and I am ashamed that an empty-headed and deficient person like [Binyamin] Netanyahu is my representative."

Geffen had made headlines for public attacks on Prime Minister Yitzhak Rabin, who was assassinated in Tel Aviv last November. Recently Geffen said that he was "afraid they would rub off the messages of mourning" left on the walls of what is now known as Rabin Square.

"To me, it is more important that the graffiti remain than that the Western Wall remain," he was quoted as saying. "That is a living human cry on those walls. The dream of peace has been destroyed."

The singer revealed his New Age philosophy when he said, "I value Judaism, but a Pink Floyd record turns me on more than the Western Wall. *I believe we have created God. I am God, you are God, John Lennon is God.*" This actually expresses one of the basic tenants of the New Age movement which is based on the views of pantheistic Hinduism and of other Eastern mystical religions. (Italics added.)

Defending the magazine's decision to print the interview. *'Maariv Le 'noarr* editor, Avi Morgenstern, said: "We absolutely dissociate ourselves from Geffen's views . . . but it was most important that the youth know what their idol thinks. We are totally opposed to his views, and I wrote an editorial expressing this." But the angry condemnations were swift in coming.

Morgenstern confirmed, in an Israel Radio interview, that there were parents who had canceled their children's subscriptions to the magazine following the publication. He said that "thousands" of angry telephone calls had been received by the paper.

Deputy Education Minister Moshe Peled called on the media not to provide someone with such views with a platform to reach the public. "It is inconceivable," Peled said, "that in a year when we are celebrating 100 years of Zionism, a Jew should call on the youth to leave Israel. I call on the youth to boycott Geffen."

"I have always believed that people who do not like Israel should just quietly leave. We can do without them," former education minister Amnon Rubinstein said.

He cautioned that Geffen might simply be seeking publicity. "We should not get over-excited about every stupid remark by one singer or another . . . because surveys carried out when I was minister showed that Israeli youth are very patriotic: The motivation to remain in this country and even to fight in combat units is higher than ever before," Rubinstein said.

In a phone-in survey conducted on Educational TV's *Erev Hadash* program, 70 percent of respondents said they "believed that the mood of the general public was not expressed by Geffen," while 30 percent said Geffen had hit the nail on the head. The program said that thousands of calls had been received, but did not give an exact number of participants."

Source: The *Jerusalem Post (International Edition).* September 21, 1996; page 32.

Chapter 13

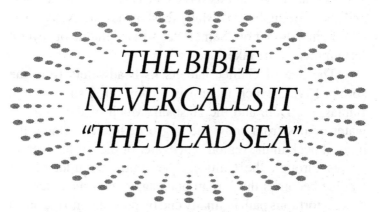

THE BIBLE NEVER CALLS IT "THE DEAD SEA"

A New Source of Life and Energy

The Bible never calls it the "dead" sea. That is a name that was visited upon this majestic body of water after the destruction of Sodom!

In ancient times towns and cities dotted the shores of the body of water the Bible calls "the Salt Sea." Thriving communities found a way to exist and support themselves in an area that became barren and lifeless.

What cataclysm brought death to the region? What lent the name the "Dead Sea" to this body of water in Israel's wilderness? For millennia this salt sea has been used as an illustration of blight and ruin. Few before Herzl had anything kindly to say about the Dead Sea. When I was attending high school in South Dakota I read an essay called "A Parable of Two Seas." I have forgotten the author's name, but as best as I can remember here is how the story goes:

Parable of Israel's Two Seas

In the north central region of Israel lies the Sea of Galilee, nestled in the rolling hills and mountains on the west and confronted with the cliffs of the Golan Heights on the east. The Sea of Galilee is a place of life and beauty. Villages and towns dot its shores. Fishermen ply their trade and take a living from it. Many feast on its bounty. Tourists delight in a dinner of "Saint Peter's Fish" in one of several restaurants on the lakeside.

The Sea of Galilee gathers its headwaters from the Jordan River, which in turn is fed by three streams, the Banias, the Dan, and the Hasbani. Much of the Jordan's water comes from snow melting off Mount Hermon, the highest peak in the region. The water of the Jordan merely passes through the Galilee. The southern outlet of the Galilee becomes the Jordan once again as it meanders on down a tortuous path to finally end by pouring into the north end of the Dead Sea.

The Dead Sea, by contrast to the Galilee, is a place of death. No villages dot its shores. No fish live in its waters. It is a bleak, dreary place shunned by all.

"What," the parable asks, "makes the drastic difference?" Both seas receive the same supply of water from the Jordan. But one body of water is a source of life and the other a dread place of death.

The answer is that the Galilee "receives and gives and lives, whereas the Dead Sea receives and holds and dies."

A New Day for the Dead Sea

The concept embodied in this parable was good for a long time (although it is a modern writing). It is no longer valid. The sea the Bible never called dead is now a source of life. There are health spas on its shores. People find healing for skin diseases and a multitude of other ills in its waters and air system. Villages now dot its shores. Crops are grown in its saline soul.

First National Bank of the Whole World

God put a deposit of mineral wealth in Israel that can hardly be comprehended. The Dead Sea may be the richest piece of real estate on the whole earth! After visiting the area over 37 times I met a man who gave me more information on the Dead Sea than I had ever before received. That man is Professor Shlomo Drori, head of the Department of Information for the Dead Sea Works of Israel.

An article written for us, by Mr. Drori, is included near the end of this chapter. It tells a part of the fascinating Dead Sea story. Drori told me how the Dead Sea has the secret of solving the world's famine problems. Potash and fertilizers for the famine-stricken areas of Africa and other regions is only the beginning of the story. When the Dead-Med canal that was prophesied by the visionary Theodore Herzl is finally realized it will enable the Israelis to more fully develop a mammoth solar pond at the southern end of the Dead Sea. This will unlock secrets for the energy crisis of the world. Cheap energy will provide for desalination of sea water for irrigation of deserts. In addition, the Dead Sea affords a host of needed minerals in abundance.

Value of the Dead Sea

I had read that the value of the Dead Sea was over six trillion dollars. I was told that this would be enough to pay the national and war debt of every nation in the world. That was before I met Mr. Drori.

In a televised interview that I conducted with Mr. Drori I asked him the question, "Has anyone ever accurately estimated the value of the Dead Sea?" He responded that attempts had been made to do so, but that they were in vain. In fact, the value is inestimable. There are enough of 11 vital minerals to supply the whole world's need for thousands of years to come.

It was the destruction of Sodom and the cities of the plains (Gen. 19) that brought death to the region. The gross sins of the Sodomites brought the wrath of God. The area lay blighted for thousands of years.

Little did anyone realize the riches that God had placed there for the Jewish people to possess when they returned to the land and were re-established as a nation in these incredible prophetic times we live in today.

A Strange Turn of Events

The return of Israel saw the blooming of the land. Jordan River water was diverted to various areas for irrigation. To a lesser degree the Jordanians have also used the Jordan's water for irrigation. This has resulted in a rather serious situation in that the waters of the Dead Sea are now dangerously low. The balance of the system is endangered. There is a great need for additional water to pour into the Dead Sea. The building of the canal from the Mediterranean Sea to the Dead Sea is now mandatory.

Unfortunately, with her financial problems Israel cannot fund the enormously expensive project. Perhaps God will raise up one of our readers to be the person to start up a worldwide campaign to help Israel build the canal. Mr. Drori's article gives more information illustrating the need for this canal.

It took the restoration of the Jewish people to the land to set in motion the chain of events that will ultimately bring the exploitation of the Dead Sea for the benefit of the entire world, as Drori indicates.

Ezekiel's Prophecy

Drori's words remind me of an ancient prophecy. I do not know exactly how this fits the picture, but the prophet Ezekiel speaks of the Dead Sea and its future state, perhaps in the Messianic Age:

> Then said he unto me, These waters issue out toward the east country, and go down into the desert, and go into the sea: which being brought

forth into the sea, the waters shall be healed. And it shall come to pass that everything that liveth, which moveth, whithersoever the rivers shall come, shall live: and there shall be a very great multitude of fish, because these waters shall come thither: for they shall be healed; and every thing shall live whither the river cometh. And it shall come to pass, that the fishers shall stand upon it from Engedi even unto Eneglaim; they shall be a place to spread forth nets; their fish shall be according to their kinds, as the fish of the great sea, exceeding many. But the miry places thereof and the marshes thereof shall not be healed; they shall be given to salt (Ezek. 47:8-11).

However this prophecy is to be fulfilled, it is interesting for you and I, through this ministry, to have a part in calling attention to the prophetic significance of the Sea the Bible never called, "Dead."

Shlomo Drori's Hopes for the Future

Shortly before the Intifada (Arab uprising) began in late 1987 a visionary concept was shared with us by Shlomo Drori. We printed it in 1988 in one of our publications, *The Jerusalem Courier*. The article was titled "The Canal of the Seas, More Amazing Facts About the Dead Sea." The following article by Mr. Drori is even more significant now, since the signing of a peace treaty with Jordan and Israel, and the ongoing negotiations between Israel and the Palestinians. Remember, as you read this essay by Shlomo Drori, that it was written in early 1987. In retrospect this gives it a prophetic quality.

Drori Writes

We usually hear evaluations of the significance of the Mediterranean-Dead Sea Canal in terms of the number of megawatts that it will be possible to extract from the hydro-electric power station in the region of Massada. This is rather like evaluating the National Water Carrier by the amount of water it provides for Jerusalem. Important as it is for Jerusalem to exist, is it in this that the importance of the National Water Carrier lies?

This is how the attitude to the canal appears to me. It is indeed very important to produce 10 percent of Israel's electricity needs without dependence on imports from abroad, but the importance of the canal goes beyond any provision of electricity to the State of Israel. Its main importance lies in five areas:

1. A solution of the Palestinian question.
2. Economic independence for the State of Israel.
3. Energy independence for the State of Israel.
4. A revival of the Zionist movement.
5. A change in the image of the State of Israel in the world.

Solution of the Palestinian Problem

This problem was not created in the aftermath of the Peace for Galilee Operation but has existed ever since the League of Nations imposed on Britain a mandate to establish a national home for the Jewish people in Palestine. This problem has undergone many transfigurations during the past 60 years and each has had its own expressions. In 1964 one such expression was created and called the PLO. The Peace for Galilee Operation did not pretend to deal with the Palestinian problem but just with that expression called the PLO. Chances are that following the Peace for Galilee Operation, the Palestinian problem will undergo a further transfiguration. The problem may attract the sympathy of the whole world to the Palestinian side.

It is thus incumbent on Israel to foresee and avert the danger by coming forward itself with a solution to the Palestinian problem, one that can be acceptable to our friends in the world, to some of the Arab countries, to some of the Palestinians, and also . . . to ourselves! Thus, the only solution that presents itself as suitable in the light of the above is concealed in the canal. Let me elaborate.

The canal between the Mediterranean Sea and the Dead Sea is not a new idea but it has not previously been considered practical. The idea is based on utilization of the differences in elevation between the two seas, but so long as the evaporation of water from the Dead Sea was balanced each year by the flow of brooks, flash floods, and underwater springs into the Dead Sea, any addition of water from the Mediterranean Sea would have flooded the Dead Sea valley and upset the concentration of salts in the Dead Sea.

Since the establishment of the Israeli National Water Carrier and the Jordanian Yarmuk Scheme, the surface level balance of the Dead Sea has been upset and water from the Mediterranean can now be allowed to flow into it in a quantity sufficient to replace the water that no longer reaches the Dead Sea from the regular sources. This quantity will not enable electricity to be produced on a scale significant for Israel's electricity consumption in ten years time.

Multiple Energy Sources

The annual evaporation of some 1.5 billion cubic meters has been replaced over the generations by the Jordan River (60%), flash floods from the Israeli side (8%), brooks and flood waters from the Jordanian side (28%), and underwater springs (4%). Thanks to the National Carrier and to the Yarmuk Scheme, a billion cubic meters of water can be allowed to flow each year from the Mediterranean Sea. this quantity will allow the production of 800 megawatts of electricity (at peak hours) which, in 10 years' time, will be some 10 percent of Israel's electricity needs.

Utilization of the resources of the Dead Sea is based on two energy sources:

> 1. Solar energy — evaporation in the system of pools of the Dead Sea Works on the Israeli side and in the system of pools on the Jordanian side.
> 2. Conventional energy in the plants on the Israeli and Jordanian sides. The cost of conventional energy restricts production in the Dead Sea industries and today permits only the production of raw material of a number of minerals from the salts of the Dead Sea. The Jordanian plant recently opened by King Hussein to produce potash will come up against three serious problems.

> 1. The flood waters coming into the Dead Sea from Arava (Nachal Arava, Nachal Zin, and Nachal Amatzia) will strike the Jordanian dams vertically and could destroy them.
> 2. The Jordanian plant is a copy of an American plant and does not answer the problems of climate and salt concentration in the solutions of the Dead Sea. The Israeli Dead Sea Works is functioning on the basis of technologies that do not exist anywhere else in the world and it can be assumed the Jordanian plant will quickly realize that they require the same technologies.
> 3. Electricity on the Israeli and Jordanian sides is produced at local power stations on the basis of diesel fuel, the cost of which is high.

Exploiting Jordanian Arava

This state of affairs will, in a short space of time, bring the Jordanians to a recognition of the need for cooperation with Israel (initially, with respect to holding back the flood waters and subsequently with technological help). Following this cooperation, which will be essential for the Jordanian plant, will come the stage in which Israel will provide the Jordanian plant with cheap electricity from the canal. And here lies the solution to the Palestinian question.

The Arava, stretching from the Dead Sea to the Gulf of Eilat, is partially in Israeli territory and partially in Jordanian territory. On the Israeli side a number of very successful agricultural experiments have been undertaken (Ein Yahav, Ein Hatseva, Neot Hakikar, Yotvata, and others), but the shortage of agricultural water has not, in fact, made it possible to develop agriculture on a serious scale. On the Jordanian side, the Arava is a near-waterless desert. The quantity of water that flows each year from the Jordanian side into the Dead Sea (through brooks and floods) comes to some 300 million cubic meters. With the help of cheap electricity (from the canal), this water could be pumped to the Jordanian Arava. It may be assumed that just as there are giant underground reservoirs of saline water on the Israeli side, they also exist on the Jordanian side. Three hundred million cubic meters of water with a saline content of 13-20 milligrams/liter could be mixed with saline water and 600 million cubic meters of agricultural quality water could be available.

With the aid of fertilizers and pesticides, cheap electricity, and 600 million cubic meters of agricultural water, it would be possible to set up in the Jordanian Arava scores of agricultural settlements on the model of Ein Yahav or Neot Hakikar, together with urban areas for the provision of services. The Palestinian refugees at present living in Lebanon and in refugee camps in Eretz Israel could then be settled in the Arava.

Jordanian industry, which would develop by virtue of the cooperation with Israel, would turn Jordan into the most industrialized of the Arab countries and would create thousands of jobs for engineers, technicians and operators. The natural candidate for these jobs would come from among the Palestinian refugees and the Arab residents of Judea and Samaria.

By virtue of Israel's contribution, the Jordanian Arava would become one of the most impressive agricultural achievements in modern history and the Palestinian question solution would become an economic dynamo of the Middle East.

Economic Independence for the State of Israel

The production of potash, phosphates, and bromide in Israel in the past year came to $250 million. All these products are raw materials for the manufacture of compound fertilizers and pesticides. The price of the finished products is almost ten times that of the raw material but the cost of energy to the State of Israel bars the manufacture of the final product and she continues to export raw material only. If the electricity for the Dead Sea Industries were considerably cheaper than electricity conventionally produced, Israel would be able to export finished products and her income would increase immeasurably.

The crisis to be expected in the world in the coming decade will not be one of energy but of food. Particularly vulnerable in the crisis will be the countries of Africa and Asia. Israel is one of the few countries in the world that has been blessed with all the components of fertilizers (potassium phosphorus and the possibility for producing nitrogen). With cheap electricity she could become the manufacturer of the cheapest fertilizers and (bromide-based) pesticides in the world. In ten years the countries of Africa and Asia will have a greater need for fertilizers and pesticides than for oil.

The concentration of bromide in the Dead Sea is the highest in the world. Cheap electricity will turn Israel into the cheapest producer of bromide in the world and the bromide reserves in the Dead Sea are sufficient for world consumption for 3,000 years. Bromide compounds have a wide range of uses (medicines, pesticides, paint industries, glass industries, fuel industries, A.D.B. for raising octane levels in petrol, etc.).

Metal of the Future

But bromide and potash, for all their importance for the economy of Israel, are only peripheral materials among the salts of the Dead Sea. The main salt is magnesium from which magnesium metal can be produced by electrolysis. This is considered to be the metal of the future since it is 50 percent lighter than aluminum and can withstand temperatures of up to 1300⁰ C. Today, magnesium metal is produced only in Norway (which has cheap hydro-electric energy but no magnesium) and in the U.S. (which has magnesium but not very cheap energy).

Magnesium reserves in the Dead Sea are the largest in the world and with the aid of cheap electricity from the canal, Israel could become the world's main producer of magnesium. Magnesium metal is considered ideal for the manufacture of airplanes, rockets, spaceships, and motor cars. It staggers the imagination to contemplate Israel's enviable position were these industries to become dependent upon the magnesium of the State of Israel.

The Canal would result in the development of energy-rich industries in the Negev and their integration with the almost inexhaustible natural resources of the Dead Sea and vicinity.

Energy Independence

Theodore Herzl viewed the canal as a hydro-electric station, as does the Ministry of Energy and Infrastructure of the State of Israel today, but it is impossible to truly evaluate the canal, the construction of which will not be completed before 1990, within the framework of 1900 concepts.

In Herzl's time the canal could only have operated a hydro-electric station, but it is already clear today that within ten years, solar pools will be economically viable and provide even cheaper electricity than thermal power stations. However, the cost-benefit factor of solar pools is questionable today for two reasons:

1. Vast areas of land are required for their construction and the price of land is a considerable factor in the costs of the pools.

2. Very large quantities of "light" water are required for the insulated water layer. This water has to flow without stop in order to prevent the layers from intermingling. Pools of a size of scores of thousands of dunams require large quantities of water, the price of which is a large factor in the costs of the pools.

Recovering Shale Oil

In the Dead Sea valley there are at least 50,000 dunams of land that are unusable (Amiaz Plain, Nachal Hever, and others).

These lands will lower the cost of solar pool construction and the "light" water will come from the canal without flowing into the Dead Sea and will thus, on its way from the Mediterranean Sea to the solar pools, produce hydro-electric energy. Not only will this not involve an outlay of money for specific imported fuels, but electricity will be created twice — 50,000 dunams of solar pools can yield 1,000 megawatts of electricity (at 200 megawatts per 1,000 dunams in the light of experience gained with solar pools at Ein Boqeq). In ten years, 1,000 megawatts of electricity will comprise 25 percent of the electricity consumption of the country.

Between Sodom and Dimona a shale oil deposit has been discovered and it is assessed that within ten years it will be economically feasible to produce energy from it. Construction of a nuclear power station near an artificial lake in the Sands of Halunsa (the lake being fed by the canal), with a production capacity of 1,200 megawatts and the increased production capacity of the hydro-electric station, thanks to the water required for the solar pools (and the replacement of 300 million cubic meters from the Jordanian side that will be pumped to the Palestinian settlement in the Jordan

Arava), will thus permit the state of Israel to attain energy independence within 15 years.

Revival of the Zionist Movement

The economic weakness of the State of Israel, its political isolation, and its social problems and inability to integrate into the Middle East, have resulted in a fading of the Zionist movement, that is to say on immigration and the transfer of Jewish capital to the state.

The financing and construction of the Mediterranean-Dead Sea Canal could be one of the most efficient responses to the problems of the Zionist movement. The Jewish people must be involved in funding the project ($150 million a year) and not only would this mean that capital could be raised under the most convenient terms, but involvement would be created by large segments of the Jewish people who are not today prepared to identify with the Zionist movement, although they would agree to participate in a revolutionary project that would mean prosperity and peace not only of the Jewish people but for the Middle East. The State of Israel bonds' success in raising $100 million for "seed money" for this project is a good augury for the future.

The subdivision of the project into zones would allow each Jewish community in the world to be involved not only financially but also in the work on the ground (volunteers, Bar Mitzvah boys, and students). Industries and their technological requirements, cooperation with Arab countries, the agriculture that would develop as a result of the Canal — all this combined would constitute a challenge to Jewish youth, their talent, and initiative. Zionism would rekindle the imagination of Jews.

A Change in the Image of the State of Israel

For all the great achievements of the State of Israel, and Operation Peace for Galilee, slanted media coverage and widespread misrepresentation by television have created a negative image of the State of Israel. This should not be ignored and this distorted image must be corrected.

The Mediterranean-Dead Sea Canal has been criticized at the United Nations in the Ecology Committee and represented as though its intention were to flood the Jordanian part of the southern basin of the Dead Sea in order, as it were, to destroy the Jordanian plant. Presentation of the project as a solution to the Palestinian problem, while cooperating with the Jordanian plant and the construction of industry and modern agriculture in the Kingdom of Jordan, could form a turning point in the attitude of the world towards us. Not only military supremacy will ensure our future but economic strength and our willingness to give!

In Herzl's vision, he saw the power of the state of the Jews as lying in its ability to give to the surroundings, and it seems to me that we have never been as close to this possibility as could be the case today.

Prime Minister Menachem Begin was awarded the Nobel Peace Prize for his willingness to find a common language with the Egyptian president. Presentation of the Mediterranean-Dead Sea Canal as a national objective both for solving the Palestinian problem and as a solution for the economic and energy problems of the State of Israel would not only create a national consensus within the country and justify again the award of the Nobel Peace prize to the prime minister of Israel, but could turn him into one of the outstanding leaders of the whole of Jewish history.

This is the conclusion of Mr. Drori's remarks.

There is also talk, now, of building the canal from the Red Sea to the Dead Sea with similar results.

Unfortunately, the canal project was delayed because of Israel's economic problems. and the Intifada. Perhaps now is the time, after the peace treaty with Jordan, the Palestinian Peace Accord, and the tragic assassination of Israel's Prime Minister Yitzhak Rabin, to begin building the

Canal of the Seas. An international consortium of investors could raise the capital for the project and bring great benefit to the entire region, and make a tidy profit for themselves. Maybe you are the person to start such a move. Or if one person would donate one billion dollars it is likely that the canal could be named (if, for example your name is Smith) the Mary/or John Smith Holy Land Canal.

Chapter 14

NEW 95 THESES

Christians and Israel

On October 31, 1517, Martin Luther nailed his 95 Theses to the door of the Castle Church in Wittenberg, Germany. Thus started the Protestant Reformation. Luther was very friendly toward the Jewish people in the beginning, thinking that in their rejection of Roman Catholic Christianity they would accept Christ in the new Protestant movement. However, after centuries of Christian persecution, slaughter, crusades and inquisition, the Jews simply were not interested in any brand of Christianity.

Late in life Luther became a hater of Jews and things Jewish. He wrote in vicious terms of the Jews: "All the blood kindred of Christ burn in hell, and they are rightly served. . . ." The result of this new Christian hatred of the Jews led directly to the holocaust. We arethankful that the Lutheran World Federation and the Evangelical Lutheran Church of America have publicly repudiated and repented for Luther's anti-Semitism. It is our prayer that the whole body of evangelical Christianity will do the same.

We now present a new 95 Theses to make up for what the Protestant and Evangelical Churches may lack in regards to the Jewish and Israel issue.

1. The Church and Israel share a common heritage in the worship of Jehovah, the one and only true God. While the Jewish people do not need the Church to explain their existence, the Church cannot explain its existence without Israel. The tragedy of the ages is that hostility has scarred the relationship between the Church and the Jewish people. It is time for us to begin searching for our real roots as Christians. The search leads us back to Jerusalem and to Israel. It is a time for healing of old wounds. This is our moment in history. Let us not miss it.

2. The Bible is the Word of God. The 66 books of the Jewish and Christian Scriptures solely comprise the written Word of God. The entire Bible is verbally inspired by God and is the revelation of God to man, the infallible, authoritative rule of faith and conduct.

3. God is sovereign, He rules over all things.

> The Lord shall reign for ever and ever (Exod. 15:18).
>
> The Lord shall reign for ever, even thy God, O Zion, unto all generations. Praise ye the Lord (Ps. 146:10).
>
> The Lord shall reign over them in mount Zion from henceforth, even for ever (Mic. 4:7).
>
> And he shall reign over the house of Jacob for ever; and of his kingdom there shall be no end (Luke 1:33).
>
> For he must reign, till he hath put all enemies under his feet (Cor. 15:25).
>
> The kingdoms of this world are become the kingdoms of our Lord, and of his Christ; and he shall reign for ever and ever (Rev. 11:15).

4. God owns the whole world. "The earth is the Lord's, and the fulness thereof; the world, and they that dwell therein" (Ps. 24).

> For the earth is the Lord's, and the fulness thereof (1 Cor. 10:26; also see, Exod. 9:29, 1 Cor. 10:28).

5. God can give any portion of the world to whomever He wills.

> When the Most High divided to the nations their inheritance, when he separated the sons of Adam, he set the bounds of the people according to the number of the children of Israel (Deut. 32:8). "And hath made of one blood all nations of men for to dwell on all the face of the earth, and hath determined the times before appointed, and the bounds of their habitation (Acts 17:26).

6. God has determined to give the land of Israel to the descendants of Abraham, through the promised line of Isaac and Jacob (Israel).

> For all the land which thou seest, to thee will I give it, and to thy seed for ever (Gen. 13:15).
> And Jacob [Israel] said unto Joseph, God Almighty appeared unto me at Luz in the land of Canaan, and blessed me, And said unto me, Behold, I . . . will give this land to thy seed after thee for an everlasting possession (Gen. 48:3-4).
> And Joseph said unto his brethren, I die: and God will surely visit you, and bring you out of this land unto the land which he sware to Abraham, to Isaac, and to Jacob Gen. 50:24).

The Abrahamic Covenant

7. The Jewish people own the land of Israel. The Church too often views Israel as merely an eschatological curiosity, a sign of the times. This misses the point that the Jews are a real people with a real future. They are not a fossil race, best ignored or placed in a museum of our dreams. They are the divinely appointed owners of the Holy Land. God's covenant with Abraham is a prophecy. It is unconditional, unilateral, and proceeds from God alone. Here is the original covenant made with Abraham:

> Now the Lord had said unto Abram, Get thee out of thy country, and from thy kindred, and from thy father's house, unto a land that I will show thee: And I will make of thee a great nation, and I will bless thee, and make thy name great; and thou shalt be a blessing: And I will bless them that bless thee, and curse him that curseth thee: and in thee shall all families of the earth be blessed (Gen. 12:1-3).

> And the Lord appeared unto Abram, and said, **Unto thy seed will I give this land**: and there builded he an altar unto the Lord, who appeared unto him (Gen. 12:7).

> After these things the word of the Lord came unto Abram in a vision, saying, Fear not, Abram: I am thy shield, and thy exceeding great reward (Gen. 15:1).

> And he believed in the Lord; and he counted it to him for righteousness. And he said unto him, I am the Lord that brought thee out of Ur of the Chaldees, to give thee this land to inherit it (Gen. 15:6-7).

> And when the sun was going down, a deep sleep fell upon Abram; and, lo, an horror of great darkness fell upon him (Gen. 15:12). *(The fact that God put Abram into a deep sleep to finalize the covenant indicates the unilateral nature of the covenant.)*

> And it came to pass, that, when the sun went

down, and it was dark, behold a smoking furnace, and a burning lamp that passed between those pieces. In the same day the Lord made a covenant with Abram, saying, Unto thy seed have I given this land, from the river of Egypt unto the great river, the river Euphrates (Gen. 17-18).

8. The Mosaic Covenant was conditional, filled with phrases like "If you obey then blessings will fall upon you." The Mosaic Covenant was bilateral, conditional, and finally fulfilled in the atoning work of Jesus Christ. "A blessing, if ye obey the commandments of the Lord your God, which I command you this day: And a curse, if ye will not obey the commandments of the Lord your God" (Deut. 11:27-28).

By contrast the Abrahamic Covenant with Israel is unconditional, unilateral, and eternal, and is based solely on the sovereign determination of God.

9. If God should break His solemn promise to Abraham, how can Christians be sure that God will not break the New Covenant, also confirmed with Israel (not the Gentiles) which assures the basis of our salvation? We former Gentiles are wild branches grafted into Israel's olive tree.

Behold, the days come, saith the Lord, that I will make a new covenant with the house of Israel, and with the house of Judah (Jer. 31:31 and Heb. 8:8).

This new covenant fulfills the Mosaic Covenant of redemption, but there is no indication that it replaces the Abrahamic Covenant. That God has more than one covenant active with various entities is shown by the everlasting nature of the Noahic Covenant, and the rainbow promise to all humankind that there will never again be a universal flood. See Genesis 9:9-17. Genesis reveals this covenant, made with Noah, to be unilateral, unconditional, and eternal.

And I, behold, I establish my covenant with

you, and with your seed after you (Gen. 9:9).

And I will establish my covenant with you; neither shall all flesh be cut off any more by the waters of a flood; neither shall there any more be a flood to destroy the earth (Gen. 9:11).

I do set my bow in the cloud, and it shall be for a token of a covenant between me and the earth (Gen. 9:13).

And the bow shall be in the cloud; and I will look upon it, that I may remember the **everlasting covenant** between God and every living creature of all flesh that is upon the earth (Gen. 9:16).

And God said unto Noah, This is the token of the covenant, which I have **established between me and all flesh** that is upon the earth (Gen. 9:17).

God's Plan for Israel

10. God's plan for Israel includes habitation of the Land of Israel. God brought Abraham out of Ur of the Chaldees and later commanded him to leave Haran and make his way to a land that would be shown to him. That new land was to be the possession of Abraham's promised descendants by the decree of the Almighty. "In the same day the Lord made a covenant with Abram, saying, Unto thy seed have I given this land" (Gen. 15:18).

And I will give unto thee, and to thy seed after thee, the land wherein thou art a stranger, all the land of Canaan, for an everlasting possession; and I will be their God (Gen. 17:8).

In response to the statement that "God is not in the real estate business," it should be noted that Genesis 1 describes the greatest land transaction of all time. See Revelation 21:1. "New earth" is real estate. In the Bible, land is mentioned 1,533 times, earth 906 times, world 248 times, heaven 678 times. Yes, God is interested in earth and all its lands.

11. The Holy Land is a title given by God to only one of earth's nations, the land of Israel. "And the Lord shall inherit Judah his portion in the holy land, and shall choose Jerusalem again. Be silent, O all flesh, before the Lord: for he is raised up out of his holy habitation" (Zech. 2:12-13). "And he showed me Joshua the high priest standing before the angel of the Lord, and Satan standing at his right hand to resist him. And the Lord said unto Satan, the Lord rebuke thee, O Satan; even the Lord that hath chosen Jerusalem rebuke thee: is not this a brand plucked out of the fire?" (Zech. 3:1-2).

Of all the cities of the world only Jerusalem is called the Holy City in the Bible, five times in the Old Testament and five times in the New (Neh. 11, Neh. 11:18, Isa. 48:2, Isa. 52:1, Dan. 9:24, Matt. 4:5, Matt. 27:53, Rev. 11:2, Rev. 21:2, Rev. 22:19. The last two references are to the New Jerusalem.)

12. God's sovereignty is called into question when the Jews are not in their land (Isa. 48; Ezek. 36).

> For my name's sake will I defer mine anger, and for my praise will I refrain for thee, that I cut thee not off (Isa. 48:9).

> Behold, I have refined thee, but not with silver; I have chosen thee in the furnace of affliction (Isa. 48:10).

> For mine own sake, even for mine own sake, will I do it: for how should my name be polluted? and I will not give my glory unto another. Hearken unto me, O Jacob and Israel, my called; I am he; I am the first, I also am the last (Isa. 48:9-12).

> And I scattered them among the heathen, and they were dispersed through the countries: according to their way and according to their doings I judged them. And when they entered unto the heathen, whither they went, they profaned my

holy name, when they said to them, These are the people of the Lord, and are gone forth out of his land. But I had pity for mine holy name, which the house of Israel had profaned among the heathen, whither they went. Therefore say unto the house of Israel, Thus saith the Lord God; I do not this for your sakes, O house of Israel, but for mine holy name's sake, which ye have profaned among the heathen, whither ye went. And I will sanctify my great name, which was profaned among the heathen, which ye have profaned in the midst of them; and the heathen shall know that I am the Lord, saith the Lord God, when I shall be sanctified in you before their eyes. For I will take you from among the heathen, and gather you out of all countries, and will bring you into your own land. Then [after the restoration of land, nation, and people] will I sprinkle clean water upon you, and ye shall be clean: from all your filthiness, and from all your idols, will I cleanse you (Ezek. 36:19-25).

13. Land for peace schemes have seldom worked. Israel possesses less than 1/2 of 1 percent of the landmass of the Middle East. The Arabs already have 99.5 percent of the land. The radicals will never rest until they have it all. This cannot be tolerated. To work with God in His determined plan calls for prayer and action on Israel's behalf. Israel may take actions that seem to be suicidal. We cannot interfere with the political process nor do we wish to do so. Even if Israel makes mistakes, we follow the principles of biblical Zionism and continue to stand by Israel in her struggle for survival.

The Early Church Was Jewish

14. The Early Church was entirely Jewish. This is reflected in Matthew's gospel, "These twelve Jesus sent forth, and commanded them, saying, Go not into the way of the Gentiles, and into any city of the Samaritans enter ye not: But go rather to the lost sheep of the house of Israel." Matthew 10:5-6.

15. The Jewish people gave us the Bible. The Bible Jesus used was the First ("old") Testament which comprises 77 percent of our Bible and is fully as inspired as the New Testament. When Jesus referred to the "Scriptures," He was referring solely to the Old Testament. "Jesus answered and said unto them, Ye do err, not knowing the scriptures, nor the power of God" (Matt. 22:29; also see Matt. 21:42, Mark 12:24, Acts 18:28, 2 Tim. 3:15). The Old Testament was the only Bible known to the earliest Church of Jesus Christ.

16. The Jewish people gave us the New Testament. All of its authors were Jewish. If Luke was of Gentile origin, then he had become a Jewish proselyte.

17. The Jewish people gave us Jesus Christ. "Therefore being a prophet, and knowing that God had sworn with an oath to him, that of the fruit of his loins, according to the flesh, he would raise up Christ to sit on his throne" (Acts 2:30).

> Concerning his Son Jesus Christ our Lord, which was made of the seed of David according to the flesh (Rom. 1:3).

> Whose are the fathers, and of whom as concerning the flesh Christ came, who is over all, God blessed for ever. Amen (Rom. 9:5).

> Hereby know ye the Spirit of God: Every spirit that confesseth that Jesus Christ is come in the flesh is of God" (1 John 4:2). The flesh he came in was Jewish flesh.

> And every spirit that confesseth not that Jesus Christ is come in the flesh is not of God: and this is that spirit of antichrist, whereof ye have heard that it should come; and even now already is it in the world (1 John 4:3).

18. Jesus made a choice. Only one person in all of time and history had the power to choose where He would be born, with what people He would be identified, who His mother would be and that person is Jesus who was born in a Judean village of a Jewish mother, of the house of David of the tribe of Judah. He will return as the lion of Judah as revealed in the Book of Revelation, chapter 5.

19. The disciples of Jesus were Jewish. They, with Jesus, worshiped in the temple, where Jesus frequently taught. Jesus said, "I sat daily with you teaching in the temple" (Matt. 26:55).

Even after the resurrection of Jesus the disciples worshipped in the temple. "And daily in the temple, and in every house, they ceased not to teach and preach Jesus Christ" (Acts 5:42).

The Tragic Split

20. The earliest Church was Jewish and was viewed as a Jewish sect until after the Bar Kochba revolt against the Roman armies in A.D. 135. The Jewish believers and the Gentile converts split on the issue of whether to support Shimon Bar Kochba in the revolt. After the split the gentile Church was Hellenized and slowly became more and more anti-Semitic. Later the apostle Paul wrote to the church in Rome:

> Boast not against the branches. But if thou boast, thou bearest not the root, but the root thee. Thou wilt say then, The branches were broken off, that I might be grafted in. Well; because of unbelief they were broken off, and thou standest by faith. Be not highminded, but fear: For if God spared not the natural branches, take heed lest he also spare not thee. Behold therefore the goodness and severity of God: on them which fell, severity; but toward thee, goodness, if thou continue in his goodness: otherwise thou also shalt be cut off.

And they also, if they abide not still in unbelief, shall be grafted in: for God is able to graft them in again. For if thou wert cut out of the olive tree which is wild by nature, and wert grafted contrary to nature into a good olive tree: how much more shall these, which be the natural branches, be grafted into their own olive tree? For I would not, brethren, that ye should be ignorant of this mystery, lest ye should be wise in your own conceits; that blindness in part is happened to Israel, until the fulness of the Gentiles be come in (Rom. 11:18-25).

Replacement Theology

21. Origenes Adamantius (Origen), an Early Church father, introduced the **allegorical** (non-literal) method of interpreting the Bible, early in the third century A.D. This laid the foundation for **replacement theology**, the idea that the Church has replaced Israel, and that there is no prophetic future for the Jewish nation. He taught against the concept of a future Millennium when Messiah shall reign over and through both Israel and the Church. He is the father of amillenialism (no millennium) which usually embodies replacement theology. **Amillenialism** is the view that there will be no literal thousand year millennial reign of Christ (see Rev. 20). They say that prophecy must be "spiritualized," as if the literal mode of interpretation were carnal, which it is not. In fact, literalism implies faith in the plain meaning of the Bible and is the truly "spiritual" approach to the Word of God. While the Bible uses symbols, we recognize that even the symbols have a literal meaning. The symbols of the Bible must be understood by internal biblical concepts, never interpreted by means of external data.

22. Augustine, author of *The City of God*, embraced and popularized allegorical interpretation, refuted the literal Millennium, which furthered the agenda of Christian anti-

Semitism expressed in replacement theology.

23. The Church became the tormentor of the Jews as demonstrated by Christian slaughter of the Jews in the Crusades and the Inquisition. The Church has been the principle source of anti-Semitism for over 1,700 years.

24. Replacement theology is inconsistent in that it puts all of the curses of the Old Testament on the heads of the Jews of today, and transfers all the blessings to the "new Israel," the Church.

25. We have come unto Zion. We have not replaced the original Zion of God. "But ye are come unto mount Zion, and also unto the city of the living God, the heavenly Jerusalem, and to an innumerable company of angels" (Heb. 12:22).

What Does Zion Mean to a Christian?

26. Zionism is the idea that the land of Israel is a national home for the Jewish people, as is stated scores of times in the Bible. One does not have to be a political Zionist to be a biblical Zionist. "Let them all be confounded and turned back that hate Zion" (Ps. 129:5). "For the Lord hath chosen Zion; he hath desired it for his habitation" (Ps. 132:13). "Oh that the salvation of Israel were come out of Zion! When God bringeth back the captivity of his people, Jacob shall rejoice, and Israel shall be glad" (Ps. 53:6).

27. Zionism did not come into existence in 1897 when Theodore Herzl convened the first Zionist Congress in Basel, Switzerland. The Zion concept is first introduced in the opening pages of your Bible, in the 12th chapter of Genesis. Moses recorded the unconditional promise of God in which the land is promised to the seed of Abraham forever. Later the promise is repeated to Jacob (Israel) as the promised seed (Gen. 35:12).

28. When some Christians say that they are biblical Zionists it says some important things about their faith. A biblical Zionist believes that God is the owner of the whole world. God is sovereign and can give any portion of the world to whomsoever He wills. He has ordained that the seed of Abraham through Isaac and Jacob (Israel) shall possess that tiny spot of land called Israel in perpetuity. This is based on a unilateral covenant made with Abraham. The covenant is unconditional. Our faith in God and His Word demands this belief. A biblical Zionist experiences a great love for Israel and the Jewish people, and will undertake legitimate action to protect Israel and to combat anti-Semitism.

29. Some charge that the Jews are evil, cursed, and more wicked than all other peoples. This is a false charge. All peoples are born in sin and are in need of salvation (Rom. 3:23).

30. Unconditional love is offered by Christians to the people of Israel. With no desire to put Jews on a pedestal, and fully recognizing all the human flaws of Israel, nevertheless we love them and support their right to their own land because of the Word of God. Paul writes to the Gentile church in Rome, "As touching the election, they are beloved for the fathers' sakes" (Rom. 11:28). Some will love a Jew only if he converts to Christianity. But we have no such prejudice. Our love to the Jewish people is based on the Word of God, and the teaching of our Jewish Saviour, Jesus.

31. Do not hesitate to identify with biblical Zionism. Let no one intimidate you. Let it be known that you are a Christian Zionist. Carry the banner boldly. We are on the winning side. We may be a minority now, but we will overcome by the sovereign will of God.

32. Christians who embrace Zion are men and women of faith and works. They believe God's Word and are willing to cooperate with the divine plan. They are people of courage, knowing that they will always be a minority in the world and in the Church. Though viewed by some as risk takers, they are confident that God's sovereign will shall prevail. They desire to participate in the end time plan of God, and not merely stand by as idle spectators.

Above all they wish to please God. Christians should coop-erate with the plan of God regarding the nation of Israel. The only thing that takes precedence over Zion is the fulfillment of the Great Commission.

33. Christians are called to be protectors of God's Zion. We believe the Bible in its most literal sense. We believe that Israel exists by the will and decree of God. There is simply no other explanation. No other nation has been driven from its homeland, endured a 19-century Diaspora, and still maintained an ethnic and national identity. The Jews have been subjected to continual pogroms and perse-cution and still they have survived. The holocaust snuffed out six million Jewish lives, yet Israel outlives her tormen-tors.

34. We are frequently accused of "sheltering the Jews from the wrath of God." It is alleged that we are the real anti-Semites, for if we would only allow God's wrath to come upon them, it would drive the Jews to Christ. This is a strange and twisted form of illogical thinking. In the first place, we should not imagine that any person or group of people could stop God from pouring out His wrath on any nation, should He so desire! Secondly, while we are not interested in interfering with the sovereign acts of God, we are determined to protect the Jewish people, God's chosen, from the wrath of man, and from any present or future "Hitlers." Thirdly, that the wrath of man dumped on the Jews would bring them to Christ has not proven to be correct as witnessed by long centuries of "Christian" anti-Semitism. Certainly the holocaust in "Christian" Germany, led by Hitler, who was a church member until the day he died, did not bring the Jews into the fold of the church.

35. Israel is God's litmus test for the Church, nations, and individuals. If you want to evaluate what seems to be a move of God, check the attitude manifested toward Israel. God will bless those who bless Israel. He will curse those who curse Israel. Do not sit in the seat of the scornful

Christian anti-Semites. They are in a dangerous place and not to be envied.

36. The church that does not resist anti-Semitism is on the road to becoming anti-Semitic. Pastor Martin Neomuller, who lived in the time of Hitler and the Nazi domination of Germany spoke out against Hitler when it was too late. He regretfully said, "When they [Nazis] came for the Jews I did not protest, for I am not a Jew. When they came for the Catholics I did not protest, for I am not a Catholic. When they came for me there was no one left to protest." Neomuller was an outstanding evangelical pastor and leader.

37. Theologians in pre-Nazi Germany were teaching the anti-Semitic doctrines of replacement and contempt. Replacement indicates that the Church has taken the place of Israel and natural Israel has no more place in the economy of God. Contempt says that since the Jews crucified Christ anything bad that happens to them is judgment and they deserve it. There is a curse upon them. I wonder how we then should view the martyrdom of Christians? We cannot afford such a double standard.

38. We must raise the question in the Church, since Israel is the apple of God's eye, why are matters relating to Israel at the bottom of the agenda in so many churches? Pastors and other Christian leaders are being told that whether or not national Israel has a place in the end-time plan of God is a low-priority item on the Church's agenda. For the sake of unity among Evangelicals, Charismatics, and Pentecostals, we are told that we really ought to be quiet about the matter. This approach is self-serving, coercive, and has no place in the Church.

39. Supporting Israel's right to exist in her own land in secure borders does not imply full agreement with actions of any political regime in Israel, any more than being a loyal American citizen demands that I agree with all the actions of my own government.

40. We are called to be a comfort to the Jews and to Jerusalem. "Comfort ye, comfort ye my people, saith your God. Speak ye comfortably to Jerusalem, and cry unto her, that her warfare is accomplished, that her iniquity is pardoned: for she hath received of the Lord's hand double for all her sins" (Isa. 40:1-2).

It is not Israel that is called to comfort Israel, but a people not yet in existence, and that people is the Church (Hos. 2:23; 1 Pet. 2:10).

41. Gentiles will assist the Jewish people in the return to the land. "Who are these that fly as a cloud, and as the doves to their windows?" Surely the isles shall wait for me, and the ships of Tarshish first, to bring thy sons from far, their silver and their gold with them, unto the name of the Lord thy God, and to the Holy One of Israel, because he hath glorified thee" (Isa. 60:8-9).

42. God will bless those who bless Israel. The very integrity of God and His Word is at stake. God is not asleep. His Word is being and shall be fulfilled. He sees the activities of people today. As individuals and as a nation we should bless Israel, for the Almighty promises to "bless those who bless and curse those who curse" the promised seed of Abraham through Isaac and Jacob (Israel).

43. "Pray for the peace of Jerusalem," Is a commandment found in Psalm 122:6. This necessitates that we pray for the peace of the nations around Jerusalem and for a normalization of relations between Israel and her neighbors. The end of the age will come in due season, but as long as the believers are here, our mandate is to pray and believe for peace in Jerusalem. Pray for the leaders of Israel. Pray for the Arabs and their leaders. Pray for the leaders of our own nation, that their decisions relating to Israel shall be divinely inspired. God does hear and answer prayer.

44. Literal Bible interpretation leads us to realize that the words Zion and Zionist have special meaning. Zion, in Scripture, first meant the city of Jerusalem. The Bible tells of King Solomon gathering the elders of Israel "In Jerusalem, that they might bring up the ark of the covenant of the Lord out of the city of David, which is Zion" (1 Kings 8:1). Later it was expanded to include the temple mountain, then the expanded city of Jerusalem, and finally the whole land of Israel (in some passages). Christians become a part of Zion by the new birth; that is, we become a part of the commonwealth of Israel. This is not replacement theology. It is rather participation theology. The Church never replaces Israel, but our spirits are bonded to the people of Israel. We pray and work for her well-being. We pray for her ultimate redemption.

45. Christian Zionism is biblical. It is not heresy. For our faith in God's Word, we are charged from pulpits, in print, on radio and television, with "vicious heresy." This is a severe charge laid to our account, for by all biblical evidence an heretic is a damned soul. We should never call our Christian opponents heretics, even though we believe they are teaching error. We leave the state of their salvation in the hands of God. We are called blasphemers and anti-Christ, by Christian ministers who disagree with us about Zion. We have been called "dirty Jew Zionist pigs" by prominent clergy (though few of us have any Jewish ancestry). Charges like this have been leveled against us over and over through the years.

46. The Church must return to her Jewish roots to be fulfilled. The late Dr. Thomas Zimmerman said at a General Council of the Assemblies of God, "The Assemblies of God will never walk the road to Rome." But we must walk the road back to Jerusalem, where it all began. Let this premise apply to all churches.

47. Israel's existence is a miracle. It is a testimony to the miracle-working power of God. Anyone who helps to insure the continued existence of Israel cooperates with the divine plan.

48. Believers in Jesus should be supportive of Israel.

The Jews have returned to the land a second time (Isa. 11:11) and they will not be driven out of the land again (Amos 9:13-15). This is the divine plan. We are not merely spectators, but we are called to end-time involvement in that plan of the Almighty. "Faith without works is dead" (James 2:20). Some things we can do nothing about . . . we must leave those things in the hands of God. When there is something you can do, put legs to your prayers. Write to both church and government leaders relating to issues concerning Israel's security and well-being. Tell them not to make demands of Israel that are suicidal for that nation.

Christian Anti-Semitism and the Holocaust

49. Anti-Semitism implies that which is against the well-being of the Jewish people, and the nation of Israel.

50. Anti-Semitism is a spiritual force. It is Satanic. It is in opposition to and an affront to God. It has no place in the Church. To battle anti-Semitism is to engage in spiritual warfare.

51. Replacement doctrines are theological anti-Semitism. They deny Israel's identity. The identity of Israel is one of the most controversial issues confronting the Church today. This is highlighted by the fact that tired old doctrines of replacement and contempt are being loudly proclaimed in certain Christian circles. Replacement is the idea that the Church has supplanted Israel, and that God has no future plans for Israel as a nation. They make it easier for the blatant, active anti-Semites to persecute and kill the Jews. The doctrines of replacement and contempt led directly to the holocaust.

52. The holocaust was Satan's effort to eradicate the Jews, break the Abrahamic Covenant and call God's sovereignty into question.

53. You cannot understand Israel without understanding the holocaust. The holocaust is never mere history to the Jews. It is forever looming and potentially could happen again. A Christian will find it exceedingly difficult without this knowledge, and a sympathetic view of what it means to a Jewish person.

54. The holocaust took place in a Christian nation whose leader, Hitler, was a church member.

55. The German churches sold out to the Nazis. With few exceptions the Roman, Protestant, and Evangelical pastors bowed to Hitler.

56. Roman, Protestant, and Evangelical churchmen were quoted by Hitler's henchmen for justification of their heinous acts against the Jews.

57. The German church was guilty of preaching and teaching theological anti-Semitism.

58. Today some deny the holocaust ever took place. General Dwight David Eisenhower gave a statement to the press on April 15, 1945, after having visited some of the Nazi death camps. He said, "The things I saw beggar description . . . the visual evidence and the verbal testimony of starvation, cruelty, and bestiality were . . . overpowering. . . . I made the visit deliberately in order to be in a position to give first-hand evidence of these things if ever, in the future, there develops a tendency to charge these allegations merely to "propaganda."

59. The Church has perpetually taught replacement and contempt. This has strengthened the false notion that there is a special curse on the Jews. Whatever evil befalls them at the hands of the Gentiles is due to them. The holocaust — good enough for them! This evil notion must be done away with. How sad that the teaching of the Church prepared the way for the Nazis, and gave legitimacy to the extermination of the Jews. Following are just a few examples of Christian theological anti-Semitism.

60. Saint Ambrose, one of the church fathers, spoke harshly when he said, that the Jewish synagogue was "a house of impiety, a receptacle of folly, which God himself has condemned." It is no wonder that his followers then went out and set fire to the local synagogue.

218 • Signs of His Coming

61. Saint Gregory of Nyssa, in the fourth century, eloquently declared the Jews to be, "Slayers of the Lord, murderers of the prophets, adversaries of God, haters of God, men who show contempt for the law, foes of grace, enemies of their father's faith, advocates of the devil, brood of vipers, slanderers, scoffers, men whose minds are in darkness, leaven of the Pharisees, assembly of demons, sinners, wicked men, stoners, and haters of righteousness."

62. John Crysostom said, "The synagogue is worse than a brothel.... the temple of demons . . . and the cavern of devils. . . . I hate the synagogue. . . . I hate the Jews for the same reason."

63. Martin Luther accused the Jews in terms that we would consider vulgar: "When Judas hanged himself and his bowels gushed forth, and, as happens in such cases, his bladder also burst, the Jews were ready to catch the Judas-water and other precious things, and then they gorged and swilled on the merd among themselves, and were thereby endowed with such a keenness of sight that they can perceive glosses in the Scriptures such as neither Matthew nor Isaiah himself . . . would be able to detect; or perhaps they looked into the loin of their God 'Shed' and found these things written in that smokehole. . . . The devil has eased himself and emptied his belly again — that is a real halidom for Jews and would-be Jews, to kiss, batten on, swill and adore; and then the devil, with his angelic snout, devours what exudes from the oral and anal apertures of the Jews; this is indeed his favorite dish, on which he battens like a sow behind the hedge." Regarding Luther, Malcolm Hay comments, "His doctrine provided many suitable texts for Hitler's program of extermination." Today various Christian and other hate groups reprint Luther's pamphlet, "The Jews and Their Lies," to support their vengeful attacks on the Jews.

64. One of the largest Lutheran synods has denounced the anti-Semitism of Luther. May God grant our evangelical and pentecostal churches the boldness to deal with the sins of our fathers. It is not enough to piously say, "but I am not responsible for the holocaust, I was not there."

Someone must finally take the responsibility for the past sins of the Church. The prophets of Israel confessed the sins of their people as if they had committed them themselves, although they had not. See Daniel 9:3-23.

65. Jodokus Ehrhardt wrote in 1558, "We ought not to suffer Jews to live amongst us, nor to eat and drink with them." Following the precedent of Saint Ambrose he also recommended that "their synagogues should be set on fire."

66. Christianity's role in the holocaust must not remain hidden or unstated. It must be faced, no matter how painful an undertaking that may be. "Two realities must be considered in our assessment of the Church's role. First the Nazis inherited a religious and social climate of anti-Semitism which had been fostered by the Church for centuries. The final solution was deeply rooted in what has been rightly described as the Church's 'teaching of contempt for the Jews.' It was relatively easy for the totalitarian state to exploit the traditional anti-Jewish teachings of the church, which said, in effect, 'You have no right to live among us as Jews,' and turned it into the murderous declaration, 'You have no right to live.' "

67. If the Church is indicted by Jewish scholars as the prime cause of anti-Semitism for the past 1,800 years, we must not be offended, it is simply the truth. It might be convenient if we could ignore the dark side of our heritage, but if we ever hope to improve conditions in the world it is imperative that we face up to history, ourselves, and our society.

68. These evil doctrines are being taught in the Church today, sometimes blatantly, sometimes subtly.

69. In response to the doctrine of replacement we offer the words of the apostle Paul in Romans 11:26, "And so all Israel shall be saved: as it is written, There shall come out of Zion the Deliverer, and shall turn away ungodliness from Jacob." Since the Church is comprised of only saved, redeemed individuals, and since Jacob never refers to the Church, but always to natural Israel, this prophecy must be recognized as God's determination for the nation of Israel. "For behold the stone that I have laid before Joshua; upon one stone shall be seven eyes: behold, I will engrave the graving thereof, saith the Lord of hosts, and I will remove the iniquity of that land in one day" (Zech. 3:9).

70. In response to the doctrine of contempt we will consider the age-old claim that the Jews were responsible for the death of Jesus. The Jews are no more responsible than any other people on earth for the death of Jesus. The apostolic prayer in Acts 4 reveals that there is plenty of blame to go around. First Herod, an Edomite is accused, next comes the indictment of the Roman governor, Pontius Pilate, then the finger is pointed at the Gentiles, and last of all Israel is on the list. After listing human factors, finally it is clarified that God himself is primarily responsible for the atoning death of Jesus. He planned it to be so.

"The kings of the earth stood up, and the rulers were gathered together against the Lord, and against his Christ. For of a truth against thy holy child Jesus, whom thou hast anointed, both Herod, and Pontius Pilate, with the Gentiles, and the people of Israel, were gathered together, For to do whatsoever thy hand and thy counsel determined before to be done" (Acts 4:26-28).

God himself takes responsibility for the death of Jesus. Jesus makes it clear that he freely gave His life for the salvation of mankind. Jesus said, "I lay down my life for the sheep. . . . Therefore doth my Father love me, because I lay down my life, that I might take it again. No man taketh it from me, but I lay it down of myself. I have power to lay it down, and I have power to take it again. This commandment have I received of my Father" (John 10:15-18).

In the Garden of Gethsemane Jesus said, "Thinkest thou that I cannot now pray to my Father, and he shall presently give me more than twelve legions of angels?" (Matt. 26:53).

71. It is incorrect to say the Jews are under a special curse. On Palm Sunday Jesus entered the Eastern Gate, leading to the Temple Mount. The people hailed him as the King of Israel, shouting, "Hosanna." How often we hear the charge that, "These fickle Jews only a short while later were shouting, 'Crucify Him, let his blood be upon us and upon our children!' " The Bible simply does not say that. By what stretch of imagination are the enthusiastic crowd of His followers and supporters identified with the rabble-rousers who later stood in Pilate's courtyard and shouted for His blood? It is not warranted.

Josephus and other scholars tell us that a vast tent city of pilgrims crowded around Jerusalem during the Passover season. They numbered upwards of a million or more. Many came from the dispersion in surrounding, and even far-off countries. How easy for the high priest to gather a crowd of rabble-rousers, most of whom had never even met or seen Jesus. The Gospel says of those living in Judea at the time, "The common people heard Him gladly." It was the high priest and his cohorts who wanted Jesus out of the way. As our Heavenly Father listens to the echoes of history, does He heed a few troublemakers shouting, "Crucify Him," or does He listen to the voice of Jesus on the cross, pleading, "Father forgive them?" The Gospels reveal that the religious leaders moved very cautiously against Jesus and His followers, because they "feared the people." "And the chief priests and scribes sought how they might kill him; for they feared the people" (Luke 22:2; also see Mark 11:32; Mark 12:12; Luke 20:19; Acts 5:26).

72. When John or Paul speak of "the Jews" being against Jesus, remember they were Jews, speaking of the leadership, not all the Jews. The JEWS refers to the leadership who were threatened by Jesus' popularity with the people of Israel. It was a Jewish family squabble. It was not a war of Gentiles against Jews. The concept of mercy was so ingrained in the followers of Jesus that the first martyr, Stephen, cried out to God, "Lay this not to their charge." This attitude is a far cry from that of the anti-Semites who want to blame the Jews for everything bad in the world.

73. Blindness in part is upon Israel, but total blindness lies on unconverted Gentiles. "For I would not, brethren, that ye should be ignorant of this mystery, lest ye should be wise in your own conceits; that blindness in part is happened to Israel, until the fulness of the Gentiles be come in" (Rom. 11:25). "In whom the god of this world hath blinded the minds of them which believe not, lest the light of the glorious gospel of Christ, who is the image of God, should shine unto them" (1 Cor. 4:4). It is interesting to note that many claim that today, proportionately more Jews are coming to Messiah Jesus than Gentiles.

Racism and Zion

74. Anti-Semitism is the oldest and most enduring form of racism. Christian Zionists have learned to despise and resist all forms of racism.

75. To be for Israel is not to be against the Arabs. Christians should manifest love and concern for all people.

76. In 1975 the United Nations voted in favor of a resolution stating that Zionism is racism. It is not — it is the Jewish national liberation movement. Although the U.N. has rescinded its slanderous 1975 resolution accusing that Zionism is racism, this false charge is still being proclaimed by the enemies of Israel, and there are those who would like to see the resolution reinstated in the U.N. If Zionism is racism, then God is a racist because He is the author of Zionism. His favor of Israel is sung in the Psalms: "The Lord doth build up Jerusalem: he gathereth together the outcasts of Israel. . . . Praise the Lord, O Jerusalem; praise thy God, O Zion. . . . He hath not dealt so with any nation" (Ps. 147:2,12-20).

Identity of the Jews

77. Robbing the Jews of their identity is a favorite activity of anti-Semites, and they are reinforced by replacement theology in the Church. Foolish people argue whether the Jews are actually the seed of Abraham. What! Do you think God is incapable of fulfilling His Word to Abraham? God means what He says. Israel is not a race, but a people, an ethnic group, a nation. That nation has descended from Abraham, Isaac, and Jacob (Israel). That nation is alive in the world today and will never be destroyed. Christian believers are grafted into the olive tree of Israel and are also counted as seed of Abraham, by adoption, but this does not disenfranchise the nation of the Jewish people, Israel (Rom., 9, 10, and 11). Theories like Anglo Israelism and Khazar identity should be studied, understood, and refuted by scholars in the Church.

Issues

78. If Israel were destroyed, the secular world and much of the Church would care little at this calamity. This attitude must be corrected. Definite steps should be taken to assure Israel's security and continued existence. There are numerous issues about which Christians should be informed. Some of the current issues include:

79. Urge the nations to move their embassies to Jerusalem, the capital of Israel. No people other than the Jews has made Jerusalem its capital. It has been the capital of Israel for 3,000 years, since the time King David united the tribes of Israel into one nation. Every nation in the world chooses its capital city, except Israel. In other nations, foreign powers set up their embassies in the designated capital, except in Israel. Almost all nations have bowed to pressure, and have placed their embassies in Tel Aviv. This is an intolerable insult to our one reliable ally in the Middle East, Israel. This should be corrected as soon as possible.

80. Yassir Arafat promised that the PLO Covenant would be revised, taking out the statements that call for the destruction of Israel. To date this has still not been done. We hope and pray for compliance.

81. Israel should not be required to leave the Golan Heights and jeopardize the security of the nation and all the Israeli people. Judea and Samaria are another case in point. Woe to those who divide the land for gain. "Thus shall he [Antichrist] do in the most strong holds with a strange god, whom he shall acknowledge and increase with glory: and he shall cause them to rule over many, and shall divide the land for gain" (Dan. 11:39). Israel may give land for peace, but will ultimately, in the Messianic Age, own the entire land described in the Bible.

82. Ethnic cleansing. We were shocked when Anwar Sadat demanded the desert to be clean of the Jews. Judenrein! The destruction of the town of Yamit in the Sinai serves as a harsh object lesson of Arab extremism. Now the world community of nations is demanding removal of all Jews from Judea and Samaria (West Bank). Next ethnic cleansing will demand that all Israel be rid of all the Jews. We are horrified at the ethnic cleansing in Bosnia, yet today the UN calls for the removal of all Jews from biblical Judea and Samaria. The plan is to have a Palestinian state that is Judenrein (Hitler's term, meaning "clean of the Jews").

There Is a Long and Honorable History of Christian Zionism

83. Increase Mather was an American clergyman who became the president of Harvard College. In 1669 Mather wrote a work titled *The Mystery of Israel's Salvation Explained and Applyed.* A Bible literalist, Mather said, "After the Jews are brought into their own land again and there disturbed with Gog and Magog (Ezek. 38 and 39) who shall think with great fury to destroy the Israelites. . . . The Jews who have been trampled upon by all nations shall become the most glorious nation in the whole world, and all other nations shall have them in great esteem and honor (Isa. 60:1-3). That the time will surely come, when the body of the 12 tribes of Israel shall be brought out of their present condition of bondage and misery, into a glorious and wonderful state of salvation, not only spiritual but temporal."

84. Pierre Jurieu, a Christian author wrote in 1686, "A time must come in which the Jewish nation shall be exalted, as has been promised, above all nations and it shall reign by its saints, its prophets and apostles. For otherwise I am bold to say that all the prophecies made to these people were delusive."

85. Rev. William Hechler, a British evangelical pastor was the person most mentioned in the diaries of Theodore Herzl, who founded the modern Zionist movement in Basle, Switzerland, in 1897. Hechler bonded his spirit to that of Herzl and dogged his footsteps all over Europe. The pastor had an uncanny ability to pry open doors that were closed to Herzl, getting him appointments with the kaiser of Germany and other European leaders. When times of depression and thoughts of failure slowed the pace of Herzl, there was William Hechler buoying up his spirits with scriptural admonition and prophetic words.

86. Dr. David Rausch, professor at Ashland College [Ohio], has written a monumental work, *Zionism Within Early American Fundamentalism, 1878-1918.* Rausch brilliantly chronicles the fundamentalist and evangelical connection to a biblical Zionist dream. We can only mention a few of the shining lights of evangelical Zionism. Dr. Elhanan Winchester wrote in 1800 that "The Return of the Jews to their own land is certain." In 1852 a Reverend Bickersteth wrote *The Restoration of the Jews to their Own Land.*

87. England's Balfour Declaration in 1917 had given hope to the Jews that they would be restored to the land. This was encouraged by Bible-believing Christians in Britain. In 1918 Dr. David Baron wrote in great detail about the coming return of the Jews to the land.

88. During the early 1900s fundamentalists were conducting prophecy conferences in New York, Chicago, London, and other cities. There was always major emphasis on the Jewish nation.

89. Dr. G. Douglas Young, founder of the Jerusalem Institute of Holy Land Studies on Mount Zion wrote, "Jerusalem has never been the capital of any people except the Jewish People.... We are struck by the fact that since the Six Day War (1967) all people are free to worship in their place of choice, unlike the situation 1948-1967. The unity of Jerusalem must be preserved . . . internationalization is an idea which has never worked in history" [1971].

90. Jaques Maritain, a Christian French philosopher on Israel: "It is a strange paradox to see disputed with the Israelis the sole territory to which, considering the entire spectacle of human history, it is absolutely divinely certain that a people has incontestably a right . . . the return of a portion of the Jewish people and its regroupment in the Holy Land (of which the existence of Israel is a sign and guarantee), this is the re-accomplishment, under our eyes, of the divine promise which is without repentance.... To wish the disappearance of Israel is to reject into nothingness this return which was finally accorded to the Jewish people and which permits it to have a shelter of its own in the world" [1975].

91. The Assemblies of God is the only church denomination with a statement in its creed that recognizes that God has future plans for the nation of Israel. This idea was amended to the AG Statement of Fundamental Truths in 1927, as an act of faith, many years before there was anything to indicate that Israel would become a nation in 1948. We urge other churches to amend their creedal statements to give recognition to God's future determination for Israel and the Jewish people.

92. The Minutes for the 1945 General Council of the Assemblies of God show the brethren and sisters of the fellowship standing guard on the ramparts, ever vigilant to oppose the forces of evil. The resolution against hatred of the Jews reads:

Anti-Semitism

WHEREAS, We have witnessed in this generation an almost universal increase in anti-Semitism and this has resulted in the greatest series of persecutions perpetrated in modern times, and

WHEREAS, Even in the United States of America there has been an alarming increase in anti-Semitism;

THEREFORE BE IT RESOLVED, That the General Council hereby declare its opposition to anti-Semitism and that it disapprove of the ministers of the Assemblies of God identifying themselves with those who are engaged in this propaganda.

BE IT FURTHER RESOLVED, That the editor of publications be instructed to prepare an article including Section I of this resolution in which our position on anti-Semitism is set forth, and that it be published in the *Pentecostal Evangel.*

Recently the *Pentecostal Evangel* published an issue entirely devoted to Israel, the Holyland. It was very positive.

I call upon my own church, especially local pastors and congregations, to live up to the spirit of the 1945 AG resolution and take a strong stance, from every pulpit, against anti-Semitism, and additionally against all forms of racism. I further urge all churches in the world to join us in this great end-time struggle against Satan, who would like to destroy both the evangelical churches and Israel.

93. Peace will come. Peace will come through God and it will unfold in His beloved Jerusalem. The Christian Celebration of the Feast of Tabernacles endeavors to fulfill the prophetic cry of Isaiah. At a time when the tide of anti-Semitism is rising and Israel is being increasingly isolated by the nations, we want to say, "Israel, you are not alone." Statement from the International Christian Embassy, Jerusalem.

94. Peace is desirable. Even though there will be a false peace under the horrible, short-lived mandate of the final Antichrist, at the present any honorable peace treaty that works, even for a time, is to be most highly desired.

95. Today there are hundreds of Christian groups that essentially hold the point of view expressed in this paper. Among them are Christians United for Israel, the National Christian Leadership Conference for Israel, the International Christian Embassy, Jerusalem, CIPAC, American Christian Trust, Bridges for Peace, Christian Friends of Israel, Voices United for Israel, Faith Bible Chapel Outreach, A Praise in the Earth, John Hagee Ministries, Israel Vistas, etc. A partial directory is in the back of the book *Can Israel Survive in a Hostile World?* by David Allen Lewis.

INDEX — 95 THESES
For Quick Reference

1. The Church and Israel common heritage.
2. The Bible is the Word of God.
3. God is sovereign.
4. God owns the whole world.
5. God can give any portion of the world.
6. God has determined to give the land.

THE ABRAHAMIC COVENANT
7. The Jewish people own the land of Israel.
8. The Mosaic Covenant was conditional.
9. If God should break His promise.

GOD'S PLAN FOR ISRAEL
10. God's plan for Israel includes habitation of the land of Israel.

11. Holy Land title given by God to only one nation.
12. God's sovereignty called into question.
13. Land for peace schemes seldom work.

THE EARLY CHURCH WAS JEWISH
14. The Early Church was entirely Jewish.
15. The Jewish people gave us the Bible.
16. Jewish people gave the New Testament.
17. The Jewish people gave us Jesus.
18. Jesus made a choice.
19. The disciples of Jesus were Jewish.

THE TRAGIC SPLIT
20. The earliest Church was Jewish — viewed as a Jewish
    sect until after the Bar Kochba revolt.

REPLACEMENT THEOLOGY
21. Origenes Adamantius (Origen).
22. Augustine.
23. The Church became — tormentor — Jews.
24. Replacement theology.
25. We have come unto Zion.

WHAT DOES ZION MEAN TO A CHRISTIAN?
26. Zionism — Israel is a national home for.
27. Zionism did not begin in 1897.
28. When Christians say that they are biblical Zionists.
29. Some charge that the Jews are evil.
30. Unconditional love.
31. Identify with biblical Zionism.
32. Christians who embrace Zion are men and women of
    faith and works.
33. Christians are called to be protectors.
34. Accused of "sheltering the Jews."
35. Israel is God's litmus test.
36. The church that does not resist A.S.
37. Theologians in pre-Nazi Germany.
38. Church agenda and Israel.

39. Right to exist — not imply . . . agreement.
40. Comfort to the Jews and to Jerusalem.
41. Gentiles will assist return to the land.
42. God will bless those who bless Israel.
43. Pray for the peace of Jerusalem.
44. Literal Bible interpretation.
45. Christian Zionism is biblical.
46. The Church must return to her Jewish roots.
48. Believers should be supportive of Israel.

CHRISTIANS AND THE HOLOCAUST
49. Anti-Semitism implies.
50. Anti-Semitism is a spiritual force.
51. Replacement doctrines.
52. Holocaust — Satan's effort destroy the Jews.
53. Can't understand Israel without an understanding of the holocaust.
54. Holocaust took place in Christian nation.
55. German churches sold out to Nazis.
56. Roman, Protestant, and Evangelical.
57. The German Church and anti-Semitism.
58. Deny the holocaust.
59. Church perpetually taught replacement.
60. Saint Ambrose.
61. Saint Gregory of Nyssa.
62. John Crysostom.
63. Martin Luther.
64. One of the largest Lutheran synods.
65. Jodokus Ehrhardt.
66. Christianity's role in the holocaust.
67. If the Church is indicted.
68. These doctrines taught in the Church today.
69. Response to replacement doctrine.
70. Response to the doctrine of contempt.
71. Incorrect to say Jews cursed.
72. John or Paul speak of "the Jews."
73. Blindness in part is upon Israel.

RACISM AND ZION
74. Anti-Semitism is the oldest racism.
75. For Israel is not against the Arabs.
76. UN says Zionism is racism.
77. Robbing the Jews of their identity.

ISSUES
78. If Israel were destroyed.
79. Urge nations to move their embassies.
80. Yassir Arafat promised PLO covenant.
81. Israel should not leave Golan Heights.
82. Ethnic cleansing.

EXAMPLES OF CHRISTIAN ZIONISM
83. Increase Mather.
84. Pierre Jurieu.
85. Rev. William Hechler.
86. Dr. David Rausch.
87. England's Balfour Declaration in 1917.
88. Early 1900s fundamentalists.
89. Dr. G. Douglas Young.
90. Jaques Maritain.
91. Assemblies of God and Israel.
92. Assemblies of God on anti-Semitism.
93. Peace will come.
94. Peace is desirable.
95. Hundreds of Christian Zionist Groups.

Chapter 15

LINCOLN'S LAST WORDS

"We could go up to Jeru —"

The Civil War was over. The country was weeping for its fallen dead and the deep scars it had sustained. The slaves were now free, but the country was in shambles.

Weary in heart and sick in spirit, President Abraham Lincoln carried a deep sense of dread. The Union was preserved but he wept for the division that still smoldered in the soul of the nation. In his last cabinet meeting before the assassination he declared that there would be no recriminations, no vengeance taken on the South. If he had lived, the history of the South would have been far different. In that final cabinet meeting he said that now the curse of slavery was ended and the next thing to deal with would be the curse of alcohol.

Lincoln had spoken privately of his plans to formally join the church and make public his testimony of faith in Jesus Christ. In his last public speech he spoke of a national day of thanksgiving that would soon be proclaimed.

The night he went to Ford's Theater he was tired, and really did not want to go, but since he had promised his wife Mary. . . . The news had just come that day that the war was over. He now looked forward to enjoying a time of peace.

A young man, John Wilkes Booth, sat in a tavern drinking the same day that Lincoln said that the scourge of alcohol should be removed. That same night another young man had left his guard post outside the president's theater box and sat across the street in a tavern, drinking. The first of these two men, in the absence of the second, was able to quietly open the door and step into Lincoln's box.

Lincoln's very last words are of great interest to us. Sitting in the theater he said to Mary, "Do you know what I would like to do now? I would like to go with you to the Near East." Booth entered the box at this point. Lincoln said, "We could go to Bethlehem where He was born." Booth stepped closer. "We could go to Bethany, we could follow in those hallowed footsteps." Now Booth lifted the gun and aimed it at the back of Lincoln's head. "And we could go up to Jeru —" **BANG!** the pistol shot rang out and a bullet pierced the head of Abraham Lincoln.

"We could go up to Jeru —" His last words, uttered as he stepped out of the theater box into the heavenly Jerusalem and the presence of our Lord.

Lincoln had written to the pastor of the New York Avenue Presbyterian Church, telling him that he had found firm faith in Jesus and wished to make a public profession of his faith, and to become a member of the church on Easter Sunday. But on Good Friday, he died.

Chapter 16

STONEHENGE TODAY

And the World Psychic Grid

On the dreary, windswept Salisbury plain, over a hundred miles west of London, stands one of the strangest monuments of all time — the Stonehenge of England. Forty-eight centuries have come and gone since an unknown people erected Stonehenge. They left no written inscription and the original purpose of the monument is not known.

Down through the ages, like a magnet, mysterious Stonehenge has drawn druids, Satanists, witches, metaphysicians, and a host of other cultists. Silent, brooding Stonehenge has been a witness to the most macabre rituals known to man, including animal and human sacrifices.

Mrs. Lewis and I visited Stonehenge in the dead of winter. The temperature was below zero. The howling winds whipping about us chilled us to the bone. We were just beginning our on-location research into one of the great mysteries of earth. We had gone to England to examine and study the original Stonehenge because of something I had seen in the state of Georgia.

Stonehenge in America

Slightly over seven miles north of the small town of Elberton, Georgia, stands a strange granite monument that is said to resemble the British Stonehenge. In fact, in a book published by the Elberton Granite Finishing Company, the likeness to the Stonehenge of England is pointed out not once, but several times.

How Did It Happen?

On a hot Friday afternoon in July 1979 a mysterious stranger arrived in Elberton. He went to the office of Mr. Joe Fendley Sr., president of a major granite company. The uninvited visitor proposed that Mr. Fendley undertake the building of a monument that would serve as a means of leading humanity into a new age of reason. This granite beacon would draw people, like a magnet, from all over the world.

No doubt Fendley, a civic-minded man, saw the possibility of a fine new tourist attraction for the area and ultimately responded favorably to the idea.

The mysterious stranger refused to give his true identity, calling himself by a pseudonym, Robert C. Christian. He claimed to represent a group of wealthy, conservative, patriotic, Christian Americans whose identity was to be forever unknown. The purpose of the stones was to give knowledge necessary for the survival of humanity.

"Mr. Christian" told Fendley that he had been chosen by the sponsors for this important task. Why Fendley? The former mayor of Elberton muses over this question, confessing that he does not know the answer. This 32-degree Scottish Rite Mason and member of the First Baptist Church is active in a long list of community organizations and activities ranging from Rotary to the VFW. He is the president and owner of both the Pyramid Quarries and the Elberton Granite Finishing Company.

Visitors from Far Places

While I was photographing the stones on my first of five research trips, I noted that people came and went continuously. There was never a large crowd, but a carload, a family, or a single individual would come from time to time. I listened as people marveled at the beauty both of the monument and its message. I felt differently, believing that the message was sinister.

I asked a young couple from Oregon, "What does that first statement mean to you?" The young man replied that it was a beautiful expression of human hope. I asked him if he would read it aloud. He read, "Maintain humanity under 500,000,000 in perpetual balance with nature," and looked at me in a puzzled fashion. When I asked him how many people there are in the world, he responded that he thought there were about five billion. I asked him how the world population was going to get down to one-half billion in order to be "maintained" at that level.

His wife exclaimed, "I didn't realize it said that. Do the other nine statements have any hidden meaning?" I proceeded to give my explanation, but when I got to the seventh statement she said, "This thing is evil, we're getting out of here." I never did get to finish my ten-point lecture!

Upon interviewing a number of people in Elberton, I found that many were frightened by the Guidestones. Some told of witch covens dancing around the stones in the nude on wicca holidays, and of Satanists who performed animal sacrifices.

Busloads of Oriental tourists-pilgrims have been drawn to the Guidestones. One of their priests was heard to exclaim, "The spirits are very strong in this place."

On a later visit to the Guidestones no visitors were present. I spent some time doing photography from many angles. Then an expensive automobile pulled up and out of it came a lady whom I can only describe as being striking in appearance. Her finely tailored clothes made a statement. Ignoring my presence, she approached the monument and knelt down. I listened curiously as she prayed in a language I could not recognize. After some time she arose and looked in my direction. I said, "Hello," and she responded coolly with the same greeting. Ever-inquisitive, I asked her who she was praying to.

Her answer was, "I am worshipping Gaia, Goddess Earth. Her presence is very powerful in this sacred place. I am a wiccan priestess and find great strength here." In our very brief conversation she revealed that she was a college professor, a teacher of anthropology. Then, agitated, she said to me, "You do not belong here, do you? There is something disturbing about you. You are not in tune with the spirits that guide me. " She strode to her Mercedes, got in, and drove away.

Church of God Pastor Comments

James Traffansted, then-pastor of Elberton Church of God, granted me a taped interview. The local press and area television had indicated that his reaction to the Guidestones was negative. He confirmed a lot of the stories I had heard about witch and Satanist cult activities in connection with the monument.

Please be careful not to blame the builder of the monument for this activity, since that was most likely not the intended purpose. It is strange, however, that the monument has exercised such drawing power for cultists.

Pastor Traffansted said that in his opinion it was only a matter of time until some crazy group would perform a human sacrifice at the site. We can only hope that this dark prognostication never sees a fulfillment.

The Message

This would all be very interesting by itself, but it is the message chiseled on the monument in eight living languages and four dead languages that really commands our attention. In addition to the ten statements in eight living languages on the sides of the huge granite slabs, there is a capstone which announces in four dead languages, *"Let These Be Guides to an Age of Reason."*

The New Ten Commandments

Reverend Traffansted said, "They are the Antichrist's ten commandments." We will give you the ten statements which Mr. Robert C. Christian and the secret sponsors say are guides to a [New] Age of Reason. Following each of the ten statements we will print a few of the words of the "sponsors" to expand understanding of each statement. These words are taken directly from a paper distributed to visitors in Elberton. This is followed by our brief comment.

The Georgia Guidestones

"A massive granite monument espousing the conservation of mankind and further generations. Sources for the sizable financing of the project choose to remain anonymous. The wording of the message proclaimed on the monument is in 12 languages, including the archaic languages of Sanskrit, Babylonian Cuneiform, Egyptian Hieroglyphics and Classical Greek, as well as English, Russian, Hebrew, Arabic, Hindi, Chinese, Spanish, and Swahili."

The guides, followed by explanatory precepts, are as follows. The words here are exactly as the sponsors provided them. The words in bold type are the statements that are seen on the Guidestones. The words following each statement, in "quotation" marks are from the printed literature which we mentioned. *Our comments follow.*

1. Maintain humanity under 500,000,000 in perpetual balance with nature. "Means the entire human race at its climax level for permanent balance with nature."

Our comment: Since there are now six billion people in the world, this raises some serious questions. How do the sponsors of the Guidestones envision the elimination of five and a half billion human beings, bringing world population down to the 500,000,000 they suggest as a maintenance level?

2. Guide reproduction wisely — improving fitness and diversity. "Without going into details as yet undiscovered, this means humanity should apply reason and knowledge to guiding its own reproduction. 'Fitness' could be translated as 'health.' 'Diversity' could be translated as 'variety.' "

Our comment: Will couples have to get a government license to have a child? Who will be permitted and who will not? Who decides? Will this involve sterilization of "undesirables?" What penalty will be meted out for those who refuse to comply?

3. Unite humanity with a living new language. "A 'living' language grows and changes with advancing knowledge. A 'new' language will be developed 'de novo' — and need not necessarily be adapted from any languages now in existence."

Our comment: This globalist call for humanity to be united through a new common language is popular in New Age circles and is another call for the New World Order to emerge in our time.

4. Rule passion — faith — tradition — and all things with tempered reason. " 'Faith' here may be used in a religious sense. Too often people are ruled by blind faith, even when it may be contrary to reason. Reason must be tempered with compassion here — but must prevail."

Our comment: Will Bible-believing Christians have to relinquish their faith for the greater good? When secular human reason mandates thoughts or actions that are contrary to our faith, how can we comply? How will this rule be enforced? Will believers who refuse to obey humanistic laws that violate our faith be fined? Will they be put in jail or concentration camps? Executed?

5. Protect people and nations with fair laws and just

courts. "Courts must consider justice as well as law."

Our comment: There is already a World Court. National sovereignty is being violated. Who decides what is justice if "law" is not the guide? Shall we be forced to do away with the Constitution?

6. Let all nations rule internally, resolving external disputes in a world court. "Individual nations must be free to develop their own destinies at home as their own people wish — but cannot abuse their neighbors."

Our comment: Here is a call for global rule. We see pictured here a United World Federation of nations. There will be a centralized world headquarters. Individual nation states will control some internal affairs, as long as they stay in line with the world government. In addition to the comment of the "sponsors" noted above, we found many references in the Georgia Guidestones book to world citizens, world government, world court, etc.

7. Avoid petty laws and useless officials. "Self explanatory."

Our comment: When there is a world government, with a dictator at its helm, he and his henchmen will decide everything for you.

8. Balance personal rights with social duties. "Individuals have a natural concern for their welfare, but man is a social animal and must also be concerned for the group. Failure of society means failure for its individual citizens."

Our comment: Seventy-five years of Soviet Russian communism demonstrated to the world that socialism does not work. This Guidestones statement declares that the state rule is superior to your individual rights. This evolutionary concept, identifying man as a "social animal," will not only fail on a monumental scale, but will lead the world into a frenzy of self-destruction in a period of time the Bible calls the Tribulation.

9. Prize truth — beauty — love — seeking harmony with the infinite. "The infinite here means the supreme being — whose will is manifest in the workings of the cosmos — if we will seek for it."

Our comment: What is the infinite? Who is the supreme being? Do you suppose for a moment that they mean our Lord Jesus Christ? I think not! "Jesus saith unto him, I am the way, the truth, and the life: no man cometh unto the Father, but by me" (John 14:6). It is this exclusivity of Bible Christianity which makes us enemies in the eyes of the world.

Commandment number nine fits very well into the Gaia hypothesis that sees the earth as a living being, a goddess, of which every material thing is a tiny part. Those who embrace the Gaia idea feel no need for individual salvation. Their goal is self-realization, discovering one's own godhood.

10. Be not a cancer on the earth — leave room for nature — leave room for nature. "In our time, the growth of humanity is destroying the natural conditions of the earth which have fostered all existing life. We must restore balance."

Our comment: Interpret this as enforced birth control, sterilization of undesirables, and as is now practiced in China, abortion forced on those bearing more than their allotment of children. "We must restore balance" simply takes us back to commandment one.

What Do You Think?

Is this monument significant or is it of no consequence? Why have people from every state and many foreign countries come to visit the monument? What about the attraction it has for far-out cultists and witches? Who or what is Mr. Robert C. Christian and the mysterious group of sponsors? Did Fendley, mayor of Elberton invent the whole thing? If so, why would he do so? Remember, there are other people involved in Elberton. Were they accomplices in a deception?

What do you think of the ten statements or commandments on the monument? What is the "Age of Reason" which they herald? Could this have anything to do with the mystery of iniquity and the spirit of Antichrist? Why do Japanese cultists become ecstatic at the monument and proclaim, "The spirits are very strong there?"

Based on the evidence we have uncovered, it is our conclusion that this was not a plot hatched out by Mr. Joe Fendley and his friends. We feel quite sure that "Mr. Christian" and the mysterious group of sponsors actually do exist somewhere in the USA. What is their motivation for undertaking this expensive project? Will we hear more from them?

Why have more Stonehenges been built in Port Perry, Ontario; Montreal, Quebec; Alliance, Nebraska; Port Townsend, Washington; Rolla, Missouri; St. Louis, Missouri; Maryhill, Washington; Arlington, Texas, etc.? These are sites I have personally visited, with the exception of Alliance, Nebraska. We hear reports of several others. Please let us know of other locations if you are aware of any. Send photographs if possible.

We will read and file all the letters you write us about this matter. Pray over your reply. Ask God for spiritual insight and revelation. Share as fully with us as you can.

If some of you researchers want to get direct information on the Georgia Guidestones there is a book available, published and copyrighted by Mr. Fendley. The book is a large 8-1/2 X 11 inch saddlestitched book. It is full of beautiful pictures. It tells the story from Mr. Fendley's point of view, and it includes a record of more information given to him by the mysterious Mr. Robert C. Christian and the sponsors. The book costs $7.00 plus $1.00 for postage. Order from Mr. Joe Fendley; P.O. Box 110, Elberton, GA 30635.

If you have negative feelings about this matter, as I am sure many do, please do not take it out on Mr. Fendley. He is simply a businessman who fulfilled a contract. I do not

244 • *Signs of His Coming*

know what he believes about the concepts portrayed by the "Guidestones." If your research turns up any new data please send us full information. We will greatly appreciate this.

Bible Belt Stonehenge

In a small mid-America community stands the second North American Stonehenge we came upon in our research. Rolla, Missouri, is the site of a Stonehenge construction on the campus of the University of Missouri at Rolla.

Clippings from the local Rolla newspaper, which we located in the public library, show the dedication of the Rolla Stonehenge. This dedication featured the services of a druid priest, brought in to perform the ceremony of the sword, and chant pagan prayers. Rolla now celebrates an annual "sunfest" centered about this new American Stonehenge.

Arlington, Texas

Between Fort Worth and Dallas stands a magnificent series of five monuments with some resemblance to the Stonehenge of Great Britain.

The monuments were given to the Caelum Moor Foundation by Jane Mathes Kelton on December 13, 1985. Caelum is another word for "Uranus," the name, not only of a starry constellation, but of an ancient pagan god.

In *The Dictionary of Classical Mythology*, author Pierre Grimal comments: "Caelus. The Sky (this personification is indicated by the use of the masculine form rather than the neuter, Caelum); this is not a Roman deity but merely a Latin translation of the name of the Greek god Uranus who played a very important part in Hellenic theology and mythology."

The dedication plaque reads in part:

> Caelum Moor represents a commitment to the concept that past and present are inextricably linked, that a meaningful future depends upon understanding our history and heritage, and that it

is through the arts that these vital connections are best expressed.

Like the megalithic monuments of prehistory [such as Stonehenge] Caelum Moor, named for a constellation suggests the relationships between material and spiritual worlds: as a work of the twentieth century it acknowledges technology while assuring the necessity of balance with nature. *[Note: If named only for the physical constellation Uranus, and not the god, why is it a link between the material and spiritual worlds?]*

Caelum Moor is dedicated to the public in the hope that it may provide a quiet place for enjoyment, contemplation, self-discovery, and rejuvenation.

Commissioned by Jane Mathes Kelton. Norman P. Hines, sculptor. Gifted to the Caelum Moor foundation December 13, 1985. Dedicated May 10, 1986.

The dedication plaque further explains that the groups of stones or "monuments" are named: Sarsen Caer; De'Danann; Morna Linn; Tolemen Barrow, and Tan Tara. The plaque expands on the definition or meaning of these terms as follows:

1. Sarsen Caer. Sarsen: Druidic stones thought to be magic. Caer: Castle.

2. De'Dannan. Celtic Divine family. Children of the Great Mother.

3. Morna Linn. Morna: Feminine name meaning beloved. Linn: Water rushing over stones.

4. Tolmen Barrow. Tolmen: Hole-stone with regenerative power. Barrow: Sacred Hill.

5. Tan Tara. Tan: Sacred fire. Tara: Home of the Celtic Divines.

The monument named De'Danann was notable for a

curious circular maze design reminiscent of the arrangement of Stonehenge.

The Tolmen Barrow monument was embellished with a curious design resembling a triangle made of three loops (mobius loop?). This symbol, a favorite of many New Agers appears on the cover of Marilyn Ferguson's book *The Aquarian Conspiracy,* considered by many to be a major "bible" of the New Age movement. Look over the advertisements in any New Age periodical and see how frequently this symbol is used. This is said to be a symbol stolen (like the rainbow) from the church. The early church is believed to have used this symbol to illustrate the eternal triune nature of God.

Maryhill, Washington

We found the Maryhill Stonehenge in Washington, two miles above the Columbia River on the Oregon border.

When we visited the site we were impressed by its towering proportions. Like other Stonehenge monuments it too has drawn cultists, witches, and Satanists into its shadows where they perform their mystical ceremonies.

Northern Neighbor

Near Port Perry, Ontario, Canada, on a lonely country road you will see the most unusual "Stonehenge" of them all. Erected by sculptor Bill Lishman, the monument is made of crushed automobiles carefully selected to approximate the size and arrangement of the original stones (in England). I call it metalhenge! The construction was funded by a major American automobile manufacturer and was used in a series of TV commercials.

Anything that resembles the Stonehenge could be looked upon as a monument of the New Age, whatever the objectives of the perpetrators. We have no indication that the builders of this Canadian "metalhenge" had any occult purpose. However, residents in the area report that cultists are drawn to it and perform ceremonies there.

Rumors

We have heard rumors of a dozen other "Stonehenge" constructs in the USA and Canada. If you know of anything of this nature please let us know. One of our research trips took us to Cahokia, Illinois, near St. Louis, Missouri. We saw the "Indian Mound Stonehenge," commonly called "Woodhenge." We also visited the Serpents Mound State Park near Cincinnati, Ohio. It is designated as a major power vortex by New Agers.

We always approach this type of research with a healthy skepticism, assuming that there is no occult meaning until it is proven (or disproved). In this way we can maintain a certain essential objectivity in our reporting. You can easily understand why our reporting of various phenomena has high credibility among the brethren. We work hard to maintain this credibility. We are not out to prove a theory, but to examine and report the facts. It is of great importance that God's people be well-informed in these strange and changing times in which we live. It is equally important that we do not become victims of Christian misinformation or fantasy. The prophecy message can be badly hurt by haphazard or irresponsible reporting.

The Millennium Society's Big Bash

The *Reader's Digest* confirmed the existence of the 6,000 member Millennium Society in the October 1996 edition. Their plan is to sponsor 24 public festivals in each of the world's time zones on the last New Year's Eve of the 20th century. Millennium parties are planned for the Taj Mahal, the Great Wall of China, Mount Fuji, and Times Square in New York, which is expected to have over one million in attendance. In addition, 250 million in the USA will watch the New York affair on television.

The Millennium Society will also have a private party to which the government leaders and the elite of the world will be invited to attend. The society has already signed an agreement with the Egyptian government for the right to hold their celebration at the Great Pyramid.

The Great Pyramid of Cheops in Egypt is a favored power vortex claimed by New Agers. At the time of the big event being planned at the Great Pyramid for the stroke of midnight, December 31, 1999, the New Age movement expects a major paradigm shift to take place. They believe it will be their great hour of victory. It will be the "dawning of the Age of Aquarius." Such psychic force will flow over the fully operational world psychic grid that all humanity will be forced to accept their new perception of reality. Only those who have a low vibratory rate will fail to make the change. They will have to be neutralized or eliminated. Guess who's hit list that puts you on!

The word paradigm means "a model." In the way it is used here it implies *the model by which you perceive reality.* Some view reality through the Gaia or goddess earth paradigm. Others choose a paradigm based on agnosticism or atheism.

Born-again Christians have a paradigm called the Bible. We interpret the world about us and our own person by the truths we find in its holy pages. The Bible is our model for understanding reality.

The paradigm shift, according to New Agers, will force all humanity to accept the new reality of the Age of Aquarius. It will be the time of the launching of the world psychic grid. Natural physical places like, Mt. Shasta, Sedona, Needles Highway, Niagara Falls, Snaefensyokle Glacier in Iceland, Rennes les Chateau in France, and manmade structures such as the pyramids, the Stonehenges, and many more things will form the Psi Grid of power vortexes, the connection nodes, all linked by mystical "ley lines."

New Agers believe that through this Psi Grid, power will flow to every point on earth. I first heard this referred to at the New Age event billed as the World Instant of Cooperation, an annual event held each December 31, starting with the Tri-Millennial Countdown which began on December 31, 1975. It was launched by anthropologist Margaret Meade; John Randolph Price, president of the Quartus Foundation; and Barbara Marx Hubbard, author of the book *Happy Birthday, Planet Earth.*

On December 31, 1986, I attended the first *World Instant of Cooperation* held in the Municipal Auditorium in Kansas City, Missouri. I was in attendance as an observer, a credentialed journalist. I did not join hands with the participants.

One of the featured speakers was former Assistant Secretary General of the United Nations Robert Muller, author of *New Genesis — Shaping a Global Spirituality.* Mueller heralds the coming of a new Christ — but it won't be Jesus. This is a familiar line with a myriad of New Age leaders who are looking for the Avatar, the Lord Mastery. It was there I first heard about the living goddess earth idea. We were told that mother goddess earth is in contact with the "ascended masters of the hierarchy of the universe" who would soon raise up a human leader from our midst. They would empower the leader with supernormal powers and knowledge. The leader would soon bring humanity into a New Age of World Order and solve all of our problems. We were told that we could prepare the way for him. As the participants left, each was given a small bag of tiny crystals. They were told to chant incantations for world peace over the crystals, then to bury them in the earth wherever they went. These crystals would be local connectors of the Psi Grid, and were an important part of the power conduits in the A.D. 2000 paradigm shift.

Another event started in August 1987 is called the "Harmonic Convergence." It was innovated by a New Age leader, Jose Arguelles. It, too, is now an annual event. It was said in 1987 that the purpose of the Harmonic Convergence was to bring 144,000 shamans, magicians, and spiritual descendants of the Mayans to many "sacred sites" for the release of massive force-energy, to usher in the next phase of the "New Age." One wonders who will attend the events at the pyramids; the Salisbury, England, Stonehenge; and hundreds of other points, for the end of the millennia event.

Let them try. Let them operate with their psychic grid. We will be ready for them. Our power grid has been operational since the Day of Pentecost. "Greater is He that is within you than he that is in the world!" Holy Ghost revival is moving all over the world. Join the Holy Spirit World Liberation Army of God. The river of God is flowing. Get in the stream today.

> Let's go forward for God and resist the foe.
> Don't give in to the man of sin.
> Our God is mighty and we're bound to win.
> Satan has an evil force to fight against the Lord.
> So, put on your armour, take up your sword,
> We're going in the name of the Lord.
> — Author unknown

I know where I will be at midnight, December 31, 1999, if Jesus has not returned. I hope that you will join me, and a host of other Bible Christians, in intercession and spiritual warfare to blunt the edge of Satan's sword. Read our publication *Prophecy Watch International* for more information. God willing, we will be conducting another prophecy conference, possibly in Springfield, Missouri. You are invited to attend.

Help us organize a thousand prayer meetings for midnight, December 31, 1999. Some people are persuaded that December 31 is when Jesus will return. We may know the season (1 Thess. 5:1), but I do not believe we can know the exact time of His return (Mark 13:33).

If the Lord Jesus has decided to come that very night, how could we be better occupied than to be engaged in prayer and spiritual battle? Please fill out the coupon in the back of the book and pledge your prayer participation. Let us know if you can conduct a meeting in a church, in a home, or in a hotel meeting room, etc. Tell us how many people you expect to be in your meeting.

We plan, God willing, to have an International Prophecy and Prayer Conference December 28, 1999 - January 1, 2000. Outstanding speakers will participate. There will be a morning, afternoon, and evening session. Let me know if you can tentatively plan to attend. We will put your name on a special mailing list and you will receive updated information as time goes by.

Chapter 17

FROM SHUNI TO SEDONA

The End-Time Struggle

A few years ago I visited the archaeological digs at Shuni, Israel, where worshipers of the Greek goddess Diana and the Earth goddess Gaia hope to erect a temple to the goddesses. This is an enormous embarrassment to the Keren Keyamet foundation which oversees the area, also to religious Jews, and several political leaders who don't like the idea at all.

Shuni is the site of the Zeev Jabotinsky Museum. He was the great Zionist revisionist and mentor of the late Prime Minister Menechem Begin. Shuni lies near the Israeli village of Benyamina, near Zichron Ya'akov, about 25 miles south of Haifa. You may want to visit the site when traveling in Israel.

Concerned Israelis report and complain to us of the advances of the New Age movement in their country. It is getting almost as bad as North America. But then no part of the world is excepted from this occultic movement, with its worrisome political connections and complexion.

Sedona, Arizona

Recently I went to Sedona, Arizona, heralded by the New Age as one of the greatest power vortex areas of the world. As we approached Sedona we saw a very unusual building under construction. It looked like a temple. In front was a sign identifying it with Xanadu. Xanadu is to the New Age an ideal, a mystical metaphysical place which does not have an open manifestation in this plane of existence. It is their equivalent to our hope for the final New Jerusalem of eternity.

World Psychic Grid

What is the connection between Sedona and Shuni? Both places are viewed by the New Agers as important connector locations in the growing psychic world grid. The Psi grid has been discussed earlier, but let's review the concept. It is the New Age theory that around the year 2000 the New Agers will have enlisted enough followers to enable them to radiate psychic, meditative, god-man energy that will effect a paradigm shift. That, in turn, will force all humans to have a new perception of reality. Finally, the age of Pisces (the Church age) will pass and in its place will stand the New Age, the Age of Aquarius. The New Age has opened an umbrella of Eastern religious philosophy under which a billion human beings feel comfortable to join hands.

War in the Spirit

Some New Age leaders have openly declared war on evangelical, Bible-believing Christians, saying that we are the people of low vibratory rate and that we must be eliminated from the earth for the New Age to succeed. Refer to the previous chapter on the Georgia Guidestones and what I have labeled "The Antichrist's Ten Commandments."

A Jewish Cartoonist

Ya'akov Kirschen told me that he is concerned about a widespread manifestation of neo-paganism in Israel. Ya'akov is the internationally acclaimed cartoonist behind the Israel-based syndicated political comic strip *Dry Bones*. From the *Jerusalem Post* to the *LA Times* and the *NY Times* his work has elucidated current events around the world for millions of people.

I first met Kirschen over two years ago when I was a speaker at the Christian Celebration of the Feast of Tabernacles in Jerusalem. He had come to hear me speak to a plenary session on the New Age movement.

After the message we talked for over an hour. I vividly recall his observations. Kirschen told me he was not a religious person, and yet I noted that the manuscript of his new book *Trees* is full of biblical references and allusions to Bible prophecies concerning Israel and the nations. He had brought me a pre-publication copy of the manuscript.

Resistance

In our initial conversation Ya'akov told me that on the way from Tel Aviv to Jerusalem he got into the worst traffic jam he had ever seen. He commented, "It was almost like something was *resisting* me from getting here." Embarrassed at his own words he added, "Of course I don't believe in that superstitious nonsense."

I replied, "Mr. Kirschen you don't have to impress me with your agnosticism, for I perceive a wellspring of faith in you just waiting to burst forth."

What was the resistance Kirschen seemed to sense? There is resistance in the world. We are in a spiritual warfare, the consequences of which effect our eternity and that of multitudes.

It Was the Devil

We went to the recently uncovered ruins of the city of Sepphoris in the Galilee region of Israel. There I purchased a video about the archaeological exploration in the ancient Roman metropolis which lies only three miles from Jesus' home in Nazareth. The video features various archaeologists who have worked on the project. Many believe that here will be revealed evidence of great facts that will enhance our understanding of Jesus, His times, and His ministry. Even our understanding of Bible prophecy may be enhanced. The research has only begun.

Mr. "Dodo" Shimhav, the chief conservator of the Israel Museum appeared on camera and explained some of the extreme difficulties in carrying out the project of moving the "Mona Lisa of the Galilee" and other mosaics.

Asked if he was afraid of damaging the mosaic, he curiously replied, "Mainly I am afraid from the devil. He is so active when you make such a complicated work that you can't imagine. You can't imagine what kind of misfortune can strike. . . . He can cause you to fall down and destroy something, and then — the devil. . . . can make you do anything. . . . they do such terrible things. . . ."

He spoke earnestly, using personal pronouns for the devil. He seemed to believe what he was saying. Or was he using, what to him, was merely a figure of speech? I may not have every word of the quotation from the video right, since there was a lot of noise and talk in the background at times, but it is close to being exact.

The Devil Is Real

I too believe that the devil is real and that we are engaged in a titanic end-time struggle against the dark powers. Not only theologians but also political cartoonists, museum conservators, archaeologists, and people from all walks of life are peering beyond the veil of the physical world into the spiritual. Just like the Bible reveals it to us.

A New Age Haven

Our recent trip to Sedona was amazing. Upon entering the town nestled amidst the red rock mountains for which it is famous we first went to the Chamber of Commerce for information. Along with maps, scenic postcards, and a magazine, we obtained many advertisements for local New Age practitioners, psychic readers, metaphysicians, astrologers, and more.

We noted that this upscale town, residence to movie stars and millionaires, is also drawing a lot of tourists, evidenced by the scores of souvenir, art, and handicraft boutiques that line the main street of the small community. We drove into the mountains where locals lay claim to more UFO sightings than any other place in the USA. New Age books, available in many of the stores, address this subject and make the connection with New Age teaching and experience (ET contacts). We purchased some of these books for research purposes.

Ordinary People Live There, Too

It should be noted that unlike Casa Daga, Florida, where each resident is a practitioner of the metaphysical, Sedona is populated with many who are not connected to the New Age. Many born-again Christians live there and are very aware of what is around them. A few years ago the New Age moved in and obtained choice properties for their establishment. Their influence is pervasive but not accepted by everyone. Whether they have a majority or not, I do not know. They are working toward that end.

We had an uneasy sense, a foreboding of gloom seems to hang over the place. We felt we were in enemy territory. That was confirmed toward the end of the day. We encountered an evil force so great that I have few experiences to compare with it.

Upon entering a very large New Age store, featuring books, idols, pictures of gurus, crystals, chimes, and Hindu elephant gods, we experienced strange things. The atmosphere was heavy with incense. Chimes and New Age music played incessantly. Several people were milling about.

None looked like tourists. I overheard one of the customers talking, and from her conversation I concluded that she was probably a local practitioner, although not a worker in the store.

Den of Confusion

From the moment we walked in, there seemed to be an air of confusion in the place. I felt extremely weak, my head began to throb. Ramona complained of a terrible headache and wanted to leave. I silently prayed and claimed the power of Jesus' shed blood. My legs "turned to rubber," and I sat in the nearest chair. Right in front of me was a Buddha idol about 2.5 feet tall. He seemed to stare up at me with malevolence. I got up and started to pick out some books, which I handed to Mona. I sat down to keep from falling down several times, in different chairs. I was ready to leave, but as I got up a force tried to overwhelm me and now I truly felt that I would fall down, my legs folding up. Instead, I continued to pray, then interrupting the prayer, I quietly rebuked Satan, saying, "Back off, devil. You have no claim. Turn your power elsewhere." Instantly a local customer fell to the floor and had to be picked up, apparently suffering no permanent damage.

We went to the counter to pay for the books we had picked out. More confusion! The computerized cash register malfunctioned as the clerk tried to prepare our bill. It just would not give the right total. Finally she muttered, "This is strange. It's never done that before. It must be haunted. Maybe there is a ghost in it."

On Assignment

Leaving the store we went to where Jim Brantley's car was parked. Since we had been driving all the way from Phoenix to Sedona, and then around the area, Jim was tired and had elected to take a nap in the car while Mona and I went into the store. We got in the car, where I sat limp. Mona said, "Let's pray again." We did and the power of evil was forced to withdraw! We sensed the power of God and complete victory.

Why did we go to Sedona? We are doing research on the New Age for this book which reveals things of which few are aware. We were there on assignment. The watchman on the wall is always pushing to the front lines for the good of the Church, Israel, and all of lost humanity.

All Over the World

It is not just Sedona, Arizona; Casa Daga, Florida; nor the Stonehenge of England and the American, Canadian, and European clones of Stonehenge, it is all over the world. The New Age lays claim to monuments, natural formations, and a host of other power nodes and vortexes for the extension of their psychic grid. They have sworn our destruction. It is good to be aware of those who have sworn themselves to be enemies of God and His church. I do not advocate that others march into the lion's den. We stand on the front lines and do battle in your behalf.

Issachar

In the days of David's struggle against wicked King Saul, the tribes of Israel sent mighty men to fight alongside David. Asher sent 40,000, from Zebulun came 50,000, and from Judah 37,000 joined David's mighty men. The tribe of Asher sent a goodly company of 40,000, *however the tribe of Issachar only sent 200,* but they were "Men that had understanding of the times, to know what Israel ought to do" (2 Chron. 12:32). The writer of the Chronicles adds that the band of 200 wise men had the help and backing of all their brethren in the large tribe of Issachar.

This research and prayer ministry labors to be like the 200 volunteers from the tribe of Issachar. Brothers and sisters, pray for us and hold us before the throne of our Lord. We are in this titanic end-time combat together and we are marching on to victory. We all need each other in this critical hour of spiritual conflict. So much is at stake!

Chapter 18

OCCULT INVASION OF ISRAEL

A Plea to All Who Respect the Torah

> And the soul that turneth after such as have familiar spirits, and after wizards, to go a whoring after them, I will even set my face against that soul, and will cut him off from among his people (Lev. 20:6).

On numerous occasions we have written articles of a most serious nature, concerning the growth of New Age influence in the USA and in Israel. We warned Israel concerning the Raelian Cult,[1] bringing it to the attention of the Government Press Office (Beit Agron), independent journalists, the Foreign Ministry, and both Jewish and Christian religious leaders. We published an article titled "End-Time Struggle" in our *Jerusalem Courier*[2] revealing the goals of the New Age Gaia cult in Israel. A new warning must now be sounded.

Jewish Plot to Rule the World?

How could this be? I read the headline with amazement! "ISRAEL CAN CONTINUE TO STRUGGLE OR IT CAN HOLD THE BALANCE OF POWER IN THE WORLD." This bold proclamation (shades of the spurious *Protocols of the Learned Elders of Zion!*) is followed with the announcement of "A Gift of Peace and Invincibility to Israel In the New Year." There is issued a call "inviting Jewish leaders in Israel and abroad to create a *Capital of One Government for One World* in Israel, creating at the same time a strong unifying in the family of nations . . . to create a *Capital of One Government for One World* in Israel and hold the balance of power in their own hands."[3]

Is it the Millennium? Is Messiah sending an announcement? Does Jehovah's voice thunder from the heavens? NO! It is none of these. The *Jerusalem Report* has sold advertising space to a religious organization which has made these promises and grandiose claims. It is actually the call of a Hindu spiritual leader, Maharishi Mahesh Yogi, a devotee of the late Swami Brahmananda Saraswati, who is commonly called Guru Dev (divine teacher). Guru Dev had instructed the Maharishi in how to formulate a meditation technique from the Hindu scripture known as the Vedas. In 1958 the Maharishi founded the Spiritual Regeneration Movement in India. In 1959 he moved to America and established the Transcendental Meditation (TM) movement, which now has millions of Americans as disciples. TM is allegedly not a religion, but in fact it is.[4]

Now the Maharishi has devised a plan to seduce Israel into embracing idol worship and Eastern cultic mysticism, under the alluring guise of TM's "natural law," a promise of peace, and even world dominance. I would hope that the Israelis will not fall for this delusion. It would be the anti-Semites' wildest dream come true, a visible Jewish plot to rule the world! More grist for the ever-grinding mill of anti-Semitism!

While in Phoenix, Arizona, I discovered that the Maharishi had made an offer to the city to solve the crime and violence of that metropolis. He would accomplish this goal by uniting hundreds of Yogic Transcendental Mediators in releasing psychic power. These people would include TM practitioners already present in Phoenix and many who would be brought in for the task. He asked the city for millions of dollars to accomplish the objective. He met with a negative response.[5]

Now the TM Yogi is asking for $175,000,000 for the Israeli Capital of One Government for One World project. This will cover only the cost of housing for the yogic flyers. The cost of the World Capital Building(s) and land on the Galilee is not mentioned. A large amount of this money, $3.5 million, had already been pledged in 1994 when the advertisement was seen in the *Jerusalem Report*. The appeal is frankly addressed to wealthy Jewish people who believe in Maharishi's plan.

Hear, Oh Israel!

SHEMA ISRAEL, ADONAI ELOHENU, ADONAI ECHAD. Hear, Oh Israel, the Lord thy God, the Lord is ONE.

Israel, I appeal to you: You do not need a psychic bag of tricks. Let us all return to Jehovah God, the source of our strength. All the Maitreyas, Krishnas, Buddhas, Imam Mahdis, Yogis, Ascended Masters, and Lords of the Hierarchy are false messiahs and lead us away from God the Creator if we follow them. We do not need their magic, mysticism, nor pseudo miracles. If we abandon Jehovah, the God of Abraham, Isaac, and Jacob we will be prey to the demons of hell who seek to destroy Israel.

Israel's need is a return to the Holy Tenach, not the mumbo jumbo of TM mantras and yogic levitation. "And when they shall say unto you, Seek unto them that have familiar spirits, and unto wizards that peep, and that mutter:

should not a people seek unto their God? for the living to the dead?" (Isa. 8:19). The latter phrase is better translated "Why consult the dead on behalf of the living?" This warning can be applied to any religious system which misinterprets the state of the dead, such as the teachings of spiritism, and Hindu reincarnation.

Shema, Israel! In the Torah, Moses, your great prophet, warns you: "If there arise among you a prophet, or a dreamer of dreams, and giveth thee a sign or a wonder, And the sign or the wonder come to pass, whereof he spake unto thee, saying, Let us go after other gods, which thou hast not known, and let us serve them; Thou shalt not hearken unto the words of that prophet, or that dreamer of dreams: for the Lord your God proveth you, to know whether ye love the Lord your God with all your heart and with all your soul" (Deut. 13:1-3).

The scheme revealed in the advertisement in the *Jerusalem Report* calls for Jewish people to donate millions of dollars to build 7,000 dwellings for the practitioners of "inner circle" Transcendental Meditation to live in and practice yogic flying (levitation), which will in turn release incredible psychic power, allegedly for Israel's benefit. The Hindu Vedas is cited as authority for these claims. The advertisement says, "The proposal you are about to read includes the construction of new homes for 7,000 Israelis, creating the 'Israeli Capital of One Government for One World.' "[6]

The ambitions of Maharishi Mahesh Yogi and his cohorts is a wonder to consider. The executive vice president of the sponsoring organization speaks of a site to be selected for the Israeli Capital of One Government for One World. He writes, "I would like to thank each one of these individuals who have inspired me deeply to begin immediately and finish this grand work. As soon as the site is finalized and sanctioned by the government, I will be conducting the ground breaking celebration for the Israeli capital of One Government for One World on beautiful land by the Sea of Galilee."[7] I am heartily in favor of choice in religious matters, but I wonder how a Jewish person can embrace Hinduism in any form?

Although it is touted as, "This non-political and non-religious solution to the problems of government, which takes recourse to the unified basis of all administration, the almighty government of Natural Law has given rise to the concept of One Government for One World," it is nevertheless a deeply religious, anti-Jewish and anti-Christian movement. A reading of the initiation prayer (Puja) of Transcendental Meditation will clearly demonstrate that the intent of TM is to bring the initiate into contact with Hindu deities. And how can the plan be non-political since the goal is to establish a world *government.* That is about as political as you can get.

David Hanna wrote in 1979, "There are reports that Maharishi . . . intends to establish a world government for the Age of Enlightenment — and its grand opening will be sparked by a special two-month course in Transcendental Meditation which will be given in Israel at a cost of $2,500 per student. The course will concentrate on levitation [yogic flying] and graduates will join 5,000 Americans who have 'gained the ability to get off the ground and fly.' "[8] The plan may be slightly altered but the goal is the same as it has always been to the Maharishi!

I believe in the freedom of religion. I would not advocate the use of any coercion to stop the followers of Maharishi Mahesh Yogi. I simply have a different point of view, based on the Tenach. I just do not want any Jewish person to think that TM's Hindu philosophy and practice is in any way compatible with the Torah. In the past I have stated this same premise for the Church. TM is in no way compatible with *biblical* Christianity. For this reason, the Bible is now considered to be an evil book by secularists, occultists, atheists, and One Worlders.

So be it. I will simply quote Israel's great prophets Isaiah and Elijah:

> Woe unto them that call evil good, and good evil; that put darkness for light, and light for darkness; that put bitter for sweet, and sweet for bitter! Woe unto them that are wise in their own eyes, and prudent in their own sight! (Isa. 5:20-21).

> Therefore as the fire devoureth the stubble, and the flame consumeth the chaff, so their root shall be as rottenness, and their blossom shall go up as dust: because they have cast away the law of the Lord of hosts, and despised the word of the Holy One of Israel (Isa. 5: 24).

In his contest with the prophets of Baal, Elijah challenged Israel:

> And Elijah came unto all the people, and said, How long halt ye between two opinions? if the Lord be God, follow him: but if Baal, then follow him. And the people answered him not a word (1 Kings. 18:21).

> Take heed to yourselves, that your heart be not deceived, and ye turn aside, and serve other gods, and worship them (Deut. 11:16).

Endnotes

1David Allen Lewis and Robert Shreckhise, *UFO 666* (Springfield, MO: Menorah Press, 1993) p. 34-49.

2*The Jerusalem Courier,* Vol. 11 #3 (Springfield, MO: David A. Lewis Ministries, Inc., 1994) p. 3.

3Advertisement, *Jerusalem Report,* (Jerusalem, Israel: Jerusalem Report Publications Limited. August 25, 1994), p. 4-5.

4Josh McDowell and Don Stewart, *Handbook of Today's Religions* (San Bernardino, CA: Here's Life Publishers, Inc., 1983), p. 80.

5Private conversations with Rev. Craig Carter and Rev. Mel Holmquist, both in the Phoenix area, October 1994.

6Advertisement, *Jerusalem Report,* (Jerusalem, Israel: Jerusalem Report Publications Limited. November 17, 1994), p. 19.

7Advertisement, *Jerusalem Report,* (Jerusalem, Israel: Jerusalem Report Publications Limited. November 17, 1994), p. 18.

8David Hanna, *Cults in America* (New York, NY: Tower Publications, Inc., 1979), p. 272.

Chapter 19

TRANSCENDENTAL MEDITATION

A Form of Hindu Religion

Maharishi Mahesh Yogi and all the leadership of the TM movement claim that TM is not a religious practice, but rather a scientific technique based on "natural law." Its purpose is to relieve tension and stress, and to raise the consciousness of the meditator. This is accomplished by quietly saying a mantra word over and over for 20 minutes, twice daily. However, even a casual examination of the TM initiation ceremony reveals how completely the system is rooted in the Hindu religion, the aim of which is to unite the mediator with Brahman, the Hindu concept of God. We have the initiation ceremony from many sources, but our primary indebtedness for this information is to a former TM instructor, Dora Gugliotta, who resides in Toronto, Ontario, Canada. Dora was trained by Maharishi Mahesh Yogi in Spain and was a very effective initiator for the TM movement up until the time of her conversion to Jesus Christ.[1]

Every potential meditator in the TM program must first submit to an initiation ceremony. It is said to be an innocent ceremony of thanksgiving to the tradition of TM masters, performed by the teacher. The initiate is only asked to witness it. The ceremony is called a *puja*, which in Sanskrit means "WORSHIP." It is chanted in Sanskrit by the TM teacher. The initiate is usually not aware of its meaning. The initiate is asked to bring offerings of fruit, flowers, and a white handkerchief. The teacher furnishes other items.

The puja is performed at a table covered by a white cloth. A picture of Guru Dev stands in the center. At the foot of the picture is a tray. Around the tray are little bowls of water, rice, sandal paste, and camphor. On one side is a candle; on the other side is incense. The items brought by the initiate are also present. Although the initiate is probably unaware of it, the table is an altar, the picture is an icon/idol, and the various items on the table are offerings.

The ceremony consists of three parts. The first is a recitation of the names of deceased Hindu masters, going back to the Hindu creator-gods, Lord Narayana and Brahma. The middle part consists of the offering of the various items on the table. As each item is offered it is moved to the foot of the icon/idol, with the refrain, "To the lotus feet of Lord Guru Dev I bow down." In the third part of the ceremony, Guru Dev is worshipped as the embodiment of deity. He is called the embodiment of Brahma, Vishnu, and Shiva (described by some as the Hindu trinity). At the end of the puja, the teacher bows to the icon of Guru Dev. The initiate is invited to bow also.

The new meditator is (perhaps unwittingly) involved in worshipping Hindu deities. The spiritual power of these gods are invoked on his or her behalf. One may wonder why Maharishi Mahesh Yogi insists on this ceremony. It seems clear that the purpose is to psychically link the initiate to the Hindu masters by worship, giving offerings to them, thus preparing the individual to receive a mantra.

The Puja

Whether pure or impure, whether purity or impurity is permeating everywhere, whoever opens himself to the expanded vision of unbounded awareness gains inner and outer purity.

The Invocation

Here is the invocation, read by the TM instructor for the initiation:

> To Lord Narayana, to lotus-born Brahma the Creator, to Vashista, to Shakti, and to his son Parashar, to Vyasa, to Shukadava, to the great Guadapada, to Govinda, ruler among yogis, to his disciple Shri Trotika and Varttika-Kara, to others, to the tradition of our masters I bow down. To the abode of the wisdom of the Shrutis, Smritis, and Puranas, to the abode of kindness, to the personified glory of the Lord, to Shankara, emancipator of the Lord, I bow down. To Sharkaracharya, the redeemer, hailed as Krishna and Badarayana, to the commentator of the Brama Sutras, I bow down again and again. At whose door the whole galaxy of gods pray for perfection day and night, adorned with immeasurable glory, perceptor of the whole world, having bowed down to him, we gain fulfillment. Skilled in dispelling the cloud of ignorance of the people, the gentle emancipator Bramananda Saraswati — the supreme teacher, full of brilliance, him I bring to my awareness.

The Offering

The Puja is followed by the presentation of offerings made on an altar, by the initiate, before a picture of Guru Dev.

Offering the invocation to the lotus feet of Shri Guru Dev, I bow down.

Offering a seat to the lotus feet of Shri Guru Dev, I bow down.

Offering an ablution to the lotus feet of Shri Guru Dev, I bow down.

Offering a cloth to the lotus feet of Shri Guru Dev, I bow down.

Offering sandal paste to the lotus feet of Shri Guru Dev, I bow down.

Offering rice to the lotus feet of Shri Guru Dev, I bow down.

Offering a flower to the lotus feet of Shri Guru Dev, I bow down.

Offering incense to the lotus feet of Shri Guru Dev, I bow down.

Offering light to the lotus feet of Shri Guru Dev, I bow down.

Offering water to the lotus feet of Shri Guru Dev, I bow down.

Offering fruits to the lotus feet of Shri Guru Dev, I bow down.

Offering water to the lotus feet of Shri Guru Dev, I bow down.

Offering betel leaf to the lotus feet of Shri Guru Dev, I bow down.

Offering coconut to the lotus feet of Shri Guru Dev, I bow down.

Offering camphor light.

White as camphor, kindness incarnate, the essence of creation, garlanded with Brahman, ever dwelling in the lotus of my heart, the creative impulse of cosmic life, to that in the form of Guru Dev, I bow down.

Offering camphor light to the lotus feet of Shri Guru Dev, I bow down.

Offering water to the lotus feet of Shri Guru Dev, I bow down.

Offering a handful of flowers.

Guru in the glory of Brahma, guru in the glory of Vishnu, guru in the glory of the great Lord Shiva, guru in the glory of personified transcendental fullness of Brahman, to him Shri Guru Dev, Shri Brahmananda, bliss of the absolute, transcendental joy, the self sufficient, the embodiment of pure knowledge which is beyond and above the universe like the sky, the goal of "thou art That" and other such expressions which unfold eternal truth, the one, the eternal, the pure, the immovable, to the very being of that which is the witness of all intellects, whose status transcends thought, the transcendent along with the three gunas, the teacher of the truth of the Absolute, to Shri Guru Dev, I bow down. To him by whom the blinding darkness of ignorance has been removed by applying the balm of knowledge; the eye of knowledge has been opened by him and therefore to him, to Shri Guru Dev, I bow down.[2]

Disturbing Words from Maharishi

Authors Josh McDowell and Don Stewart quote the words of Maharishi Mahesh Yogi which reveal a sinister side to the TM movement. "There has not been and there will not be a place for the unfit. The fit will lead, and if the unfit are not coming along, there is no place for them. In the place where light dominates there is no place for darkness. In the age of Enlightenment there is no place for ignorant people, the ignorant will be made enlightened by a few orderly, enlightened people moving around. Nature will not allow ignorance to prevail. It just can't. Nonexistence of the unfit has been the law of nature."[3]

A Federal Court Declares TM to Be a Religion

After a two-year federal court battle in New Jersey, the verdict was that in every sense of the word Transcendental Meditation is religious in nature, and cannot be taught in state-operated schools. The decision of the Federal District Court was upheld by the United States Court of Appeals, in Philadelphia, October 19, 1977. The presiding judge ruled that TM was clearly a part of Hindu religious practice and that this Hindu meditation practice could not be used in public schools.

The Mantra

At the initiation each inductee to TM is given a secret, personalized mantra. This mantra is repeated, under the breath, two times a day for 20 minutes. This relieves stress and raises the meditators consciousness. "A mantra is chosen according to a six thousand year old tradition, say the followers of TM," writes John Butterworth in *A Book Of Beliefs*. According to Butterworth, "Actually there are only 16 mantras and the present tradition goes back only to 1973. All the mantras are the names of, or close to the names of Hindu Gods. . . . Maharishi is a Hindu Bhakti monk and evolved his technique while studying the Hindu Vedic Scripture."[4]

Dora Gugliotta, a former TM instructor and initiator has spoken at our conferences on several occasions. This Christian lady is fearless and forthright in her exposé of TM. She called to our attention, that like so much in TM, the true meaning of the mantra is kept hidden. Only a few mantras are actually used, dealt out to particular age-groups. Over the years, Maharishi has shifted the mantras and age groups around. Bob Larson reports, "Recent investigation has shown that only 16 TM mantras actually exist." Later Larson writes, "To counter such criticism and to legitimize his efforts, the Maharishi has tried to further refurbish his image. God-name mantras have been dropped."[5]

The mantras, according to Dora and other researchers, is called a *bija* (seed), names used in the worship of Hindu deities. In his Vedic studies Maharishi teaches that in Sanskrit, *a word creates its form* because of its vibration at a subtle level of existence. One taps this subtle level in TM. Maharishi says, "Meditating leads one to contact the gods, thereby gaining their help, and . . . one sins if one does not contact these gods."[6] This is more than superstitious nonsense. Behind every idol is a demonic force, which can react to the call or prayer of the supplicant.

Researching the mantras reveals that Maharishi believes they are not merely names that invoke the power of the deity. *The mantra is the deity itself:* The real (hidden) purpose of Transcendental Meditation is to produce the gradual transformation of the personality of the meditator into that of the deity. As one progresses, he or she takes on more of the nature of the deity and worships less and less of self. The passivity that results from TM helps this process.

Dora Gugliotta pointed out that all idols and gods are in opposition to Jehovah and are demon spirits!

All idol worship is forbidden in the Bible. This is so important that the first two commandments deal with it: "Thou shalt have no other gods before Me. Thou shalt not make unto thee any graven image. . . . Thou shalt not bow down thyself to them" (Exod. 20:3-5). We are not to invoke other gods or *even speak their names.* "And in all things that I have said unto you to be circumspect: and make no mention of the name of other gods, neither let it be heard out of thy mouth" (Exod. 23:13).

It is difficult to understand the command not to mention the names of the false gods. Of course, the prophets did speak the names of false gods such as Baal, Ashtaroth, Beelzebub, and Moloch, in order to instruct and warn the children of Israel. Never did they direct prayer or worship to an idol or wicked false deity! I take it that this is the solution to the question.

King David's insight into the nature of the spiritual force behind an idol is sobering to contemplate. "But [they] were mingled among the heathen, and learned their works. And they served their *idols:* which were a snare unto them. Yea, they sacrificed their sons and their daughters unto *devils*" (Ps. 106:35-37). William MacDonald, in writing about the confrontation between Moses and Pharaoh's magicians, Jannes and Jambres, observes, "When Aaron cast down his rod and it became a serpent, Pharaoh's magicians and sorcerers were able to duplicate the miracle through demonic powers."[7]

Both Christians and Jews who believe in the inspiration of the Bible are forced to make exclusivist claims. This brings a lot of pressure upon us.

In addition to the quotations from the Jewish Scriptures (Tenach, the First Testament), Christians must be made aware of promises and warnings regarding the spiritual warfare we are facing. The apostle John wrote: "And we know that we are of God, and the whole world lieth in wickedness. And we know that the Son of God is come, and hath given us an understanding, that we may know him that is true, and we are in him that is true, even in his Son Jesus Christ. This is the true God, and eternal life. Little children, *keep yourselves from idols.* Amen" (1 John 5:19-21; emphasis added).

Chapter 20

PSYCHOTRONIC WEAPONS OF WAR

Update on an Aspect of Spiritual Warfare

I believe that we are noted for moderation and sensibility in interpreting prophecy, and avoiding extremism, date setting, and other wild speculations. Sometimes, when we deal with a legitimate subject that has, by its nature, an element of "sensationalism," our readers are a bit shocked. Let me assure you that in these areas we are as cautious as in other, better-known areas of Bible truth. The Bible is a great book with areas unexplored as yet. Further, while the revelation of God in the 66 books of the two testaments of the Bible is complete, our illumination of that revelation increases as time goes by. The very nature of our calling places us on the leading edge of biblical exploration into spiritual truth.

Gaylord, Michigan - 1955

I am sure that congregants of the church in Gaylord, Michigan, that I spoke to in 1955 on the topic of "Psychic Warfare Prophesied in the Bible" were puzzled by my startling presentation. There was no scientific or historic evidence to which I could refer to buttress my seemingly radical predictions.

It must have been nearly impossible at that time, to grasp the idea that military leaders would actually try to harness the power of the mind and use psychic energy as a weapon of war. We had only vaguely heard of these types of things in connection with voodoo and witchcraft, as reported by missionaries from dark pockets of far continents.

Our Concept Originated from the Bible

For months I had wrestled with concepts derived from statements by three great prophets — Daniel, Paul and John. I was led to the inescapable conclusion that the world of the end times would be very unlike anything that has preceded this period of history. On this basis I spoke to the Gaylord church, where Herbert David Kolenda was the pastor.

In 1975 John Weldon and Zola Levitt wrote: "The Book of Revelation presents quite a different world from that which we are accustomed to. . . . At this time, most expectedly that parallel world, the province of the demons and the forces of good, is very restless. . . . Christianity is realizing a tremendous revival; so are occultism and the forces of evil."[1] Both Weldon and Levitt are conservative evangelical scholars, well-known, and highly respected.

Faithful to my understanding of the Word of God, I continued warning the church of the dangers of Psi-War. We wrote two chapters on this subject which were first published as a booklet titled *Psychotronic Warfare* (Menorah Press). In 1987 the content of the booklet was incorporated into our book *Smashing the Gates of Hell in the Last Days*.[2]

My warnings then and now fall, mostly, upon deaf ears. I have to some extent been an object of ridicule from Christian skeptics and reviewers of books. Nevertheless, I stand firm on my careful interpretation of God's Word.

Confirmation from Secular World

When syndicated columnist Carl Alpert wrote of the findings of Avraham Shifrin, a Russian researcher, it brought confirmation from the world of science. Since reading Alpert's article, I have met Shifrin on numerous occasions. An interview with Shifrin is printed in my book *Smashing the Gates of Hell in the Last Days*. Since meeting Shifrin in 1985 (and many times subsequently) I have also talked to six more Russian psychics on this subject.

My booklet, and the inclusion of its contents in *Smashing The Gates of Hell,* constitute a call to spiritual warfare. It is my impression that very few Christians take this matter seriously. I can only hope that more will wake up and assist us in binding the powers of Satan, which are now masquerading as humanistic psychic powers and forces. It is an end-time parade of deception and delusion. Those who try to use paranormal force become bond slaves to demons.

Noted Scientist Confirmed Our Ideas

It is gratifying to find that we do not stand alone in our notification of the dangers of Psi-War. Lambert Dolphin, who for over 20 years was senior research physicist at Stanford Research International, one of our nation's major think tanks, furnished us with documentation of American efforts to duplicate and counteract the Russian Psi-War.

Dolphin also confirmed the idea that psychotronic generators are a reality. The idea that manmade devices could amplify psychic energy and use it as a weapon was documented by ABC-TV on March 25, 1993. The hour-long documentary *World of Discovery — Powers of the Russian Psychics* not only told of these Russian creations but showed pictures of the Psi-generators.

ABC-TV — World of Discovery

We saw and heard the ABC-TV narrator as he said, "Until recently such [Soviet] demonstrations of psychic powers were virtually inaccessible to scientists in the West. For the greatest part of this century an icy veil of secrecy has obscured our view and knowledge of the wondrous place called Russia. Subjects like parapsychology have been shrouded in rumor and mystery, but today all that has changed. With glastnost, perestroika, and the fall of the Soviet Union, a vital new sense of freedom has overtaken Russia. There is new hope for the future — an unprecedented access to once secret and hidden aspects of the past. The mood is brave and hopeful and Russians can openly say things never possible before. Today for the first time Russian scientists, researchers, and psychics themselves are able and willing to share their work in the paranormal."

ABC-TV was able to secure films of Russian psychics at work, demonstrating powers of levitation, telekenesis, and thought transfer.

At one point in the hour-long documentary it was stated, "For Dr. Ganady Segeyev, the neuro-physiologist who devised the experiment, the applied use of psychic energy is a plain and proven fact. Many Russian scientists agree, and in the early 1970s began creating devices to harness psychic power. They are known as psychotronic generators, instruments designed to capture and accumulate psychic energy and then release it on command. It is believed that psychotronic generators create a union between mind and matter, transforming human psychic power into a practical and controllable resource. In theory, the power originates from somewhere inside the brain, and is emitted most effectively, directly through the eyes. Once accumulated and concentrated by a psychotronic generator the power can be released and used for a multitude of purposes.

The field of psychotronics remains vital to this day. Russian para-psychologists have developed more advanced and sophisticated devices. Psychotronic generators which in theory, at least, have powers to heal — or harm."

One of the Russian experts interviewed for the ABC-TV production said, "A psychotronic generator can influence a whole crowd of people. It can affect a person's psyche, memory, or attention span. A psychotronic device can cause physical fatigue, disorientation, and even alter a person's behavior."

Edward Molvov and many others believe that the Soviet military and KGB conducted intensive secret research to harness psychotronic power, as a weapon of mass mind control and psychic warfare:

> Major General Oleg Kalugin was in charge of foreign counter-intelligence for the Soviet Union. He is the youngest general in the history of the KGB and a former minister of the Soviet Parliament. He said, "Obviously the Soviet security services could not stay indifferent to those efforts to produce a new deadly or mysterious weapon. So they tried to explore the mysteries of human power over other people and simulate a generator of the same nature which produces similar effects. . . . The military did produce something of that nature and according to my knowledge it was very successful."

The TV special then showed a chess match taking place in the Philippines in 1978. It was the contest for the World Chess Championship. Here a major "crucial Soviet experiment in psychic mind control" took place.

Anatoly Karpov was the Soviet defending world chess champion. He arrived in the Philippines with a large entourage of specialized aids. Men who specialized in mind control and psychotronics. That team was headed up by Dr. Vladimir Zukov, a leading Russian para-psychologist. His specialty was and is telepathic hypnosis.

The challenger who hoped to defeat Karpov was Victor Kortchnoy, a Russian grand chess master who had defected to the West two years earlier.

Kortchnoy recognized Zukov and hotly protested the presence of Dr. Zukov in the playing hall. Kortchnoy claimed that Zukov was dulling his playing ability with psychic force. Kortchnoy said, "Dr. Zukov forced me to make blunders." It was the longest match in the history of chess. Finally Kortchnoy conceded defeat. Karpov won the match. An angry Kortchnoy said, "I came to the Philippines to play one against one. It was not quite right. The whole red army was against me."

It was a great and prestigious victory for the Russian. On the ABC-TV documentary it was said that in a major institute of para-psychology in Moscow there was, at the time, a banner saying, "Let us help Karpov to retain the title of world champion."

The Soviet military and KGB had goals much larger than chess. In the cold war competition to tip the balance of power, elements in the Soviet defense establishment looked to para-psychology as a source of exotic weapons for which Western powers were unprepared.

A classified U. S. intelligence report stated, "Many scientists, U.S. and Soviet, feel that para-psychology can be harnessed to create conditions where one can alter or manipulate the minds of others." Dr. Nikolai Koklov, a former KGB agent who defected to the West was hired by the CIA in 1976 to investigate and report on secret para-psychological research in the Soviet Union.

He uncovered more than 20 clandestine laboratories, staffed by hundreds of top scientists and technicians. Research included well-funded experiments in negative telepathy and mind control as well as investigations into the biophysics of mind to mind communication, which involved the electrocution of newborn rabbits." In other words the Russians were trying at methods for remote murder by the use of psychic force.

At heavily guarded military facilities, psychotronic generators were developed and tested. The hearts of lab animals were stopped telepathically. . . . The sinister specter of psychic power as a destructive and harmful weapon is still present in Russia today.

This government laboratory in Moscow manufactures psychotronic generators. It is the type of equipment which many believe could pose a present-day threat to the new democratic Russia.

One of the Russian experts interviewed for ABC-TV said, "The minister of . . . in the KGB and other organizations did build psychotronic generators. I know that over half a billion rubles were spent in developing psychotronic equipment, which brings up the question, where are all these devices?

ABC suggested that in the coup of 1991 these weapons may have been used to influence the military.

It was reported that Boris Yeltsin was likely the target of a psychotronic attack which was the cause of the heart attack he suffered. Extensive testimony to this was given on the TV special, which also suggested that these weapons could be used to affect an entire population. ABC's narrator said, "There are those who now perceive a grave and terrible threat from psychic warfare."

We have long contended that the real power behind psychic warfare is demonic. Every new piece of evidence lends credibility and strength to this point of view. One must, of course, believe the Bible and its powerful witness to the supernatural realm to understand this concept fully.

U.S. intelligence agencies report that the Russians spent thirty million dollars a year in developing these bizarre weapons systems. A great deal of time, money, and effort were spent in trying to develop new means of telepathy for remote spying and other purposes. The Russians call this "bio communication."

Overcoming Dark Powers by God's Power

In *Smashing the Gates of Hell* we outline the means by which intercession and spiritual warfare can effectively nullify the power of paranormal, demonic, psychotronic weapons. Don't be amazed. This revelation is clearly outlined, in principle, in Paul's letter to the Corinthian church:

> For though we walk in the flesh, we do not war after the flesh: (For the weapons of our warfare are not carnal, but mighty through God to the pulling down of strong holds;) Casting down imaginations, and every high thing that exalteth itself against the knowledge of God, and bringing into captivity every thought to the obedience of Christ; And having in a readiness to revenge all disobedience, when your obedience is fulfilled (2 Cor. 10:3-6).

This is a new problem of warfare facing our nation. Most people are unaware of the dangers of the spirit world, though it is now documented by Bob Rosio and myself that Hitler did try to harness these forces during World War II.

The joint chiefs of staff at the Pentagon have no defenses, except for those who may be praying Christians. I propose that only the church can effectively defeat these demonic forces and hold them at bay until God removes the restrainer (2 Thess. 2:3-10). The apostle Paul teaches us that our weapons are powerful against the dark powers:

> Finally, my brethren, be strong in the Lord, and in the power of his might. Put on the whole armour of God, that ye may be able to stand against the wiles of the devil. For we wrestle not

against flesh and blood, but against principalities, against powers, against the rulers of the darkness of this world, against spiritual wickedness in high places. Wherefore take unto you the whole armour of God, that ye may be able to withstand in the evil day, and having done all, to stand. Stand therefore, having your loins girt about with truth, and having on the breastplate of righteousness; And your feet shod with the preparation of the gospel of peace; Above all, taking the shield of faith, wherewith ye shall be able to quench all the fiery darts of the wicked. And take the helmet of salvation, and the sword of the Spirit, which is the word of God:

Praying always with all prayer and supplication in the Spirit, and watching thereunto with all perseverance and supplication for all saints; And for me, that utterance may be given unto me, that I may open my mouth boldly, to make known the mystery of the gospel (Eph. 6:10-19).

Peace be to the brethren, and love with faith, from God the Father and the Lord Jesus Christ. Grace be with all them that love our Lord Jesus Christ in sincerity. Amen (Eph. 6: 23-24).

To help equip yourself, your church, friends, and family for the end-time struggle on many fronts, please read or re-read my book *Smashing the Gates of Hell in the Last Days*. Pay special attention to the chapters on end-time Holy Spirit world liberation.

Endnotes
[1] Weldon, John; Levitt, Zola, *UFOs — What On Earth Is Happening?* (Eugene, OR: Harvest House, 1975), p. 121.
[2] David Allen Lewis, *Smashing the Gates of Hell in the Last Days* (Green Forest, AR: New Leaf Press, 1987), chapters 24 and 25.

Chapter 21

EUROPE, THE USA, AND THE NEW WORLD ORDER

The Kingdom of the Beast

The Antichrist will look good. The apostate world will see him as a saviour, not a monster. But a beast he is, wearing an almost impenetrable disguise. He is for peace, not war. But he wages war to obtain elusive peace.

> The words of his mouth were smoother than butter, but war was in his heart: his words were softer than oil, yet were they drawn swords (Ps. 55:21).

The final human effort to produce a New World Order is described in Revelation 13. John, on the island of Patmos, described it as the Antichrist beast kingdom. His regime is doomed from the start. Proclaiming world peace, the beast brings havoc and ruin. He is called Aberdeen, the destroyer. The beast kingdom will never succeed. Daniel, whom Jesus called a prophet (Matt. 24), spoke of a coming "king of fierce countenance" whom we understand to be the very Antichrist: "And through his policy also he shall cause craft to prosper in his hand; and he shall magnify himself in his heart, and *by peace shall destroy many:* he shall also stand up against the Prince of princes; but he shall be broken without hand" (Dan. 8:25).

Most scholars agree that the beast kingdom represents a last-days emergence of the Roman Empire. European leaders have dreamed of reviving the Old Roman Empire and forging a United Europe for centuries. One reflects for but a moment to recall the exploits of Charlemagne, Charles the Fifth, Louis the Fourteenth, Napoleon, Kaiser Wilhelm the Second, Mussolini, and Hitler. By force or intrigue, these and a score of others have sought to fulfill their dream of the ages, the revival of the Roman Empire.

When six European nations signed the Treaty of Rome on March 27, 1957, and launched the EEC — the European Common Market, there was a feeling of exaltation throughout the Western world. Jean Gabriel Monnet declared, "Once a common market interest has been created, then political union will come naturally."

A national news magazine in the USA described the final ratification of the Treaty of Rome on December 28, 1958, with these words: "When the history of the 20th century is written, last week is likely to prove one of its watersheds. For in the seven days which spanned 1958 and 1959, Western Europe began to flex its economic muscles for the first time in a decade, and took its biggest step toward unity since the death of Charlemagne 1,145 years ago" (*Time*, January 12, 1959, p. 23). We have that copy of *Time* magazine in our research files.

The following quote is from Dr. Wilmington's book *The King is Coming* (p. 116):

> On Capitoline Hill in Rome, nearly 2,000 years ago, Caesar's legions went forth to bring the first unified rule to Europe's warring tribes. Since

the Roman Empire's fall the unification of Europe has been a dream which neither the sword of Napoleon nor Hitler could realize. But on Rome's Capitoline Hill last week six statesmen, with the peaceful stroke of a pen, took the biggest step yet made toward this dream of centuries.

Wilmington attributes this quote to *Life* magazine, January 9, 1959. We found that issue of *Life* in the public library in the microfilm files, but could not locate the quote. Perhaps someone can help us pinpoint the primary source of this colorful quote.

About 20 years ago I was invited to participate as an observer in a conference on "European Unity and American Destiny." The conference was sponsored by the University of Cincinnati. Present at that meeting were such luminaries as Alterio Spinelli of Rome who headed the committee that drafted the treaty of Rome, which in 1957 brought six member nations into a Common Market, now simply known as the European Community (E.C.).

There was David Schoenbrun, political analyst and commentator, and many others. One evening at dinner, Sir Geoffrey DeFrietas, who was serving at that time as the president of the Council of Europe, and is to this day a member of the British Parliament, graciously answered many of my questions. At one point he looked into my eyes and slowly said, "You know, Lewis, what we are actually trying to do in Europe is to bring the old Roman Empire back to life again."

Both Daniel and John, writer of the Book of Revelation, predict a revival of the Roman Empire in the last days prior to the establishment of the visible millennial kingdom of Jesus Christ on earth. The kingdom of God is not brought through human effort. As Dr. Stanley Horton so often says, it comes through a period of judgment and the outpouring of the wrath of God on earth, climaxed by the personal return of Jesus, who comes to save the world from self-destruction.

Before every knee bows to the Son of God and recognizes His supremacy, there will be a vile ruler, the Antichrist, who defies the God of heaven and tries to fulfill the ancient vision of Babel/Babylon. That final Antichrist is foreshadowed by Nimrod, Nebuchadnezzar, Antiochus, Hadrian, Hitler, and a host of others (1 John 2:18). The Antichrist will not look like a monster. He will be the most appealing secular man ever to walk on the face of the earth.

His humanist New Age religion will exalt man as the divinity. "He opened his mouth in blasphemy against God, to blaspheme his name, and his tabernacle, and them that dwell in heaven" (Rev. 13:6). Paul clearly describes "the man of sin . . . the son of perdition; Who opposeth and exalteth himself above all that is called God, or that is worshipped; so that he as God sitteth in the temple of God, shewing himself that he is God" (2 Thess. 2:3–4).

Like John, Daniel saw visions of far tomorrows. He described how the coming man of evil would "speak great words against the most High, and shall wear out the saints of the most High, and think to change times and laws: and they shall be given into his hand until a time and times and the dividing of time" (Dan. 7:25). The latter means three and one-half years, or half of the seven years tribulation.

Daniel's foreview of the beast-king is parallel to that of the apostle Paul:

> And a mighty king shall stand up, that shall rule with great dominion, and do according to his will. . . . The king shall do according to his will; and he shall exalt himself, and magnify himself above every god, and shall speak marvelous things against the God of gods, and shall prosper till the indignation be accomplished: for that that is determined shall be done. Neither shall he regard the God of his fathers, nor the desire of women, nor regard any god: for he shall magnify himself above all (Dan. 11:3–37; compare 2 Thess. 2:3–4).

His program is peace, but war dogs his footsteps. He fails, how miserably he fails. "He shall magnify himself in his heart, and by peace shall destroy many: he shall also stand up against the Prince of princes; but he shall be broken without hand" (Dan. 8:25; also see 1 Thess. 5:3).

Strange that so few knew the name Jean Gabriel Monnet until now. He is truly the father of the "European Idea," and architect of the E.C. He is one of the most important figures in modern history. When the global World Federation finally emerges out of the Union of Europe, Monnet will be a hero known and lauded by every school child.

Paul Henri Spaak, living in exile in London during the Second World War, was inspired by Jean Gabriel Monnet, and into his mind came the Benelux idea, which materialized when the war was over. Before there was a six-member Common Market there was the economic union of Belgium, Netherlands, and Luxembourg, hence "Benelux." The Benelux Union provided a model for the Common Market, which, when finalized and reduced to a ten-member federation, will provide a model for a world government, probably divided into ten regions or kingdoms.

On January 1, 1981, Greece became the 10th member nation of the EEC. "This is it," exclaimed excited prophecy students. But no, this was not it, for as I had earlier predicted on national television, Spain and Portugal became the 11th and 12th member nations and there will be more. There will be adjustments, unions, dropouts, but finally there will be the ten kingdoms prophesied in the Bible.

The now-famed treaty that was brought into being at Maastricht, Netherlands, is now very close to approval by the 12-member nations of the EEC. The Danish government rejected the treaty, refusing to sign. This was followed by a media blitz that many believe brainwashed enough of the Danes that when it was put to a referendum vote, it passed by a slim margin. But surely England would continue to steadfastly reject the treaty. The House of Commons passed it by a healthy majority. Would not the iron lady, Margaret Thatcher, prevail with powerful arguments before the House of Lords? It was not to be. The *News Leader* carried the following report datelined, "London:"

> From the seclusion of their ancestral estates or tax havens, bluebloods rallied Wednesday behind a newcomer to the House of Lords, Baroness Thatcher, as she vainly sought to derail a bill on closer European Union.
>
> Her successor and fellow Conservative, Prime Minister John Major, averted a government defeat with the support of most opposition peers, loyal Conservatives, and a rival clutch of aristocrats making rare appearances in the chamber.
>
> Supporters of the bill voted overwhelmingly against the Thatcher-led motion late Wednesday. The vote was 445-176. Thatcher's motion demanded that Britain's 43 million voters hold a referendum before the government could ratify the Maastricht treaty on closer union for the 12-nation European Community.

It was a long, long road to Maastricht, mein Herr? How much further to Babylon? And, what groping beast, slavering as he goes, is this that lurches toward Rome and Ur of Chaldee? Lurching through the dimming gloom of earth's twilight, and night cometh.

Thank God that after the darkest night of earth's history there comes the dawning of a new day, the Day of Messiah and the Regnum Millennium (Kingdom of 1,000 years).

Before me is a fascinating book by Merry and Serge Bromberger, published in French in 1968, then in English in 1969. It is titled, *Jean Monnet and the United States of Europe.*[1]

The Brombergers wrote of Jean Gabriel Monnet's

devout Christian sister who never ceased witnessing to him, trying to convert him to Christ. But, say the Brombergers, "He, too, is a mystic in his own fashion, dedicated to achieving understanding among his fellowmen, to a quest for the mechanisms of international integration."[2]

In 1992 I posed the question, "Will the January 1993 European agreement only work to abolish tariffs and open borders? Will it affect only the economy of Europe?" I put the question to Wolfgang Behrends, the German ambassador to Canada. The late George Spaetzel and I were having lunch at the Confederation Club in Kitchener, Ontario, where we met with Behrends. "Mr. Ambassador," I queried, "Will the union in Europe remain economic or should we expect a political federation?" With a look of great satisfaction the Honorable Mr. Behrends replied, "To be sure, what we are moving toward is a political federation in Europe."

The year 1950 was one of fervent activity in Europe. Economic treaties were proposed. It was the year of the Schumann Plan, launched at a big press conference engineered by Jean Gabriel Monnet. Later Monnet lamented to Professor Paul Reuter, "Look here. In 1950 we were wrong. We should have organized Europe politically right from the start. We should have taken advantage of Adenauer's suggestion of a joint Franco-German government, a joint parliament. . . . We probably could have initiated a United States of Europe as easily as we launched the Coal and Steel Community."[3]

Toward the end of his life, French General de Gaulle made an unusual comment: "In order to have a European army — in other words, an army of Europe — Europe must first exist as a political, economic, financial, administrative, and *above all, spiritual entity* . . . millions of men would be willing to die for it"[4] (emphasis added).

Former President George Bush launched in the minds of men the concept of a New World Order. There is no doubt that he meant a world government. His successor, President

Clinton, is no less enthusiastic in promotion of the federation of all mankind. Only his tactics and rhetoric differ.

Seldom is the agenda of the One Worlders more clearly declared than in the *Time* magazine article, "The Birth of the Global Nation" by Strobe Talbott.[5] Noting that in the recent past, "The advocacy of any kind of world government became highly suspect. By 1950 'one-worlder' was a term of derision for those suspected of being woolly-headed naïfs, if not crypto-Communists."

But Talbott points out that times are changing. "The internal affairs of a nation used to be off-limits to the world community. Now the principle of 'humanitarian intervention' is gaining acceptance." Talbott cites U.N. authorized action against Saddam Hussein both in the action to help the Kurds in the north, and, of course, the Desert Storm in defense of Kuwait (or was it in defense of oil?).

Strobe Talbott notes that the Rio Environmental World Summit held in June 1992 "signified the participants acceptance of what Maurice Strong, the main impresario of the event, called 'the transcending sovereignty of nature.' " In other words, the main agenda of Rio was actually the promotion of globalism. The environmental issue simply provided a convenient vehicle to ride down the yellow brick road to the land of Super Oz. Dorothy, I don't think we are in Kansas any longer.

No doubt the New World Order will be called a democracy, that most abused and misunderstood of terms. Strobe Talbot sums it up: "The best mechanism for democracy, whether at the level of the multinational state or that of the planet as a whole, is not an all-powerful Leviathan or centralized superstate, but a federation, a union of separate states that allocate certain powers to a central government while retaining many others for themselves. Federalism has already proved the most successful of all political experiments, and organizations like the World Federalist Association have for decades advocated it as the basis for global

government. Federalism is largely an American Invention.
. . . If that model does indeed work globally . . . [it would be]
a special source of pride for a world government's American
constituents."

The spirit of this pride can be seen in the remarks of
former President George Bush:

> Out of these troubled times, our fifth objec-
> tive — a New World Order — can emerge. . . . We
> are now in sight of a United Nations that performs
> as envisioned by its founders" (September 11,
> 1990, TV address to the people of the USA).

> The United Nations can help bring about a
> new day . . . a New World Order and a long era of
> peace (October 1, 1990).

Regarding the U.N. sanctions Bush said, "When we
succeed . . . we will have invigorated a U.N. that contributes
as its founders dreamed. We have established principles for
acceptable international conduct and the means to enforce
them" (October 26, 1990).

Two days after the air offensive was launched against
Iraq, he spoke to the Arab nations that were not part of the
coalition: "Look, you're part of this New World Order. . . .
You can play an important part in seeing that the world can
live at peace in the Middle East and elsewhere" (January 18,
1991).

When President Bush spoke to the U.S. Reserve Offic-
ers Association he said, "From the day Saddam's forces first
crossed into Kuwait, it was clear that this aggression required a swift response from our nation and the [world
community]. What was, and is at stake is not simply our
energy or economic security, and the stability of a vital
region, but the prospects for peace in the post-Cold War era
— the promise of a New World Order based on the rule of
law" (January 23, 1991).

In His address on the State of the Union, January 29,

1991, Bush said, "What is at stake is more than one small country; it is a big idea: a New World Order, where diverse nations are drawn together in security, freedom, and the rule of law."

"There is no room for lawless aggression in the Persian Gulf for this New World Order we are trying to create, and Saddam Hussein will know this" (January 1, 1991).

We heard our president talking about "our friends and fellow members of the coalition." Some of these friends are the most dangerous cutthroats of modern history. They are the creators and supporters of world terrorism. Blood flows from their hands. They rank with Hitler, Antiochus Epiphanes, and Nero. Allied intelligence reports that our Soviet "allies" continually helped launch the SCUDS which they had furnished to Saddam in the first place. The Soviets refused to recall their advisors who were doing this. The USSR kept right on shipping materials to Iraq. Up to the time of the actual attack, the USSR was flying twelve AN-124 and AN-22 transports into Baghdad daily. Gorbachev admitted to President Bush that this was happening and said, "The Soviets need cash."

The role of public education in promoting the New World Order must not be overlooked. In 1955 I was preaching in a midwestern church during the first year of my evangelistic teaching ministry. From the pulpit I boldly proclaimed that, potentially, the public education system was the most dangerous anti-Christ force, and could be used to brainwash the generation that would herald and welcome the prophesied world ruler.

With no thought of being unkind, the pastor's wife chided me for making such a rash statement. Being a school teacher herself, it was hard to receive such a concept. It did seem unlikely in 1955. A year ago I saw that lady again. She brought the subject up saying, "David, you were right about the educational system in this country."

Kenneth DeCourcey's *Intelligence Digest* is a London,

England, based research publication dealing with global affairs. In the September 1963 edition there is an article on UNESCO, United Nations Educational, Scientific, and Cultural Organization. The author quotes William Benton, U.S. Assistant Secretary of State.

Benton said the following while chairing the charter forming meeting for UNESCO on September 23, 1946. "We are at the beginning of a long process of breaking down the walls of national sovereignty. UNESCO must be the pioneer. The Department of State has fathered this national commission. Now you give for the first time a collective brain to the whole nervous system of American science, culture, education, and means of communication." This speech was given before the first meeting of the U.S. National Commission for UNESCO.

DeCourcey also cited UNESCO publication number 356. "As long as the child breathes the poisoned air of nationalism, education in world-mindedness can produce only precarious results. As we have pointed out, it is frequently the family that infects the child with extreme nationalism. The school should therefore use the means described earlier to combat family attitudes that favor jingoism [those who favor warlike aggressive foreign policy]. . . . We shall presently recognize in nationalism the major obstacle to development of world-mindedness." (In 1985 the USA withdrew from UNESCO because of its anti-Western bias.)

Parents are hearing that a new thought system of schooling our children known as Outcome Based Education (OBE) is taking over our schools. Every Christian teacher I have talked to about OBE declares that it is a brainwashing system to turn our children into globally minded candidates for world citizenship. Sound radical? Look at what Pam Shellenberger, area representative for the Christian Women's Association wrote about OBE: "The education goals proposed have nothing to do with testing based on self-worth, information and thinking skills, learning independently, adaptability to change, and ethical judgment. I'm not quite sure how this program could improve our academic excellence." A citizens OBE task force in Wisconsin has declared that Outcome Based Education has identified one of its desired "outcomes" to be "global awareness."

Janet Parshall writes, "In this new age of politically correct thought and speech, it is not too difficult to imagine how the classroom could become the great social factory, churning out boys and girls who all think the same way. . . . Perhaps the most repugnant aspect of OBE is the overriding philosophy that children belong to the state. More and more schools have tried to assume the role of co-parent with all the vestiges of that high calling. The movement toward collaboration of all social service agencies through the public school can be readily fostered through anti-parent and subjective programs like OBE."

No OBE in your local school? Look again, it may be called America 2000, Success-Based Education, Criterion-Based Education, Mastery Learning, and a host of other names attached to the New Think Education.

If George Bush was a prophet of the New World Order, what about Bill Clinton? Is the William Clinton administration any different from that of the preceding presidential regime? Indeed not, in fact the race toward one world speeds up under his leadership.

What really goes on in that murky, almost hidden bureaucracy of underlings in Foggy Bottom? Let me pull back the veil and give you an inside look. Scenes like this unfold each day in the nation's capitol. C-Span 2 Television cable service pulls the curtain for us. On July 15, 1993, under the banner of U.N. peacekeeping, the Parliamentarians for Global Action held a congressionally sponsored, and we assume tax dollar-funded, conference.

The moderator of the conference was Kennedy Graham, secretary general of Parliamentarians for Global Action.

In his rambling preliminary remarks Graham revealed

that "Global Action is a worldwide network of politicians, that is of congresspersons and parliamentarians.... We now have 900 members from 70 countries, including 45 members from the United States Congress, both the Senate and the House. . . ."

Graham stated that members of P.F.G.A., which has been in existence for 14 years, are committed to "approaching global problems as a coordinated network working across national boundaries." They are, "politicians who take the interest of the planet into account, along with the traditional national interest.

"We have been working on issues such as sustainable development and democracy, peace, and security, focusing especially in the 1980s on nuclear disarmament issues, and of course, more recently on peacekeeping itself.

"I think in the post Cold War era all of us are now searching for new structures of peace, new structures of security to replace the strategy of nuclear deterrence that underpinned global security for the better part of four decades. Perhaps somewhat paradoxically that new structure of peace and security is, in fact, not especially new — it is the 20th century concept of peace, namely collective security. Collective security through the United Nations."

Collective security means a world army which would override the authority of national sovereignty or the authority of national armies. In short, we are looking at a United Nations World police force, the ultimate Gestapo.

Kennedy Williams charmed the group:

It was, as you will recall, a Wilsonion idea in the 1920s, it has had a checkered career through the thirties, in the face of blatant aggression. . . . It was revived and strengthened in the 1940s, in the second cut, through the U.N. charter, put into cold storage as a result of the cold war for four decades. Now in the 1990s we have a third opportunity to make collective security through the U.N. work.

When one looks at the hot crisis spots of Somalia, Bosnia . . . also the more traditional tension areas of Golan Heights, Cyprus, and Kashmir, which have not been resolved politically and which remain potential explosive spots . . . it is urgent that we succeed . . . in insuring that collective security becomes the reliable replacement to deterrence for securing the peace around the world. Collective security is fraught with problems, teething problems. We are on the frontier of progress in this respect — in making global cooperation work in terms of self governance . . . problems of political decision making, and the legitimacy of powers of primary principle organs of the UN, [there are] problems of judgments to be made [as to the] degree of intervention in sovereign states, and levels of engagement. . . .

That is the reasoning behind our decision to convene this workshop in the Congress, to enable congresspersons and their staff to listen to recognized experts in the field.

The first speaker introduced by Graham was David Scheffer, senior advisor and council to the U.S. ambassador to the United Nations.

Scheffer's topic was peacekeeping. His thinking and expression was not only New Age, it sounded like something straight out of George Orwell's classic *1984*.

"We are in a new era [new age] . . . of multilateralism . . . now in era of engagement on global agenda."

Multilateralism simply indicates that our armies must coordinate with U.N. forces and commanders and in fact, be subjected to them. Never again should the USA act as an independent agent. Of course, many alleged benefits from this were described.

We were told that in this age of complexity we must come up with a "new agenda," one that would have a "policy of assertive multilateralism." Of course there has to be a totally new mindset and if "we are going to be engaged in conflicts multilaterally must have multilateral perspective."

Scheffer assured us that the "Soviet threat has expired," and that a new kind of engaging multilateral diplomacy on an hourly basis is going on in the U.N. These new tactics, "focus on preventive diplomacy."

With up-to-date statistics, Scheffer let us know that the USA is currently involved in 14 peacekeeping operations in various parts of the world, and our hard-working U.N. officials are in continual sessions seven days a week from early in the morning until late each night. New Think, à la Orwell, is the avenue for progress to world tranquillity. Scheffer said, "We cannot express strongly enough . . . have to get ourselves out of the old think of the Cold War and into the new think of the new era [era = age = New Age]."

Scheffer made a point of the fact that Vice President Al Gore and other leading politicians stress the New Think idea. According to Scheffer the three steps to peace involve

1. Peacemaking
2. Peacekeeping
3. Peace enforcement

Chapter seven of the U.N. charter deals with peace enforcement according to Scheffer. He said, "Peace enforcement is a much tougher sword . . . authorizes the use of military force pursuant to however the Security Council resolution sets forth in the resolution. . . . We must bring political pressure to bear on the belligerents."

But what if, one day, the U.N. decides that because the USA sides with Israel they are the belligerents? Can the United Nations forces be used to straighten us out? Why not?

I will share one more pithy observation from the Parliamentarians for Global Action symposium. James Sutterlin, former political advisor to U.N. Secretary General de Cuellar strengthened the idea of multilateralism: "This is a time of great change in the world . . . if we are to meet the challenges we face in the world it requires . . . changes in national thinking particularly on the allocation of national resources and I include in that very specifically the allocation of military force."

There will be a world government. We all understand that there can be no peace without it. It is true that the Saddam Husseins and the Slobodan Milosevichs of this world can only understand a superior power with the will to enforce peace in a region. Someone must "rule with a rod of iron."

Windswept House — More Truth than Fiction

I think you could profit from reading Malachi Martin's new book *Windswept House,* remembering that this man writes truth in a docu-story form, changing names to protect himself and some of those he writes about. He is a Vatican insider, a close associate of Pope John XXIII. He describes the movement toward world government. You do not have to agree with his theology to benefit from his knowledge.

This is a shocking book. It pulls aside the veil and gives you a clear and detailed view into the European Union, the Church, the Masonic Lodge, and the conspiracy between religion and international politics. Linkage of homosexual clergy and Satanism is portrayed. Gorbachev and Yeltsin of Russia come into the spotlight for their role in the globalist agenda. The Mafia is not ignored. This 646-page book is an exciting read. Once you get into it, it is hard to put down.[6]

U.S. News and World Report interviewer Jeffery L. Sheler asked Malachi Martin, "Why write this as fiction? Why not name names?" The author replied, "Some of the cardinals involved are well-respected and loved. Understandably, many people would react emotionally in defense of the cardinals and would miss the larger point. I plan to write a monograph in the fall that names some names."

Go to the library and read the short review of *Windswept House* in *U.S. News and World Report,* June 10, 1996, page 66. Better yet, check out the book at your local library.

The Choice Before Humanity

There are two ways set before the human race. One way leads to the Antichrist and his short-term, weak, shaky world coalition. The other leads to Jesus Christ and His glorious and peaceable kingdom on earth, the Regnum Millennium — the Kingdom of a Thousand Years. It takes faith to accept either one. To put it in terms a secular person can understand, "I am willing to bet the farm on Jesus." We have staked our all on Him and His Divine Word. He will return. He will not fail us. The world's politicians have always failed us, but Jesus never fails. He keeps His campaign promises. It's not a bet at all, we have a sure thing.

> There is no peace, saith the Lord, unto the wicked" (Isa. 48:22).

> And he shall judge among the nations, and shall rebuke many people: and they shall beat their swords into plowshares, and their spears into pruninghooks: nation shall not lift up sword against nation, neither shall they learn war any more (Isa. 2:4).

> I will both lay me down in peace, and sleep: for thou, Lord, only makest me dwell in safety (Ps. 4:8).

Endnotes

[1] Merry and Serge Bromberger, translated by Blaine P. Haplerin, *Jean Monnet and the United States of Europe* (New York, NY: Coward-McCann, Inc., 1969).

[2] Ibid., p. 11.

[3] Ibid., p. 104.

[4] Ibid., p. 118.

[5] *Time* magazine, "The Birth of the Global Nation," Strobe Talbott, July 20, 1992, p. 70.

[6] Malachi Martin, *Windswept House* (New York, NY: Doubleday, 1996).

Chapter 22

LOOMING WORLD GOVERNMENT

State of the World Forum

What went on in San Francisco, in September 1995 was nothing less than extraordinary. Mikhail Gorbachev and a bevy of politicians, futurologists, and New Agers took the world a giant step closer to global dictatorship. From September 30 to October 1, 1995, a landmark meeting, headed by Marxist Mikhail Gorbachev, former head of the Soviet Union was conducted at the Fairmont Hotel and a nearby Masonic Auditorium in San Francisco. Billed as the State of the World Forum — Toward a New Civilization, it was one of the most significant steps forward in implementing the coming world government, which President Clinton recently referred to as the "global village." It was previously hailed as the New World Order by former President George Bush in many speeches made while he was president of the USA.

Jim Garrison, executive director of the Gorbachev

306 • Signs of His Coming

Foundation, made a very revealing statement in the May 31 issue of *SF Weekly*, a far-left San Francisco newspaper: "Over the next 20 to 30 years we are going to end up with the world government . . . it's inevitable." Garrison writes of the problems of violence in the USA and the rest of the world, proclaiming that "In and through this turbulence is the recognition that *we have to empower the United Nations and that we have to govern and regulate human interaction.*" Garrison is from the New Age Esalen Institute and Soviet American Exchange Program, San Francisco. (Emphasis is added, here and throughout this chapter.)

Yes, the Cold War is over, but looming before us is the ideological Hot War of hegemony (domination) and oppression. The globalists know that the human race must be blinded to the real intentions of these elitist one-worlders if they are to succeed. They must endeavor to use the media to brainwash you into thinking that they have your best interests at heart.

I have no doubt that history will record the World Forum as a momentous occasion in the annals of the coming Antichrist.

And the world lies in darkness, ignorant, blindly stumbling along, vaguely uneasy but nonetheless apathetic. "Woe unto them that call evil good, and good evil; that put darkness for light, and light for darkness; that put bitter for sweet, and sweet for bitter!" (Isa. 5:20).

> We wait for light, but behold obscurity; for brightness, but we walk in darkness (Isa. 59:9).

The Presidio

The U.S. Army has handed Gorbachev a key to the Presidio in San Francisco. The Presidio was one of our major military bases closed down by the Pentagon. It is the former headquarters of the 6th Army. It was a major military intelligence center. One prestigious building was turned over to Gorbachev for his USA headquarters. The Presidio has been divided into over 350 choice areas and will be handed over to various globally minded organizations. Gorbachev got first choice.

The *Los Angeles Times* recorded, "In an event that would have been unfathomable a few years ago, former Soviet President Mikhail Gorbachev opened an office Friday on one of America's most hallowed military posts, the Presidio of San Francisco.

"Gorbachev, who resigned from office in 1991 as the Soviet Union crumbled, was given the key to the office for his pro-democracy*[sic]* foundation by the Presidio's commanding general.

" 'Please accept this key as a gesture of our good will and our best wishes to you as the newest Presidian,' Lt. Gen. Glynn C. Mallory Jr. told Gorbachev.

" 'I assure you this key is in reliable hands,' the world's former top communist replied."[1]

The article said that the Presidio would be a base of operations for "prestigious organizations with an international focus." And, "the creation of a center for global environmental studies. . . . The [Gorbachev] foundation's staff will occupy a stately white house that was formerly home to a Coast Guard commandant. Ringed by cypress trees and just a few steps from the surf, it commands views of the Golden Gate Bridge and San Francisco's skyline.

" 'The entire Presidio is spectacular, but he sure got one of the best spots, that's for sure,' said Park Service spokesman Howard Levitt."

Mikhail Gorbachev

Just what is the driving force that motivates Mikhail Gorbachev? Gorbachev is a Communist, a dedicated Marxist, former president of the Soviet Union and general secretary of the Communist Party. His own words indicate that he still adheres to the Marxist theory of the *inevitability of world conquest*. The methods may change but the goal remains the same, and that is world domination. They may no longer call it communism, substituting world socialism, but the leopard has not changed his spots.

Here are a few quotes from Gorbachev's speeches and from the pages of his best selling book *Perestroika*. "In October 1917 we parted with the Old World, rejecting it once and for all. We are moving toward a New World, the world of communism. We shall never turn off that road." The new word for Marxism or communism is "socialism." Gorbachev said in June 1990, "I am now, just as I've always been, a convinced Communist." He wrote, "I am a Communist, a convinced Communist. For some that may be a fantasy. But for me it is my main goal."

Gorbachev stated, "Today we have perestroika, the salvation of national socialism, giving it a second breath, revealing everything good which is in this system." Now we understand. The Cold War is over and the hottest war of all, the ideological war for the very soul of humanity is upon us. The title of Gorbachev's book *Perestroika* means "restructuring." I have read and re-read *Perestroika*. It is credited with bringing about the collapse of the Soviet Union. Long live the new Russian Empire! Russia is now the strongest military force in the world, according to European intelligence sources.

Is the old Soviet Empire still functioning? Yes, it is, although now in disguise, as the new Commonwealth of Independent States (CIS). In the *Jerusalem Report* magazine for October 19, 1995, Lawrence Kohn demonstrates keen insight in a letter to the editor. Referring to an article in the *Report* for September 21 on Israel's new ties to the CIS republic of Azerbaijan, he points out the dangers of trusting this predominately Muslim nation. Kohn wrote, "Israel is making a grave mistake working closely with the regime in Azerbaijan. Any brief claim the state had to independence disappeared when President Haidar Aliyev took over. Aliyev was a Communist Party boss under Brezhnev and a KGB general. The lack of independence of certain CIS republics is particularly obvious when the likes of Aliyev are in charge. The trappings of capitalism simply mask the continuity of the 'former' Soviet Union and re-baptized Russia. Neither Strauss ice cream nor Israeli cellular phones will change these facts." Yes, Virginia, Magog is still Magog.

"The New Russia is haunted by the old Russia. Devastation, industrial pollution, corruption, and a bizarre nostalgia provide a harrowing glimpse of a society in free fall." *Life* magazine, July 1995 continued portraying a horrifying vision of the new Russia, "Pollution, poverty and caricatures of capitalism . . . a menacing swirl of corrupt capitalism, nuclear plague, and civil and gang wars. . . . Societal decay spreads unchecked. Half the drinking water is unsafe; birth defects have increased fivefold; and more than 70 percent of Russian businesses have Mob ties. . . . It should be no surprise [that] when a society crumbles, its people frequently turn to despotic solutions."

While these awful conditions take their daily toll on the republics of the CIS, including Russia, the building of an ever stronger military machine continues on apace. *Life* displayed graphic photos of soldiers in futuristic garb, "Members of an elite tank division train near Moscow for chemical and atomic warfare." Worldwide military intelligence services report that Russia still has tens of thousands of nuclear weapons, and while junking obsolete bombs, new advanced bombs are being manufactured.

President Reagan was not wrong when he called the former Soviet Union the "Evil Empire." We refer to the Communist leaders and ideologues, not the people of Russia, when we quote Reagan. "For we wrestle not against flesh and blood, but against principalities, against powers, against the rulers of the darkness of this world, against spiritual wickedness in high places" (Eph. 6:12).

In a recent essay, *New Priorities for the World* Gorbachev wrote, "It is increasingly clear that the ideological foundations of the Western world are becoming outdated." Note that it is the Western world, not the Communist-Socialist world that is outdated.

In *Perestroika* (p. 49) Gorbachev says, "Perestroika is a revolution. . . ." and, "No revolutionary movement is possible without revolutionary theory — this Marxist precept is today more relevant than ever." On page 54 he says, "We are not going to change Soviet power, of course, or abandon its fundamental principles. . . . Perestroika requires Party leaders who are very close to Lenin's ideal of a revolutionary Bolshevik. We must heed Gorbachev's words when he writes, ". . . the guarantee of the irreversibility of perestroika. The more socialist democracy there is, the more socialism we will have. This is our firm conviction, and we will not abandon it. . . . The creativity of the masses is the decisive force in perestroika. There is no other, more powerful force."

By reading *Perestroika,* one gets a strong message: The Soviet Union is in trouble and they must make short-term compromises with the Western nations in order to achieve their ultimate objectives.

With America plunging headlong down the Socialist road we must recognize that powerful people, backed by enormous wealth, are formulating changes that will alter the course of human lives and destiny. Gorbachev wrote in *Perestroika* (p. 95). "We are preparing the masses for radical change." On page 100 he reaffirms the very core of Marxism, saying "This will be under communism." On page 151 Gorbachev calls scientific socialism the *"inevitable evolution of the world.* Let the West think capitalism is the highest achievement of civilization. It's their prerogative to think so. We simply do not agree with this. And let history decide who is right."

The Document — We Meet Dr. Paul Busiek

There were about 50 people at the Ozarks Breakfast Club meeting at the Heritage Cafeteria in Springfield, Missouri. The speaker was Dr. Paul Busiek, M.D., a notable researcher in Marxist thought, and an infiltrator of Communist organizations. His topic was the proliferation of Marxist socialism on the local, national, and international levels. In his heavily documented presentation, which riveted all of our attention, Dr. Busiek referred to a lengthy document that he called "Gorbachev's Plan." After the meeting I was asking Paul some questions. He handed me the document for my examination. It was the only copy he had with him. He surprised me by offering to let me have it for my own further research.

I am the only person in the meeting who received the document, labeled, *State of the World Forum — Towards a New Civilization;* September 27 - October 1, 1995, San Francisco, California. So far Busiek is the only person I have been able to find who is aware of the existence of this document. Evidently, he was never intended to have it. We presume that the document was for those invited to attend the *State of the World Forum.* Fasten your seatbelts! Here we have a statement of purpose, the plan and program for the conference. The list of speakers and attendees is notable. You will be shocked! We have the document in a secret place.

The words of Vaclav Havel, president of the Republic of Czechoslovakia, appear on page one of the document: "There are good reasons for suggesting that the modern age has ended. Many things indicate that we are going through a transitional period, when it seems that something is on the way out and something else is painfully being born. It is as if something was crumbling, decaying, and exhausting itself, while something else, still indistinct, was arising from the rubble."

One might wonder if that "something else" will it be an idealistic Utopia or will it be an *Evil Empire*, the Fourth Reich of the World?

We reveal to you that it will be the doomed Antichrist attempt at world domination. After a short success, it will fail. "And the beast [Antichrist] was taken, and with him the false prophet that wrought miracles before him, with which he deceived them that had received the mark of the beast, and them that worshipped his image. These both were cast alive into a lake of fire burning with brimstone" (Rev. 19:20).

After the fall of the beast kingdom we will see the true Theocratic Regnum Millennium that will be ushered in and governed by the Messiah, Jesus Christ, whose visible return we anticipate.

On page three of the document the mission of the conference is clearly stated. "The State of the World Forum is the launching of a multi-year global initiative to focus on the fundamental challenges and opportunities confronting humanity as we enter the next phase of human development. It is being held in the belief that at this momentous juncture in history — between the ending of the Cold War and the dawn of the new century — *we are experiencing the birth of the first global civilization.*"

> Raging waves of the sea, foaming out their
> own shame; wandering stars, to whom is reserved
> the blackness of darkness for ever (Jude 13).

The document states further, "The goal of the Forum is to articulate a clearer vision of new international priorities. Its product will be an on-going process to generate innovative approaches to the challenges facing human society.

"This historic gathering will (1) Analyze the current state of the world; and (2) Launch a multi-year process, culminating in the year 2000, to articulate the fundamental priorities, values, and actions necessary to constructively shape our common future.

"Ultimately, the State of the World Forum is an invitation. It is a call to individuals throughout the world to join in this dialogue and to work directly with the convening of committed individuals as an active member of an historic and timely global initiative."

On the last page of the document we read, "The State of the World Forum is a project of the Gorbachev Foundation/USA, an international non-partisan, non-profit educational foundation created in 1992 to address the immediate challenges of the post Cold War world and assist in the process of *building global consensus for our common future.*"

Participants

On page five of this inner circle document we read: "Mikhail Gorbachev is the convening Chair and will be joined by co-chairs: President Askar Akaev [Republic of Kyrgyzstan], President Oscar Arias [Costa Rica], Prime Minister Tansu Ciller [Turkey], Prime Minister Ruud Lubbers [Netherlands], Former Prime Minister Yasuhiro Nakasone [Japan], Secretary of State George Shultz [USA], Ted Turner [CNN], Archbishop Desmond Tutu [S. Africa]. Some of the titles of these persons indicate maximum title, and may be a former position held."

It is also stated on page five that this initiative will bring together, from all over the world "senior statespeople, current political leaders, business executives, scientists, artists, intellectuals, spiritual leaders, community activists, and youth."

"At the center will be approximately 100 Fellows, chosen for their internationally recognized contributions to designing our emerging global civilization. Working directly with the fellows will be other participants, comprised principally of senior executives from around the world who are actively committed to fulfilling this historic mission."

Among the speakers were Mikhail Gorbachev, former New York Governor Mario Cuomo, former Prime Minister Margaret Thatcher, former President George Bush, and New Age futurologist John Naisbit. These were speakers at major sessions. In addition, at least 500 international business leaders paid $5,000 as round table sponsors. Only these were allowed to participate in the secret round table discussions. Many more speakers and participants are listed, here are the names of just a few of them. The list is part of the document, and some had not confirmed attendance at the time the document was printed: As time goes on we will discover many others who were at the forum. Obviously these elitists are considered allies by Gorbachev and associates, or they would not have been invited.

Michael Alexander; director, Sierra Club Presidio Task Force.

Hanan Ashrawi; founder, Palestinian Commission for Citizens Rights.

Zbigniew Brzezinski; national security advisor to the president, (1976-1980).

George H.W. Bush, former president of the USA, New World Order advocate.

Fritjof Capra, New Age leader.

Deepak Chopra, New Age leader.

Alan Cranston; U.S. senator (1968-1992). Director, USA Presidio base of the Gorbachev Foundation.

John Denver; musician, New Age leader.

Matthew Fox, New Age leader.

William Gates III, chairman, Microsoft Inc., Richest man in America!

Thich Nhat Hanh; Vietnamese Buddhist leader.

Willis Harman, New Age leader.

Mahbub ul Haq, special advisor, UN Development Program.

Vaclav Havel; president of the Czech Republic (taped message).

Theodore Hesburgh; president, University of Notre Dame (1952-1987).

Morohiro Hosokawa; former prime minister, Japan. Member of parliament.

Sheikh Ahmed Kuftaro; grand mufti, Syria.

Richard Leakey; anthropologist.

Amory Lovins; president, Rocky Mountain Institute.

Wilma Mankiller; principal chief (former) Cherokee Nation.

Fred Matser; Chairman, Gorbachev Foundation, the Netherlands.

Akio Matsumura; founder, Global Forum of Spiritual & Parliamentary Leaders.

James Miscoll; vice chairman (ret., Bank of America).

Gertrude Mongella; secretary general, fourth U.N. Women's Conference.

Robert Muller, former assistant secretary general, U.N. Linked to Lucis Trust. New Age guru. Author of *New Genesis, — Shaping a Global Spirituality.*

Thabo Mbeki, ANC terrorist.

Brian Mulroney; prime minister of Canada (1984-1993).

Rupert Murdock, international media mogul.

Michael Murphy; founder, Esalen Institute.

Ralph Nader, consumer rights advocate.

John Naisbit; futurist; author.

Mohammed Naki; chairman, Kuwait Industries.

David Packard; founder, Hewlett-Packard Corporation.

Martin Palmer; president, International Consultancy on Religion, Education, and Culture.

Shimon Peres; minister of foreign affairs, Israel.

K. S. Raju; managing director, Nagarjuna Fertilizers and Chemicals.

Tony Robbins, author of *Unlimited Power* (walk on fiery coals, etc.) TV motivation, infomercial superstar.

Carl Sagan; astronomer, author, Cornell University.

Georgi Shaknazarov; director, Center for Global Programs, Gorbachev Foundation, Moscow.

Hisham Sharabi; Omar al-Mukar professor of Arab culture, Georgetown University.

George Shultz; secretary of state of the United States (1982-1989).

316 • Signs of His Coming

Jeremy Stone; president, Federation of American Scientists.

Oliver Stone; Hollywood director, producer.

Maurice Strong; chairman, Ontario Hydro, Canada.

Prince Sultan; Saudi Arabia.

Margaret Thatcher; prime minister, United Kingdom (1979-1990).

Alvin Toffler; futurist; author, *Future Shock, the Third Wave, Coming EcoSpasm and Power Shift.*

Ted Turner; chairman of the board, Turner Broadcasting Systems, Inc.

A carefully selected group of children and youths were present at the forum. They were there to be trained as the next generation of world leadership.

This list of names is from the document that was printed in advance of the event. We may never know who all were there, as the list of participants will not be released to the public.

Hot Line News Flash!

The phone rang here at the D.A.L. Research Center. It was from an information base in Louisiana. "T" reported to us that infiltrator "S" had gotten into the World Forum for the purpose of intelligence gathering. Names are not used here for security reasons. "S" had reported to "U" at an information base in Indiana with instructions to pass data to "T" in Louisiana, who reported to us several times during the World Forum. The following bits and pieces were passed on to us while the forum was in progress. It has passed through two channels, and we await firm documentation on some items.

"S" reports, "New world headquarters will finally be somewhere in Asia [China?]. . . . International elitists I have seen here: President George Bush, Prime Minister Margaret Thatcher, George Schultz, Jane Fonda, Bill Gates, John Naisbitt, a host of multinational corporate heads, New Age leaders. . . . I had a hotel room assigned to me . . . had phone, FAX line . . . then I was moved into a room no FAX line connection. . . . Phone line tapped . . . I am calling from lobby phone. . . . They are on to me . . . please pray . . . I am probably the only Evangelical Christian here . . . estimate 2,000 in attendance at Masonic Hall. . . . Most meetings at Fairmont Hotel . . . on Sunday the TV show will be in Masonic Hall . . . Buddhist meditation on Saturday . . . TV show will air on CNN on Sunday . . . Gorbachev, Thatcher, and Bush will be interviewed live by Bernard Shaw. . . . Masonic Hall located next to FEMA [Federal Emergency Management Agency]. . . . They say that U.S. must network with Asia-political, economic, religious . . . 220 press people here . . . Gorbachev said we must reinvent the world together . . . we need unity in diversity . . . they claim that Clinton and Gore say we must wire educational system into the worldwide computer INTERNET . . . California school system will be the test market. . . . Leadership at forum includes Mafia, New Age, and Eastern religions but no Evangelical Christian [except "S"] . . . Gorbachev setting up global brain trust . . . citizen world court and jurist association . . . emphasize environmental concerns, relationship with mother earth . . . move to world population . . . earth charter . . . new legal center for international law . . . U.N. world court . . . 32 children and teens, handpicked delegates at forum, meeting separately across the street, leaders here speak of setting up United Nations children's organization . . . occult. . . ."

Many months have passed since these reports from "S" reached us via "U" and "T." We still do not have confirmation on some details [referring only to the "T" reports], and must be viewed as hearsay until firm documentation is available.

Anatoly Golytsin — We Were Warned!

Anatoly Golytsin was a high-ranking KGB officer who became a Soviet defector to the United States. Long before the events of 1990-1991 he had predicted the breakup of the

Soviet Union, the fall of the Berlin wall, and 146 other predictions, of which 139 were fulfilled by 1993. He has given testimony to our intelligence services consisting of more than 1,500 pages of explosive information. He began to bear this witness in 1969. At one time his strongest supporter was CIA Chief of Counterintelligence James J. Angleton who took Golytsin very seriously.

Golytsin came here to warn of a Soviet plot to deceive the West, by apparently reforming. At the time of his predictions, the Soviet Union was strong, the Berlin Wall firmly in place, and we had never heard of perestroika or glastnost. The goal of the Soviet plan, formulated in 1958, was to effect the convergence of communism and capitalism into a new world socialism. The Western nations must be deceived into thinking that communism was done and democracy had taken its place. This simply has not happened. The final goal of Gorbachev's perestroika and glastnost is world convergence, international socialism, and a global government dominating a New World Order.

New Lies for Old is the title of a book Golytsin wrote in 1984. Every serious student of world affairs and Bible prophecy should read it. It documents the major political deception of our times. Golytsin says the Russian plan was formulated in 1958-1960 under the Communist guidance of the late KGB chief, Aleksandr Shelepin.

Now Golytsin has written a new book, *The Perestroika Deception.* You may find a copy in the library or local bookstore. This is vital reading.

The TV Whitewash

On Sunday, October 1, 1995, at 1 p.m., Central Standard Time, a live television program on CNN was broadcast from the Masonic Hall in San Francisco. The State of the World Forum was nearing its conclusion, and there on camera were George Bush, Margaret Thatcher, and Mikhail Gorbachev being interviewed by Bernard Shaw. It was a program of pablum, a cover-up.

My analysis of the situation is twofold. First, they knew that the meeting could not be kept secret, so Ted Turner, one of the co-chairmen of the State of the World Forum, had exclusive TV rights nailed down for CNN. This allowed absolute insider control of what the public was to be told about the forum.

Second, the TV program dealt with topics such as Bosnia, world peace, democracy, and other common subjects. No new knowledge was forthcoming, and little of the real nature of the forum revealed. There was just enough mild difference of opinion (e.g., role of the UN) among the three participants to spice up the media event and make us think that real substantive issues were being discussed.

Words of Hope

Ye are all the children of light, and the children of the day: we are not of the night, nor of darkness (1 Thess. 5:5).

To open the blind eyes, to bring out the prisoners from the prison, and them that sit in darkness out of the prison house (Isa. 42:7).

And I will bring the blind by a way that they knew not; I will lead them in paths that they have not known: I will make darkness light before them, and crooked things straight. These things will I do unto them, and not forsake them (Isa. 42:16).

World Religion and the Presidio

So he carried me away in the spirit into the wilderness: and I saw a woman sit upon a scarlet coloured beast. . . . And the woman . . . had a golden cup in her hand full of abominations (Rev. 17:3-4).

The woman in this passage is the final apostate world

religion. This is beyond any vision of ecumenism (united world church). This is religious synchretism, a coming together of all world religions into a "synchronized" world religious body. The harlot in Revelation rides on the back of the beast, hoping to dominate him. The new world, new age religion is in league with earth's political henchmen, but they clash and the beast destroys the woman. "And the ten horns which thou sawest upon the beast, these shall hate the whore, and shall make her desolate and naked, and shall eat her flesh, and burn her with fire" (Rev. 17:16).

After destroying the last vestiges of religion, the Antichrist (beast) then claims to be God, himself. The final New Age deity is man himself. The beast makes himself the focal point of humanities self-worship. The apostle Paul wrote of a coming "man of sin" who would be "the son of perdition." This human Satan's intentions are clear. "Who opposeth and exalteth himself above all that is called God, or that is worshipped; so that he as God sitteth in the temple of God, shewing himself that he is God" (2 Thess. 2:4).

Many prominent religious leaders no doubt have good intentions when they promote the New World Order united religion, but the end of their efforts spell disaster.

The *San Francisco Chronicle* reported that "Bishop William Swing's proposal for a United Religions headquarters at the Presidio will reach a new stage in February when the San Francisco Episcopalian embarks on an ambitious, round-the-world pilgrimage to sign up spiritual leaders from Rome to Dharmasala." Swing is collaborating in this effort with the World Conference on Religion and Peace, the Gorbachev Foundation, and private foundations (which he declined to identify).

He is proposing to build a "United Religions" (UR) complex — consisting of a "Hall of Speaking," "Hall of Listening," "Hall of Action," and "Hall of Meeting," at the Presidio site now occupied by the Letterman Hospital highrise building.

"This is not about creating one big religion. This is about inviting religions to be responsible for global good," Swing insists. "Up to now, the world's religions have been co-opted by tribes and ethnic groups, and end up in murderous postures that violate the teachings they inherited." The UR would dispatch *"conflict-resolution teams'"* to areas "where religious extremism leads to violence" (emphasis added).

Swing announced plans to hold an interfaith summit conference in San Francisco, with the objective of holding a charter-signing ceremony for the new organization.

> And there came one of the seven angels which had the seven vials, and talked with me, saying unto me, Come hither; I will shew unto thee the judgment of the great whore that sitteth upon many waters (Rev. 17:1).

> And he saith unto me, The waters which thou sawest, where the whore sitteth, are peoples, and multitudes, and nations, and tongues (Rev. 17:15).

Bold New World — Evidence Everywhere

> And the ten horns which thou sawest are ten kings, which have received no kingdom as yet; but receive power as kings one hour with the beast. These have one mind, and shall give their power and strength unto the beast (Rev. 17:12-13).

Twenty-two years have passed since Richard Gardner, writing in *Foreign Affairs,* flagship publication of the globalist Council on Foreign Relations, advised that "the 'house of world order' will have to be built from the bottom up rather than from the top down . . . [by way of] an end run around national sovereignty, eroding it piece by piece." *Bold New World: The Essential Road Map to the*

Twenty-First Century, a recently published book by business heavyweight William Knoke, enthuses that this "end
run has been nearly completed."

Knoke is founder and president of the Harvard Capital
Group, which advises "global corporations" on *technological innovations.*

Bold New World bears effusive jacket endorsements
from motivational guru Tom Peters and "Third Wave"
oracle Alvin Toffler. The message of the volume could be
distilled into this directive: "World government is not only
coming, it is essentially here — and businessmen had better
learn the discipline of "global citizenship."

According to Knoke: "In the 21st century, we will each
retain our 'indigenous' cultures, our unique blend of tribal
affiliations, some acquired by birth, others chosen freely.
Many of us will live in one place for most of our lives and
take pride in the local region. Yet our passion for the large
nation-state, for which our ancestors fought with their
blood, will dwindle to the same emotional consequences of
county or province today. A new spirit of global citizenship
will evolve in its place, and with it the ascendancy of global
governance."

NAFTA, the European Union, and developing trade
blocs in Asia and elsewhere are preparing for full-scale
global government. Notes Knoke: "As each bloc forms,
regional trade heightens and the need for a common cur-
rency, uniform product labeling, and commercial regulation
rises. In each case, we are experimenting with new ways to
link countries, to yield sovereignty in exchange for something more than what is lost."

The socialist European Union, according to Knoke, "is
showing us the next step. . . . What happens in Europe will
very much be the model for world consolidation in the 21st
century, not just economically, but politically and socially
as well." Enthuses Knoke, "Historians looking back on us
today will view regional blocs as mere steppingstones

toward the world as a trading bloc, perhaps one political unit. . . . It will only be a matter of time before these blocs, in turn, merge into a whole." He acknowledges that "The foundations to such a re-ordering have already been laid in the path-breaking World Trade Organization," which he describes as "a limited world government with sovereignty over world trade." Through the WTO, *"member governments have voluntarily yielded sovereignty over domestic laws governing the environment, food, safety, and way of life"* (Emphasis added.)

In predictable fashion, Knoke urges that the U.N. be equipped with taxing authority, a standing army, and "*a world police force* with special training and equipment usually not found in armies" and manned with "peacekeepers" who are "a combination of social worker, policeman, riot police, and Rambo-style SWAT commandos." (Emphasis added. Attribution for information: *New American* magazine).

> Thy riches, and thy fairs, thy merchandise, thy mariners, and thy pilots, thy calkers, and the occupiers of thy merchandise, and all thy men of war, that are in thee, and in all thy company which is in the midst of thee, shall fall into the midst of the seas in the day of thy ruin (Ezek. 27:27).

> The merchants of these things, which were made rich by her, shall stand afar off for the fear of her torment, weeping and wailing (Rev. 18:15).

> For thy merchants were the great men of the earth; for by thy sorceries were all nations deceived (Rev. 18:23).

Endnotes
[1] *LA Times,* cited in the *Kansas City Star.*

Chapter 23

TWO
WORLD WARS —
AND NO MORE

A Biblical View of
History and Prophecy

The biblical story of planet earth is the saga of one long, long war involving God, His angelic and human subjects battling against Satan and his evil hordes. This epic drama begins on page one of your Bible. God states His divine intention to destroy the works of the serpent, the devil (Gen. 3:15). There is actually only one universal war, and it concludes with the devil's final incarceration in the Lake of Fire (Rev. 19:20, 20:10). That takes place after the Millennium and the Great White Throne Judgment (Rev. 20:11).

There is one universal war, which began in eternity past with the rebellion of Lucifer, the devil. The universal war ends, after a last battle at the close of the Millennium, with the final judgment and eternal imprisonment of Satan.

Peace at Last

Then dawns an eternity of peace at last. War, cruelty, death, sickness, pain, and suffering will be a dim memory if remembered at all. "There will be peace in the valley for me, some day, oh yes. . . ." No more cruelty, terrorism will be done, no more false accusations, no injustice, no prejudice, no more misunderstanding, no more lonely days or nights, for "God shall wipe away all tears from their eyes" (Rev. 21:4).

Within the scope of the one universal war there will be two planetary or earthly world wars with a thousand years of peace between them. This is a bigger picture than can be conveyed by speaking of two, so called, "world wars" of the 20th century.

To miss this overview is to fail to understand the message of the Bible prophecy. It is our premise that there are *two world wars* described in the Bible. These two wars are separated by 1,000 years of divinely mandated peace on earth. Understanding this should make end-time prophecy much easier to understand.

Under Observation

For I think that God hath set forth us the apostles last, as it were appointed to death: for we are made a spectacle [theater or drama] unto the world, and to angels, and to men (1 Cor. 4:9).

Note: *Spectacle* (Strong's + On Line Bible notes).
Strong's GR. #2302 theatron {theh'-at-ron}.
KJV- translated "theater twice; "spectacle" once.
1) a theater, a place in which games and dramatic spectacles are exhibited, and public assemblies held (for the Greeks used the theater also as a forum)
2) a public show

> And having spoiled principalities and pow-
> ers, he made a shew of them openly, triumphing
> over them in it (Col. 2:15).

Please bear with me if I seem to be repeating my theme,
for I am doing it deliberately. I am strongly convicted that I
must make you understand the magnificent revelation in this
chapter.

The Bible Describes Two World Wars

The First World War did not begin in 1914 nor did it
end in 1918. The encyclopedia tells us, "The assassination
of the Austrian archduke Franz Ferdinand in Sarajevo in
1914 proved to be the spark that ignited World War I (1914-
18).

"Called 'the Great War,' it quickly came to involve all
the great powers of Europe and eventually most countries of
the world, and cost the lives of more than 8 million soldiers."[1] That was a major conflict, but it was not the first
world war. It was only a part of the first world war.

The Second World War Did Not Begin in 1939

Grolier's Encyclopedia says, "World War II com-
menced as a localized conflict in eastern Europe and expanded until it merged with a confrontation in the Far East
to form a global war of immense proportions. The war began
in Europe on September 1, 1939, when Germany attacked
Poland."[2]

This recent war brought on the holocaust which snuffed
out the lives of six million Jewish people, among them one
and a half million children. Altogether, 52 million people
were sacrificed on Moloch's burning altar as a result of the
struggle.

The Second World War did not end on September 2,
1945, with the formal surrender of Japan, aboard the U.S.
battleship Missouri, in Tokyo Bay. I now make use of
emphasized type and italics. I want these words to shout at
you:

The *First World War* began with the fall of Adam and concludes at the Battle of Armageddon.

Then comes the *Millennium.*

After the Millennium comes the *Second World War,* called the Battle Of Gog and Magog (Rev. 20:8). It is a world war and, apparently, is of short duration.[3]

Two World Wars

Let me briefly review a *third time* the concept that Bible prophecy reveals two world wars. World War One began with the fall of Adam, and it ends at Armageddon when Christ returns and defeats the Antichrist.

Then comes the 1000 year visible Kingdom — the Millennium. The Second World War will be at the end of the Millennium when Satan is loosed for a season. This war is called Gog and Magog (II).

Prophecy begins on the first pages of your Bible. Here, in Genesis 3 we find both the declaration and outcome of the First World War. This passage is called the protoevangelium, the first declaration of good news to a fallen race of mankind:

> And the Lord God said unto the serpent [Satan[4]] Because thou hast done this, thou art cursed above all cattle, and above every beast of the field; upon thy belly shalt thou go, and dust shalt thou eat all the days of thy life: And I will put enmity between thee and the woman, and between thy seed and her seed; it shall bruise thy head, and thou shalt bruise his heel (Gen. 3:14-15).

Planet earth's World War I is not over yet. We are in the midst of it.

> Have your eyes caught the vision?
> Has your heart felt the thrill?
> To the call of the Master
> Do you answer, I will?

For the conflict of the ages,
Told by prophets and by sages
In its fury is upon us,
Is upon us today.[4]

The Outcome of the War Is Already Determined

We are not losing the battle, for Jesus Christ is the captain of our salvation and the winner of the end-time conflict.

> For it became him, for whom are all things, and by whom are all things, in bringing many sons unto glory, to make the captain of their salvation perfect through suffering (Heb. 2:10).

Jesus took the disciples to a place called Caesarea Philippi, at the foot of old Mount Hermon. This place has the stench of hell about it. Here the evil gods Baal and Moloch demanded human sacrifices, and were worshiped. Human sacrifices were offered up to the pagan god Pan during the early Greek period. In Jesus' day a temple of Caesar Augustus deified that Roman ruler. Yet it was at Caesarea Philippi that Jesus made a most sublime statement, a declaration of victory. Here Jesus shook his fist in the devil's face and announced the ultimate victory of His church.

> When Jesus came into the coasts of Caesarea Philippi, he asked his disciples, saying, Whom do men say that I the Son of man am?
> And they said, Some say that thou art John the Baptist: some, Elias; and others, Jeremias, or one of the prophets.
> He saith unto them, But whom say ye that I am?
> And Simon Peter answered and said, Thou art the Christ, the Son of the living God.
> And Jesus answered and said unto him, Blessed art thou, Simon Barjona: for flesh and

blood hath not revealed it unto thee, but my Father which is in heaven. And I say also unto thee, That thou art Peter, and upon this rock I will build my church; and the gates of hell shall not prevail against it. And I will give unto thee the keys of the kingdom of heaven: and whatsoever thou shalt bind on earth shall be bound in heaven: and whatsoever thou shalt loose on earth shall be loosed in heaven (Matt. 16:13-19).[5]

God's Purpose Revealed

Whenever God speaks of His foreordained purposes we had better pay attention. God says Jesus came to destroy Satan's works.

He that committeth sin is of the devil; for the devil sinneth from the beginning. For this purpose the Son of God was manifested, that he might *destroy the works of the devil"* (1 John 3:8).

This was accomplished through Jesus' identification with fallen humanity, culminating with His atoning death on the cross of Calvary (Heb. 2:14-3:5). Jesus victory was openly manifested in His resurrection from the dead.

But now is Christ risen from the dead, and become the firstfruits of them that slept. For since by man came death, by man came also the resurrection of the dead. For as in Adam all die, even so in Christ shall all be made alive. But every man in his own order: Christ the firstfruits; afterward they that are Christ's at his coming. Then cometh the end, when he shall have delivered up the kingdom to God, even the Father; when he shall have put down all rule and all authority and power. For he must reign, till he hath put all enemies under his feet. The last enemy that shall be destroyed is death (1 Cor. 15:20-26).

Our Warfare Is Spiritual in Nature

For though we walk in the flesh, we do not war after the flesh: (For the weapons of our warfare are not carnal, but mighty through God to the pulling down of strong holds;) Casting down imaginations [Gr., reasonings], and every high thing that exalteth itself against the knowledge of God, and bringing into captivity every thought to the obedience of Christ (2 Cor. 10:3-5).

For we wrestle not against flesh and blood, but against principalities, against powers, against the rulers of the darkness of this world, against spiritual wickedness [Gr., wicked spirits] in high [Gr., heavenly] places (Eph. 6:12).

Rapture and the Tribulation

The rapture of the church is a victory in the war. Far from being an escapist message, the rapture is a proclamation of the coming victory over Satan and death. It is *by force* that God resurrects those who have died in the faith and removes the church from earth before the Tribulation. "Then we which are alive and remain shall be caught up together with them in the clouds, to meet the Lord in the air: and so shall we ever be with the Lord" (1 Thess. 4:17).

The words "caught up" do not give the full meaning of the Greek "harpazo." See Strong's Gr. #726 harpazo (har-pad'-zo) Meaning: catch up, take by *force*.

> 1) to seize, carry off by *force*
> 2) to seize on, claim for one's self eagerly
> 3) to snatch out or away

After the Rapture, the earth is rocked with judgment after judgment (Rev. 6-16). This is the time of the fulfillment of Daniel's 70th week of seven years. The last three and one-half years are called "great tribulation" (Matt. 24:21; Rev. 2:22, 7:14).

Through the witness of the 144,000 (literal) saved and sealed Israelite servants of God (Rev. 7) multitudes are saved in the Tribulation. Many are martyred by the wicked beast, the Antichrist.

The Millennium will not be not brought about through human effort. As my college professor and mentor Dr. Stanley Horton often says, "The Kingdom comes on the heels of earth's greatest tribulation and the outpouring of the judgment of God on this rebellious world. Jesus Christ will establish the thousand year Kingdom at the time of His second coming."[6]

The End of the First World War

The first world war ends with the battle of Armageddon at the time of Christ's return with the glorified, raptured church.

> And I saw three unclean spirits like frogs come out of the mouth of the dragon, and out of the mouth of the beast, and out of the mouth of the false prophet. For they are the spirits of devils, working miracles, which go forth unto the kings of the earth and of the whole world, to gather them to the battle of that great day of God Almighty. Behold, I come as a thief. Blessed is he that watcheth, and keepeth his garments, lest he walk naked, and they see his shame. And he gathered them together into a place called in the Hebrew tongue *Armageddon* (Rev. 16:13-16).

Last Campaign of World War I: Target — Israel

Note in the following three translations of Zechariah 12:3 that all nations follow the Antichrist, sending armies to conquer Jerusalem:

> *Zechariah 12:3;KJV.* "And in that day will I make Jerusalem a burdensome stone for all people:

all that burden themselves with it shall be cut in pieces, though all the people [Strong's #01471 gowy {go'-ee} nations] of the earth be gathered together against it." (KJV, frequency of use of "gowy" - nation, 374 times; heathen, 143 times; Gentiles, 30 times; people, 11 times).

Zechariah 12:3;NIV. "On that day I will make Jerusalem a heavy stone for all the peoples; all who lift it shall grievously hurt themselves. And all the *nations* of the earth shall come together against it."

Zechariah 12:3;NRSV. "On that day, when all the nations of the earth are gathered against her, I will make Jerusalem an immovable rock for all the *nations*. All who try to move it will injure themselves."

Jesus Returns with the Glorified Church

Only the Jews stand with God against Antichrist. Zechariah writes:

Behold, the day of the Lord cometh, and thy spoil shall be divided in the midst of thee. *For I will gather all nations against Jerusalem to battle;* and the city shall be taken, and the houses rifled, and the women ravished; and half of the city shall go forth into captivity, and the residue of the people shall not be cut off from the city. Then shall the Lord go forth, and fight against those nations, as when he fought in the day of battle.

And his feet shall stand in that day upon the mount of Olives, which is before Jerusalem on the east, and the mount of Olives shall cleave in the midst thereof toward the east and toward the west (Zech. 14:1-4).

And the Lord shall be king over all the earth:

in that day shall there be one Lord, and his name one (Zech 14:9).

And Judah also shall fight [Heb. lacham — make war] *at Jerusalem;* and the wealth of all the heathen round about shall be gathered together, gold, and silver, and apparel, in great abundance (Zech. 14:14).

And it shall come to pass, that every one that is left of all the nations which came against Jerusalem shall even go up from year to year to worship the King, the Lord of hosts, and to keep the feast of tabernacles (Zech. 14:16).

(Italics added.)

The Shout of Victory

In the Book of Revelation we see a wondrous scene:

And I heard as it were the voice of a great multitude, and as the voice of many waters, and as the voice of mighty thunderings, saying, Alleluia: for the Lord God omnipotent reigneth. Let us be glad and rejoice, and give honour to him: for the marriage of the Lamb is come, and his wife hath made herself ready. And to her was granted that she should be arrayed in fine linen, clean and white: for the fine linen is the righteousness of saints [the company returning with Jesus is the raptured church saints] (Rev. 19:6-8).

And I fell at his feet to worship him. And he said unto me, See thou do it not: I am thy fellowservant, and of thy brethren that have the testimony of Jesus: worship God: for the testimony of Jesus is the spirit of prophecy.

And I saw heaven opened, and behold a white horse; and he that sat upon him was called

Faithful and True, and in righteousness he doth judge and make war. His eyes were as a flame of fire, and on his head were many crowns; and he had a name written, that no man knew, but he himself. And he was clothed with a vesture dipped in blood: and his name is called The Word of God.

And the armies which were in heaven followed him upon white horses, clothed in fine linen, white and clean. And out of his mouth goeth a sharp sword, that with it he should smite the nations: and he shall rule them with a rod of iron: and he treadeth the winepress of the fierceness and wrath of Almighty God. And he hath on his vesture and on his thigh a name written, KING OF KINGS, AND LORD OF LORDS.

And I saw an angel standing in the sun; and he cried with a loud voice, saying to all the fowls that fly in the midst of heaven, Come and gather yourselves together unto the supper of the great God; That ye may eat the flesh of kings, and the flesh of captains, and the flesh of mighty men, and the flesh of horses, and of them that sit on them, and the flesh of all men, both free and bond, both small and great.

And I saw the beast, and the kings of the earth, and their armies, gathered together to make war against him that sat on the horse, and against his army. And the beast was taken, and with him the false prophet that wrought miracles before him, with which he deceived them that had received the mark of the beast, and them that worshipped his image. These both were cast alive into a lake of fire burning with brimstone. And the remnant were slain with the sword of him that sat upon the horse, which sword proceeded out of his mouth: and all the fowls were filled with their flesh (Rev. 19:10-21).

Thus concludes the First World War.

One Thousand Years of Peace

In Revelation 20 we view the binding of Satan for a thousand years. The earth will know a thousand years of true peace. This is the Regnum[7] Millennium.

> And I saw an angel come down from heaven, having the key of the bottomless pit and a great chain in his hand. And he laid hold on the dragon, that old serpent, which is the Devil, and Satan, and bound him a thousand years, And cast him into the bottomless pit, and shut him up, and set a seal upon him, that he should deceive the nations no more, till the thousand years should be fulfilled: and after that he must be loosed a little season (Rev. 20:1-3).

The Second World War
Gog and Magog (II) — the Final Victory

When the devil is released at the end of the Millennium he makes war against God one final time. *This conflict is the Second World War.*

The second world war begins when Satan is released from the pit or abyss, after having been bound and imprisoned there during the one thousand years.

At the end of the Millennium, Satan is loosed for a little season, deceives the nations one final time, heads up the Second World War — Gog and Magog. He is defeated and cast into hell forever. The wars are over, never to be known any more for all eternity.

That war is described, briefly, in Revelation 20:

> And when the thousand years are expired, Satan shall be loosed out of his prison, And shall go out to deceive the nations which are in the four

quarters of the earth, Gog and Magog, to gather them together to battle: the number of whom is as the sand of the sea. And they went up on the breadth of the earth, and compassed the camp of the saints about, and the beloved city: and fire came down from God out of heaven, and devoured them. And the devil that deceived them was cast into the lake of fire and brimstone, where the beast and the false prophet are, and shall be tormented day and night for ever and ever (Rev. 20:7-10).

Revelation 21 is God's portrait of the eternal state. We will be free from war at last — forever!

And I saw a new heaven and a new earth: for the first heaven and the first earth were passed away; and there was no more sea. And I John saw the holy city, new Jerusalem, coming down from God out of heaven, prepared as a bride adorned for her husband. And I heard a great voice out of heaven saying, Behold, the tabernacle of God is with men, and he will dwell with them, and they shall be his people, and God himself shall be with them, and be their God. And God shall wipe away all tears from their eyes; and there shall be no more death, neither sorrow, nor crying, neither shall there be any more pain: for the former things are passed away.

And he that sat upon the throne said, Behold, I make all things new. And he said unto me, Write: for these words are true and faithful (Rev. 21:1-5).

Dear friends, the long war is almost over. Never give up! The final victory is worth any sacrifice in the now season. We have read the last page of the grand old, yet ever-new book, the Bible. And there we find out that we are going to win!

> Let's go forward for God
> And resist the foe
> Don't give in to the man of sin
> Our God is mighty
> And we're bound to win
> Satan has an evil force
> To fight against the Lord
> So put on your armour
> Take up your sword
> We're going in the name of the Lord!
> — Author unknown.

Isaiah gives a vivid description of the millennial age in the book that bears his name.

> And he shall judge among the nations, and shall rebuke many people: and they shall beat their swords into plowshares, and their spears into pruninghooks: nation shall not lift up sword against nation, neither shall they learn war any more (Isa. 2:4).

> And there shall come forth a rod out of the stem of Jesse, and a Branch shall grow out of his roots: And the spirit of the Lord shall rest upon him, the spirit of wisdom and understanding, the spirit of counsel and might, the spirit of knowledge and of the fear of the Lord; And shall make him of quick understanding in the fear of the Lord: and he shall not judge after the sight of his eyes, neither reprove after the hearing of his ears: But with righteousness shall he judge the poor, and reprove with equity for the meek of the earth: and he shall smite the earth with the rod of his mouth, and with the breath of his lips shall he slay the wicked. And righteousness shall be the girdle of his loins, and faithfulness the girdle of his reins.

The wolf also shall dwell with the lamb, and the leopard shall lie down with the kid; and the calf and the young lion and the fatling together; and a little child shall lead them. And the cow and the bear shall feed; their young ones shall lie down together: and the lion shall eat straw like the ox.

And the sucking child shall play on the hole of the asp, and the weaned child shall put his hand on the cockatrice' den. They shall not hurt nor destroy in all my holy mountain: for the earth shall be full of the knowledge of the Lord, as the waters cover the sea.

And in that day there shall be a root of Jesse, which shall stand for an ensign of the people; to it shall the Gentiles seek: and his rest shall be glorious (Isa. 11:1-10).

And God shall wipe away all tears from their eyes; and there shall be no more death, neither sorrow, nor crying, neither shall there be any more pain: for the former things are passed away. And he that sat upon the throne said, Behold, I make all things new. And he said unto me, Write: for these words are true and faithful (Rev. 21:4 -5).

The Prince of Peace is coming. He will end all wars.

Endnotes

[1] Grolier Electronic Encyclopedia. 1995.

[2] Ibid.

[3] Not to be confused with the battle of Gog and Magog (1), in Ezekiel chapters 38 and 39.

[4] A chorus by Mrs. C.H. Morris, 1912.

[5] I hope you will study this idea very carefully. You may wish to order a copy of my book, *Smashing the Gates of Hell in the Last Days.* ($10.00 + $2.00 postage and handling). Or you can order a 4-page pamphlet *Holy Spirit World Liberation.* (Free, postpaid).

[6]From a message given by Dr. Horton at the Springfield Regional Eschatology Club.

[7]Regnum: Latin, Kingdom. The word Millennium is derived from two Latin words, mille (1,000) and annum (years). Therefore, every time you read "one thousand years" in the Book of Revelation *you are reading Millennium!*

Chapter 24

Beware
This Symbol

The prophet Isaiah heralded the coming Messiah as the "prince of peace," the true liberator of mankind. The age of true peace on earth is near at hand. It is not the Age of Aquarius but the Age of Jesus Christ we await.

The devil tries to counterfeit the acts of God, but the end result is always a perversion. The coming Antichrist will be a pseudo-peacemaker. The reason the world will accept him is that he will have a plausible peace plan.

Antichrist will not be some hideous monstrosity. He will be a charming, wise, appealing person. He will seem like an angel of light. He will come at a time when the cry of the world is for peace. Our day appears to be the time when "these things are fulfilled." Remember that while the man of sin comes to the world with a peace program, yet he shall honor the "god of forces" and "by peace shall destroy many" (see Dan. 8:25; 11:21, 24, 38).

The cry of humanity is for peace. Symbols of this longing are seen everywhere. However, Paul warns "For when they shall say, Peace and safety; then sudden destruction cometh upon them . . . and they shall not escape" (1 Thess. 5:3). The supposed symbols of peace interest me. I have carefully researched the history of the so-called peace symbol at the Library of Congress and other research centers. Some interesting facts come to light.

The symbol I refer to is the familiar one resembling a swept-wing airplane in vertical flight, enclosed in a circle. Or as someone has said, "It looks like a chicken track." The radical World Without War Council claims: "The Peace Action Symbol was designed on February 21, 1958, for use in the first Aldermaston Easter Peace Walk in England. The symbol is the composite semaphore signal for the letters 'N' and 'D' standing for Nuclear Disarmament. The meaning of the symbol has broadened as other groups (Committee for Non-Violent Action, Student Peace Union, American Friends Service Committee, etc.) have used it. . . ."

It is claimed that the symbol was designed by Bertrand Russell. The fact is that the sign is a very ancient one and has an evil, anti-Christian meaning. Perhaps one wonders why Lord Russell chose a symbol which is a perversion of the Christian cross to be used in a program aimed at the radicalization of British youth. The answer becomes quite clear when one reviews the life and writings of the anti-Christian Russell, who wrote in *The Will to Doubt:* "I am a dissenter from all known religions and I hope that every kind of religious belief will die."

Senator Strom Thurmond reported on the Aldermaston March: "The program was manipulated by pro-Communists whose objective was to involve British students in something they do not fully comprehend." The organizers of the march are identified by DeCourcey's *Intelligence Digest* as being affiliated with European Communist enterprises.

The controversial "peace" symbol has a long history. It has been called the broken cross, devil's trident, witch's foot, the death rune, sign of the defeated Christ, Nero's cross, sign of the broken Jew, Satan's eye — to name a few of the descriptions connected with its usage.

In every case it has an evil concept. It is anti-Christ and anti-God. Anton LaVey, high priest of the Satanist cult of San Francisco pointed out: "A Black Mass consists of such things as saying the Lord's Prayer backwards, interspersed with obscenities; also trampling the cross underfoot or *hanging it upside down* . . . ." The sign has long been associated with Satanism and witchcraft.

A 16th century woodcut depicting the devil, by John Knox, founder of Scot Presbyterianism, shows the peace symbol for the eyes of the devil. Knox was aware of the usage of the symbol by Antichrist forces of his day. The sign was cited by Knox as "the mark of the beast" — a concept connected with Antichrist in the Book of Revelation. Today the sign is promoted by not only a lot of radical groups, but by world society in general.

An observer states that in the fall of 1968 he "attended a four-hour acid-rock festival in a darkened auditorium in downtown Seattle. Sprawled throughout the hall were more than 300 young radicals, many on drugs and all bathed in the eerie and subliminal patterns being flashed in stroboscopic colors on the curtain serving as a backdrop for the entertainers. In the center of that curtain, upon which were flashed the faces of Ho Chi Minh, Che Guevara, and Mao Tse-tung, was a huge Aldermaston peace symbol. When the performance ended at precisely midnight, the curtains parted to reveal a huge symbol of the Goat of Mendes. And there on that stage in Seattle, to the applause of hundreds of radical youths, a Black Mass was performed at the altar of Satan. It was positively Medieval." Rollo Ahmed's *Complete Book of Witchcraft* published in 1936 tells that the Goat of Mendes is a concept from the realm of Satan worship, the Goat of Mendes being Baphomet or the devil.

The Museum of Witchcraft in Bayonne, France, has several wood-cuts illustrating the Black Mass and Witch

Sabbath with the symbol of anti-God (the peace symbol) adorning the altar as an unholy relic. This is referred to by the Marquis de Concressault in *Symbol of the Anti-God.*

In 1866 an international team of archeologists uncovered an ancient Roman villa which incorporated the "peace" symbol in the mosaic designs of the floor. In 1608 Francesco Maria Guazzo referred to the emblem as both "witch foot" and "Nero cross." We recall that Nero's persecutions of the church earned him the title of "antichrist" in the writings of the Early Church fathers. According to Nestorius, the Patriarch of Constantinople (fifth century), Nero is said to have designed a cross, the arms of which were broken, upon which many Christians, including the apostle Peter were crucified. From then on the symbol was known as "the sign of the broken Jew" or the "symbol of the Antichrist."

The Nero cross was later adopted as an appropriate sign by the Satanists of the dark ages. The sign has been painted on the doors of churches closed by the Communists in Russia. It was branded on the bodies of some Jews during the Spanish Civil War of 1936-1939. Now Communists, globalists, and radicals are promoting the use of this evil sign. The Palestine Liberation Front has worn the sign on red armbands. Remember, the Russian writer Tutchcov wrote, "If there is a devil, we Communists are on his side."

One of the nation's most sophisticated magazines, The *New Yorker,* had some interesting things to say about the symbol. The *New Yorker* says that the emblem was adopted by various youth organizations on direct orders from the Communist party. This, they indicate, is part of a long-range program of propaganda to encourage youth to express contempt for adults, for authority, and the ideals that built the United States. The magazine indicates that the symbol is old, but never before associated with peace. It has always been a sign of evil.

I am sorry to see American youth duped into wearing the sign of our enemies, the sworn enemies of Jesus Christ.

I have even seen this sign prominently displayed in the youth annex of one of our own churches, not by evil intention, but out of ignorance, I am quite sure.

How easy it is to relax our diligent resistance to the evil one! Here are wise words from John E. Roberts, editor of the *Baptist Courier,* state Baptist publication of South Carolina:

> So young people, wear it if you must. Draw it, stitch it into your clothing. But be sure you know what it really means. Do not be so naive as to follow the crowd without thinking for yourself ... the so-called peace symbol is an enemy flag of godless tradition, cleverly foisted on the unsuspecting.
>
> This is the most critical hour of world history. It is important that you know what side you are on. I hope you will reject the signs of the enemy, and inform others of the true meaning and background of the peace symbol.

It is not a sign of peace but of evil, hate, war and chaos. There is something missing in the whole peace movement today. The missing something is Jesus Christ, the Prince of Peace. The words of Isaiah have meaning for today: "There is no peace, saith my God, to the wicked" (Isa. 57:21). But there is peace for the righteous. "For the kingdom of God is not meat and drink, but righteousness and peace, and joy in the Holy Ghost" (Rom. 14:17). Note that righteousness comes first. Without righteousness there is no peace. James instructs us that wars arise from the sinful, unrighteous nature of man. Concerning Melchizadec, King of Salem (Salem means peace) the writer of Hebrews says, *"First* being, by interpretation, King of righteousness, and *after that* also King of Salem, which is, King of peace" (Heb. 7:2).

We have peace with God now through our Lord Jesus Christ. Further we anticipate being with Him in His peaceable kingdom of the Millennium.

But with righteousness shall he judge the poor, and reprove with equity for the meek of the earth. . . . And righteousness shall be the girdle of his loins, and faithfulness the girdle of his reins. The wolf also shall dwell with the lamb and the leopard shall lie down with the kid; and the calf and the young lion and the fatling together; and a little child shall lead them. . . . They shall not hurt nor destroy in all my holy mountain: for the earth shall be full of the knowledge of the Lord as the waters cover the sea (Isa. 11:4-9).

By accepting Jesus Christ as your Saviour you will know personal peace. In anticipating His coming you will not disassociate yourself from the realities of the "now season." You will strive to "live peaceably with all men" (Rom. 12:18). Your witness to others will help to bring peace to our nation, for "Righteousness exalteth a nation" (Prov. 14:34). Only a revival of righteous living will bring peace to our nation.

Chapter 25

END-TIME
REVIVAL —
BROWNSVILLE

God is sending true revival to our land. Dead churches are coming to life. This is a sovereign move of God. Suddenly all my past studies of historical revivals are coming back to my heart and mind. From the day of Pentecost to Azusa Street, to the Welsh and the Wesleyan revivals, to the New Hebrides outpouring of the 1950s, and now to churches in our day, revival fires are burning again! I sat in my doctor's office a few days ago and told him about the move of God in Pensacola, Florida. The power of God was great and we began to pray together. I am still trembling at the awesomeness of God's mercy. In Pensacola we were "between the porch and the altar."

> Let the priests, the ministers of the Lord, weep between the porch and the altar, and let them say, Spare thy people, O Lord, and give not thine heritage to reproach, that the heathen should rule over them: wherefore should they say among the people, Where is their God? (Joel 2:17; also,

please read 2 Chron. 7:14 and 15:8).

On September 18-22, 1996 my family and I attended services at Brownsville Assembly of God in Pensacola, Florida. We stayed for five services. What we saw there was the most remarkable thing we had ever beheld in our 42 years of ministry. In the 53 years I have been serving Jesus, since I was saved at the age of ten, this is the greatest outpouring of the Holy Spirit I have witnessed. Revivals like this had broken out around the turn of the century in "God's Bible College" in Topeka, Kansas, under the leadership of Charles Fox Parham, and the Azusa Street revival in Los Angeles in 1906-1909, under the leadership of Brother William Joseph Seymour.

During that time, Pentecostal revival, accompanied by gifts of the spirit, signs and wonders, and many unusual manifestations, broke out all over the world. Most of these revivals were spontaneous. There was little or no contact with other groups experiencing the revival. The contacts and awareness of the vast work God was doing came later. Now I have seen it with my own eyes, in my own day.

We had been asked, "Is the Pensacola phenomenon a real revival? Is it from God or is it manmade and man-promoted? How is it influencing the Church?" This is my attempt to give an objective answer to these and other questions. I had been greatly encouraged in phone conversations with Richard and Deanne Reuben to come and see for myself. I give that same advice to anyone reading this who has an interest in seeing true revival in our times.

The June 4, 1996, Meeting at Central Assembly

On June 4, 1996, I attended a service at Central Assembly of God in Springfield, Missouri. The meeting started at 10:00 a.m. and continued until mid-afternoon. There was anointed preaching, singing, and worship. The Word was preached by Pastor John Kilpatrick and Evangelist Stephen Hill.

During the prayer time at the end there was an unusually strong anointing as hundreds of pastors and church leaders came forward to cry out to God for revival in these last days.

Ramona, my wife of 42 years, was with me along with our daughter Sandy, her husband, Neil Howell, and our grandchildren Elizabeth and David Ben Joseph. As the message went forth, nine-year-old David turned to me and said, "Papa, this is the end-time revival you have been preaching about." "Out of the mouth of babes . . ." (Matt. 21:16).

I decided to go to Pensacola to personally witness this amazing outpouring of God's Spirit. Now I can answer the critics, "This is a heaven-sent revival, sent from our Heavenly Father to refresh and empower us in a desperate world. This is the only answer to the deepest problems we face in our personal lives, in the churches and in society in general."

Some cannot handle the move of the Spirit, so in an effort to justify their Laodicean outlook, they must criticize. One gentleman even went so far as to say that it was New Age. If you think that, in the first place you cannot even define the New Age. The central doctrine of the New Age movement is the deity of man. Never will you find New Agers glorifying our Lord Jesus Christ, proclaiming salvation through His blood atonement, and calling lost sinners to repentance. In the second place, you had better be wary lest you ascribe the works of the Holy Ghost to the devil. See Mark 3:28-30. We must avoid sitting "in the seat of the scornful" (Ps. 1:1). King David danced with abandon before the ark of the covenant. His wife, Michal, mocked him for his "disgraceful behavior."

> And David danced before the Lord with all his might; and David was girded with a linen ephod. So David and all the house of Israel brought up the ark of the Lord with shouting, and with the sound of the trumpet. And as the ark of the Lord

came into the city of David, Michal, Saul's daughter, looked through a window, and saw King David leaping and dancing before the Lord; and she despised him in her heart" (2 Sam. 6:14-16).

The tragic result for Michal was that God judged her. She was smitten barren, and bore no child. Barren! That is what happens spiritually to those who mock the move of God.

Father's Day

On Father's Day in 1995 revival fires from God began to fall in Brownsville Assembly of God. For over two years Pastor John Kilpatrick had led his congregation in intercessory prayer, crying out to God for revival. Some genuine spiritual warfare was involved. During that same period of time a new church sanctuary seating 3,000 people was under construction. Finally the church building was finished. The people were tired, the pastor was weary. Nevertheless, intense prayer went on as the people were crying out to God for a time of revival.

On Father's Day, June 18,1995, it happened. Evangelist Stephen Hill had been invited to speak for one service only, in the evening. However, Pastor John Kilpatrick was exhausted and since Hill had arrived early he was invited to speak in the morning service. Pastor Kilpatrick was glad that Stephen Hill was there to preach for the service. He was anticipating a "normal" dismissal time, then a nice Father's Day dinner with his family. The pastor was grieving for his mother who had recently passed away. I watched a video of that service, and could see exhaustion written on his face.

At the end of his message Steve began to give an extended altar call. That did not seem to thrill Pastor Kilpatrick, *at first*. Steve kept pleading with sinners and backsliders to come forward for prayer. It started with a trickle, and then a flood of about 1,000 people came to the altar. The power of God began to fall amid cries of repentance and as pleas for salvation went up. Pastor Kilpatrick became animated, thrilled that the Lord was moving, his weariness washed away by the moving of the Holy Spirit. It was a good thing that he was newly invigorated since the revival that started that morning was to continue for many months (in the 19th month at the time of this writing, and no end in sight).

Time

Each night, Tuesday through Saturday, there is a service that begins at 7:00 p.m. and usually concludes around 1:00 a.m. Some meetings, I am told, actually lasted until 4:00 or 5:00 a.m. Sunday morning the service starts at 10:00 a.m. and runs until 1:00 or 2:00 p.m. Very few people leave before the meetings are over. The church is filled, as well as three overflow auditoriums furnished with large screen television where people can see the service. Those who have a seat in the main sanctuary or the overflow areas feel so fortunate they are not about to leave early. When the Sunday morning service I attended was over most people stood to their feet. I stood, having lost track of time. I thought we were taking a break. In the previous evening meetings there was a short break at around 8:00 or 9:00 p.m. To my amazement, when I finally turned around I saw that most of the people were gone! I was ready for more. I looked at my watch and saw that it was about 1:30 p.m. It was actually hard for us to leave.

If people are clock-watchers there is little hope of this kind of revival breaking out in a local church. There *may* be times of refreshing, but without an investment of intercession and time these "showers of blessing" cannot be sustained. We long to move out into Ezekiel's river where there are "waters to swim in" (see Ezek. 47:1-5). There is a price to pay for the blessing and power of God. Some church members simply are not interested. They are members of the lukewarm Laodicean church. Some are on the church board of the bored. The Book of Revelation contains a severe warning to the Laodiceans and a challenge to the overcomers:

> And unto the angel of the church of the Laodiceans write; These things saith the Amen, the faithful and true witness, the beginning of the creation of God; I know thy works, that thou art neither cold nor hot: I would thou wert cold or hot. So then because thou art lukewarm, and neither cold nor hot, I will spue thee out of my mouth. Because thou sayest, I am rich, and increased with goods, and have need of nothing; and knowest not that thou art wretched, and miserable, and poor, and blind, and naked: I counsel thee to buy of me gold tried in the fire, that thou mayest be rich; and white raiment, that thou mayest be clothed, and that the shame of thy nakedness do not appear; and anoint thine eyes with eyesalve, that thou mayest see.
>
> As many as I love, I rebuke and chasten: be zealous therefore, and repent. Behold, I stand at the door, and knock: if any man hear my voice, and open the door, I will come in to him, and will sup with him, and he with me.
>
> To him that overcometh will I grant to sit with me in my throne, even as I also overcame, and am set down with my Father in his throne. He that hath an ear, let him hear what the Spirit saith unto the churches (Rev. 3:14-22).

They Come from Far and Near

Housewives, students, politicians, businessmen, teachers, white and blue collar workers, preachers, Bible teachers, evangelists, denominational leaders, Pentecostals, Baptists, Episcopalians, Methodists, Presbyterians, Catholics, etc., all come for salvation, spiritual refreshing, and a renewed vision. They come by airplane, car, pickup truck, tour bus, and a few have hitchhiked. The rich, the poor, the middle class come from far and near. Some are local people, others are from all over the USA and Canada as well as foreign countries. They have one thing in common, they have come to meet with God. They have a divine appointment.

Men, women, teens, and children come with a predetermined plan to get saved. Someone told them they could meet God in Brownsville in a real and special way. God met Israel at Sinai. In the gospel we read, "And go quickly, and tell his disciples that he is risen from the dead; and, behold, *he goeth before you into Galilee; there shall ye see him: lo, I have told you*" (Matt. 28:7, also Mark 16:7).

A wealthy man steps out of his luxury automobile and says to the parking attendant, "I have come here to get saved and to give my life to God." A ragged addict comes with a heart-wrenching cry for salvation and deliverance. What is it that draws these people from all strata of society, so that they all sit together and listen to the gospel, then respond to the altar call? It is the power of God and the promise of the forgiveness of sin and of a transformed life. They come to meet with Jesus, who is always glorified and uplifted in these meetings.

One of the members of Brownsville Assembly asked a waitress, "Are you a Christian, have you ever been saved?" She replied, "I'm not saved yet, *but I will be Thursday night.*" "What do you mean, Thursday night?" The waitress replied, "I have been invited to go to Brownsville Church on Thursday night. So I am going and I will be saved."

A teenage addict came to the revival and accepted Christ as her Saviour. She had not been in church. She did not know the names of the four Gospels, nor who Peter and Paul were. But she accepted Jesus as her Saviour and Lord. Her mother strongly objected to her going to the revival, even though she had stopped taking drugs. She was ordered to stay home. This brought a siege of depression on the teen girl, but she did not turn back to narcotics. Rather, she went to her room, stood on her bed and shouted at the top of her lungs, "Devil, you get out of my house." The next day her mom went out and bought her a beautiful, expensive leather-bound Bible and gave her permission to attend the revival.

I was talking to Steve Hill in the pastor's lounge. Steve had just gotten a call from a man who "checks in" with him frequently. The man said that he is so happy his wife and children have gotten saved and their lives are straightened out. Then he said, "Reverend Hill, I haven't gotten saved yet, but don't give up on me. I am coming."

As long as this revival continues, people will come. God will use converts, pastors, evangelists, and missionaries alike to spread the revival fires across this nation and around the world. Many churches report revivals breaking out. God is moving by the power of the Holy Spirit. Sometimes God uses a pastor that has visited Brownsville. In other cases, a pastor hungry for the moving of God is employed by the Holy Ghost to bring revival to a local church. Sometimes a revival starts in a church that has never even heard about Brownsville. Later they are delighted to hear how God is moving everywhere that there are hungry hearts. A close friend just called me from a town in Arkansas. He described what he called "continuous revival" that is going on in the church he attends. We hear good reports from many churches in Missouri. Salvation of souls is the keynote, uplifting Jesus the emphasis, and this is accompanied by miraculous manifestations of the Spirit. Deliverance from demons is no longer a rarity. A new understanding of biblical spiritual warfare is being birthed.

Come Early

As early as 8:00 a.m. people start lining up in front of Brownsville Assembly of God for the evening service which begins at 7:00 p.m. There they stand for hours in the hot sun, patiently waiting for the doors to open. Some bring picnic coolers with snacks, soda pop, and water. Some have brought beach umbrellas, books, Bibles, tape players, but most important of all they come with hungry hearts.

Many pagan sinners come with one intention in mind — to get right with God. Some call the church and ask when they can come and get saved. Others are brought, reluctantly, by friends or family, but once there the Holy Ghost convicts, and many are redeemed and taste the sweet wine of forgiveness, cleansing, and salvation.

Young People

There are people of all ages involved in the Brownsville revival. It is especially encouraging to see so many young people in attendance, adding their youthful zeal and strength. Their response to prayer and witnessing is notable. Teenagers are being asked to speak to groups in public schools where altar calls are given and more teens are saved. Some are brought to the revival for deliverance from drugs, immorality, atheism, occultism, and a host of other spiritual maladies. New prayer meetings and Bible study groups have been launched. Many of the young people wear t-shirts with brightly colored, well-designed logos bearing gospel messages. Some shirt messages shout at you. Others are cleverly created to invite questions. People are visibly carrying their Bibles to school. Some read a chapter at lunch time. Most openly ask God's blessing on the food. This teenage army of witnesses has real impact. Miracles are wrought as shattered lives are rescued from misery, fear, crime, immorality, pornography, violence, and drugs.

The church runs a bus from some schools to bring unsaved youth to the revival. If a Christian young person wants to ride the free bus, they must bring an unsaved person with them.

Flagpole rallies at schools that would have attracted a half-dozen participants a couple of years ago, now serve as a magnet to gather large groups of young people for prayer and preaching. The results are awesome. Teachers, frustrated by the failure of psychology and other secular means to aid troubled teens, are now turning to young Christian evangelists for Bible advice and prayer. The revival is spreading in wondrous ways.

The Meetings

Each night the service is the same — yet completely different. Every night I know there will be an extended time of praise, worship, and singing. Powerful testimonies of salvation and deliverance will be given. There will be a break of about ten minutes around 8:00 or 8:30 p.m. Pastor Kilpatrick and others will say a few words of exhortation. An offering will be received. Someone sings a solo or a group sings. Sometimes the choir sings a special song or hymn. Evangelist Steve Hill delivers a powerful, challenging, simple salvation message filled with Bible truth. There is always a distinct call to holiness accompanied by strong denunciation of sin in general and specific sins in particular. Redemption through the blood of Jesus is the remedy offered by the anointed evangelist. Then there is the altar call, and sinners and backsliders come to the cross of Jesus for salvation and deliverance.

Purple Badge

The altar counselors all wear a purple badge. People are cautioned not to let anyone without the purple badge pray with them. There have been infiltrators, New Agers, witches, warlocks, and even Satanists who have tried to disrupt the work of the Holy Spirit by offering to lay hands on and pray for people. Serious precautions are taken. Watchful security people are scattered throughout the sanctuary and overflow buildings. We appreciate these safeguards and the concern they reflect. The altar workers spend quality time with each seeker. Each case is different and is treated individually. This insures a greater success rate.

No personal picture taking is allowed, as the flashes could be distracting. Video cameras operated by a church team record everything for posterity.

Statistics

Over a million people passed through the doors of the Assembly during the first 16 months of the revival. Over 65,000 souls were saved.

Richard Reuben told me that this is a conservative estimate. Actually over 150,000 came forward in 16 months, most of whom signed decision cards. I asked Richard how the 65,000 figure was determined. He explained that the number was divided by three and only one-third is reported. This is to make sure that no exaggeration creeps in.

Revival or Apostasy in the Last Days?

Frequently I am asked, "Does the Bible teach that there will be apostasy or revival in the Church of the end times, before the return of our Lord Jesus Christ?"

The answer is, "Definitely, YES!"

There is apostasy. There is and will be revival. This is not an either/or situation. There is and will be both. You must determine with which camp you will be identified.

Those who preach only apostasy play right into the enemy's hands. If you tell a church enough times that all they can experience is a "falling away" you have preached faith in reverse, negative faith. You allow no room for God to move and work in your midst. That is exactly what the devil wants. He loves pessimistic preachers who hold forth no hope for revival.

God Is Greater

Some people's problem is that their devil is bigger than their God. Many good, sincere Christians are rendered ineffectual by pagan fatalism. Whatever will be, will be. But that is not necessarily true. God answers prayer. He will not alter His overall plan, but prayer moves the hand of God and helps mold the course of future events in the short term. We have no desire to thwart or change the plan of God. Rather we seek to understand and implement the plan of God for tomorrow's world. What we want to do is to gain an understanding of God's will and then implement His will through intercession and action.

> But wilt thou know, O vain man, that faith without works is dead? . . . But be ye doers of the word, and not hearers only, deceiving your own selves. . . . For as the body without the spirit is dead, so faith without works is dead also" (James 2:20; 1:22; 2:26).

We can conclude that belief without action is self-deception. The devil is not bothered as much by what a Christian believes, but rather what he *does* about what he believes.

Last Days — Perilous Times

We are not blind. We know that our nation is in the depths of degradation. We weep with you over millions of aborted babies murdered by their own mothers, assisted by the greedy abortion/death industry. Abortion is worship of Moloch and Baal, both of which pagan gods demand human sacrifice. We see the growing acceptance of euthanasia. Acceptance of assisted suicide is shocking. Sin is rampant. Lives are devastated by drugs, alcohol, tobacco, immorality, pornography, and sins of the flesh too horrible to mention. Read Paul's warning list in the second letter to the young pastor Timothy. This is found in 2 Timothy 3:1-4:8. In this long passage, I am leaving the verse numbers in place for easy reference.

> 1 This know also, that in the last days perilous times shall come.
> 2 For men shall be lovers of their own selves, covetous, boasters, proud, blasphemers, disobedient to parents, unthankful, unholy,
> 3 Without natural affection, trucebreakers, false accusers, incontinent, fierce, despisers of

those that are good,

4 Traitors, heady, highminded, lovers of pleasures more than lovers of God;

5 Having a form of godliness, but denying the power thereof: from such turn away.

6 For of this sort are they which creep into houses, and lead captive silly women laden with sins, led away with divers lusts,

7 Ever learning, and never able to come to the knowledge of the truth.

8 Now as Jannes and Jambres withstood Moses, so do these also resist the truth: men of corrupt minds, reprobate concerning the faith.

9 But they shall proceed no further: for their folly shall be manifest unto all men], as theirs also was.

10 But thou hast fully known my doctrine, manner of life, purpose, faith, longsuffering, charity, patience,

11 Persecutions, afflictions, which came unto me at Antioch, at Iconium, at Lystra; what persecutions I endured: but out of them all the Lord delivered me.

12 Yea, and all that will live godly in Christ Jesus shall suffer persecution.

13 But evil men and seducers shall wax worse and worse, deceiving, and being deceived.

14 But continue thou in the things which thou hast learned and hast been assured of, knowing of whom thou hast learned them];

15 And that from a child thou hast known the holy scriptures, which are able to make thee wise unto salvation through faith which is in Christ Jesus.

16 All scripture is given by inspiration of God, and is profitable for doctrine, for reproof, for

correction, for instruction in righteousness:

17 That the man of God may be perfect, throughly furnished unto all good works.

4:1 I charge thee therefore before God, and the Lord Jesus Christ, who shall judge the quick and the dead at his appearing and his kingdom;

2 Preach the word; be instant in season, out of season; reprove, rebuke, exhort with all longsuffering and doctrine.

3 For the time will come when they will not endure sound doctrine; but after their own lusts shall they heap to themselves teachers, having itching ears;

4 And they shall turn away their ears from the truth, and shall be turned unto fables.

5 But watch thou in all things, endure afflictions, do the work of an evangelist, make full proof of thy ministry,

6 For I am now ready to be offered, and the time of my departure is at hand.

7 I have fought a good fight, I have finished my course, I have kept the faith:

8 Henceforth there is laid up for me a crown of righteousness, which the Lord, the righteous judge, shall give me at that day: and not to me only, but unto all them also that love his appearing.

Now add to these things, the warning that believers can also fall away and become apostate: "Now the Spirit speaketh expressly, that in the latter times some shall depart from the faith, giving heed to seducing spirits, and doctrines of devils" (1 Tim. 4:1).

Thank God, this is only one aspect of the end times! There is hope for a great end-time revival, as I have taught in my book, *Smashing the Gates of Hell in the Last Days.*[1]

Bible Basis for End-Time Revival

Many powerful passages of Scripture show that God desires to pour out of His Spirit in the last days.

> And it shall come to pass afterward, that I will pour out my spirit upon all flesh; and your sons and your daughters shall prophesy, your old men shall dream dreams, your young men shall see visions: And also upon the servants and upon the handmaids in those days will I pour out my spirit (Joel 2:28-29).

The apostolic declaration on the Day of Pentecost, almost 2,000 years ago, refers to the prophecy of Joel, indicating a partial fulfillment at that time:

> For these are not drunken, as ye suppose, seeing it is but the third hour of the day. But this is that which was spoken by the prophet Joel; And it shall come to pass **in the last days**, saith God, I will pour out of my Spirit upon all flesh: and your sons and your daughters shall prophesy, and your young men shall see visions, and your old men shall dream dreams: And on my servants and on my handmaidens I will pour out in those days of my Spirit; and they shall prophesy (Acts 2:15-18).

> Then Peter said unto them, Repent, and be baptized every one of you in the name of Jesus Christ for the remission of sins, and ye shall receive the gift of the Holy Ghost. For the promise is unto you [those present], and to your children [some present, some not yet born], and to all that are afar off [includes people today], even as many as the Lord our God shall call" (Acts 2:38-39; comments in brackets added).

Christ is greater than Antichrist. How can some people read the Book of Revelation and see more Antichrist than Jesus Christ? There is something perverted in such a point of view. Let's get our priorities in order!

By the way, there is no Book of Revelations (plural) in your Bible. The last book of your Bible is "The Revelation (singular) of Jesus Christ, which God gave unto him, to shew unto his servants things which must shortly come to pass; and he sent and signified it by his angel unto his servant John" (Rev. 1:1). The Apocalypse is the Revelation of Christ Jesus triumphing over all His enemies.

The Two Greatest Prophecies

Over 30 percent of your Bible is prophecy. I have read that there are 2,712 details of prophecy which can be divided into 839 major categories. Every one of these prophecies are very important. Prophecy already fulfilled proves the authority of the Word of God. Prophecy gives us a road map in the present. Future prophecy gives us hope for tomorrow and eternity. We are, "Looking for that blessed hope, and the glorious appearing of the great God and our Saviour Jesus Christ" (Titus 2:13).

There are two passages of Scripture that are not always noted as being prophetic, and yet Matthew 16:18 and Matthew 24:14 tower above every other prophecy in significance. One guarantees the future victorious destiny of the Church, and the other assures the successful completion of the Great Commission.

The first prophecy quotes Jesus, "And I say also unto thee, That thou art Peter [Greek: Petros, a small stone], and upon this rock [Gr: Petra, a huge rock] I will build my church; and the gates of hell shall not prevail against it" (Matt. 16:18). This is God's absolute, 100 percent guarantee that there will never be a "post-Christian era" and that contrary to the ranting of some modernist theologians, God is *not* dead. Put your trust in Jesus, for He never falters nor fails. He did not establish His Church to fail or go down in defeat.

Jesus is more powerful than the devil and all of his horde of demons. His Kingdom shall prevail. We are not defeated. Lambert Dolphin, a renowned scientist who is a strong believer in Jesus, sent us information he got off the Internet. It is a declaration by an organization blaming Christianity for all the world's problems. The declaration calls for the killing of 200,000,000 Christians by the year 2000. This is nothing new! The devil always tries to kill God's people, but the Church survives. We will live for Jesus and we can die for Him, but we will never bow to the devil.

This is war, folks! God is our only hope. But He is the Sovereign Majesty of the universe. Time to wake up to the harsh realities of what this world has become. We must have a mighty worldwide revival. We need a move of the Holy Spirit as never before.

What I saw happening in Brownsville Assembly in Pensacola encourages me to hope that the great end-time revival has begun, and is spreading everywhere. Don't miss the greatest opportunity of your lifetime. Please read my book *Smashing the Gates Of Hell in the Last Days.*[1] Pastor Kilpatrick has mentioned several times that people should read this book. He also told how much the book meant to his life personally.

The Greatest of All the Prophecies

The second of the two great prophecies may be the greatest of all, however, this is hard to evaluate since the two are interdependent on the fulfillment of each to fulfill God's plan for the redemption of earth's people. This prophecy is found in the context of Jesus' Olivet Discourse, in Matthew 24 and 25.

> And this gospel of the kingdom shall be preached in all the world for a witness unto all nations; and then shall the end come (Matt. 24:14).

Fifty percent of earth's people have never heard the gospel even one time. It will take a mighty Holy Ghost revival with manifestations of God's power to finish the task.

> And he said unto them, Go ye into all the world, and preach the gospel to every creature. He that believeth and is baptized shall be saved; but he that believeth not shall be damned. And these signs shall follow them that believe; In my name shall they cast out devils; they shall speak with new tongues; They shall take up serpents [not deliberately]; and if they [accidentally] drink any deadly thing, it shall not hurt them; they shall lay hands on the sick, and they shall recover. So then after the Lord had spoken unto them, he was received up into heaven, and sat on the right hand of God. *And they went forth, and preached every where, the Lord working with them, and confirming the word with signs following. Amen"* (Mark 16:15-20; italics and words in brackets added for emphasis and clarification).

What to Expect If You Go to Brownsville Assembly

Expect an encounter with God. Expect to be touched by His mighty power. But this revival is not about manifestations, tongues, or falling under the power, nor healing the sick. These things all happen, but the main event is the salvation of souls. That is the principal emphasis of the revival. You will see hundreds of people saved, delivered from drugs, alcohol, and immorality. People will sing enthusiastically, praising God with loud shouts.

Dick Reuben may blow the shofar and sound the call to war against the powers of darkness. If you have any spiritual sensitivity you must be aware of the intensification of satanic activity. The devil is trying to destroy the Church and all humanity. He wants to destroy you. We have declared war on hell, and it is a fight to the finish.

The Church is not going to be raptured out of here lukewarm, half backslidden, pale and washed out, whimpering in defeat. NO! When the rapture trumpet sounds we will leave here with a shout of triumph. Look out, Lucifer, here comes the invincible Church of Jesus Christ, marching down the road of time into eternity with victory banners unfurled. Jesus served notice on you, devil, at Caesarea Philippi, almost 2,000 years ago. For 20 centuries you have tried to wipe us out, but here we are at the end of the age. Devil, it is more and more apparent that you are the loser of all time. So just back off and get your filthy, slimy hands off the people of God.

What Kind of Preaching Will You Hear at Brownsville?

Each night Steve Hill preaches a clear gospel message that anyone can understand. He quotes a lot of Scripture, and Christ Jesus is uplifted and glorified. The preaching is strong, confrontational, and wrapped in compassion. Steve will tell of people who have been saved and delivered. He pointedly mentions several times that there will be an altar call at the end of the message, and sinners should be ready to come forward for prayer. There is a powerful anointing on the evangelist as he holds forth the Word of life.

Preaching the Word

This is a revival based on the Scripture. Jesus is declared and given supremacy. Both Pastor Kilpatrick and Evangelist Steve Hill teach and read from the Bible in a responsible fashion. I heard no abuse of the Word. One thing different is the passion with which the salvation message; denunciation of sins of the flesh, mind, and spirit; call to repentance; and holy living, were declared in every service.

I detected no false doctrine being preached at any time. There were numerous references to the Rapture of the Church and the Second Coming of Christ. On Sunday morning, Pastor John Kilpatrick brought a strong doctrinal message on hell, heaven, and life after death. Oh! With what anointed fervor and compassion he spoke.

Manifestations

There were powerful manifestations of the Spirit as the power of the Holy Ghost fell on convicted sinners and repentant believers. Some wept, some expressed holy joy and worship. Some, under conviction, fell to the floor. Others experiencing deliverance were slain in the Spirit.

Over and over the preachers cautioned, "This is not about falling under the power, but about Jesus and His salvation for sinners." Yes, there are miracles and healings, but that is not the primary emphasis. Jesus and salvation of the lost take first place.

Sinners come with one intention and that is to get right with God. Already convicted of their wretched sinful ways, they quickly respond to the altar call.

Some people literally shook under the power of God. Many fell to the floor. Some of the critics charge, "There is danger of getting in the flesh." Or, "Maybe it is demonic." The pastors at Brownsville are the first to recognize these pitfalls. Whenever the Spirit moves there is always fleshly mimicry. Demons always try to creep in and disrupt.

My answer is, "I never saw a counterfeit $52 bill. There are counterfeit $50 bills, but no counterfeit $52 bills. Only what is real gets counterfeited."

I was told that if I went to Pensacola I would see people barking and growling like dogs and chattering like monkeys. I had my eyes wide open and I saw none of this. I did see one thing. I saw a woman who was obviously demon-possessed, growling. She came close to me as two believers physically assisted her in leaving the sanctuary. She was taken to a private place for prayer and exorcism, if necessary. That was all I observed of this type of activity. In my own meetings in churches through 42 years we have encountered demonic activity and even possession in some services. When God's Spirit moves, evil spirits will try to disrupt, sow confusion and in general, oppose the work of God.

I witnessed no Spirit-anointed believers acting or making noises like animals. This would seem to me to be out of order. Barking like a dog offends the sense of Scripture. Dogs are always pictured as wild, vile, unclean beasts. These were not like our domesticated dogs we have today. I have not seen believers barking like dogs, but I have heard that it takes place in some places. The following Bible verses should be read:

> But against any of the children of Israel shall not a **dog** move his tongue (Exod. 11:7).

> Thou shalt not bring the hire of a whore, or the price of a **dog**, into the house of the Lord thy God for any vow: for even both these are abomination unto the Lord thy God (Deut. 23:18).

> Why should this dead **dog** curse my lord the king? Let me go over, I pray thee, and take off his head (2 Sam. 16:9).

> Him that dieth of Baasha in the city shall the **dogs** eat; and him that dieth of his in the fields shall the fowls of the air eat (1 Kings 16:4).

> Thus saith the Lord, In the place where **dogs** licked the blood of Naboth shall **dogs** lick thy blood, even thine (1 Kings 21:19).

> For **dogs** have compassed me: the assembly of the wicked have enclosed me: they pierced my hands and my feet (Ps. 22:16).

> Deliver my soul from the sword; my darling from the power of the **dog** (Ps. 22:20).

> Thou therefore, O Lord God of hosts, the God of Israel, awake to visit all the heathen: be not

merciful to any wicked transgressors. Selah (Ps. 59:5).

They return at evening: they make a noise like a **dog**, and go round about the city (Ps. 59:6).

Swords are in their lips: for who, say they, doth hear? (Ps. 59:7).

But thou, O Lord, shalt laugh at them; thou shalt have all the heathen in derision (Ps. 59:8).

And at evening let them return; and let them make a noise like a **dog**, and go round about the city (Ps. 59:14).

As a **dog** returneth to his vomit, so a fool returneth to his folly (Prov. 26:11).

His watchmen are blind: they are all ignorant, they are all dumb **dogs** (Isa. 56:10).

Yea, they are greedy **dogs** which can never have enough (Isa. 56:11).

And I will appoint over them four kinds, saith the Lord: the sword to slay, and the **dogs** to tear, and the fowls of the heaven, and the beasts of the earth, to devour and destroy (Jer. 15:3).

Give not that which is holy unto the **dogs**, neither cast ye your pearls before swine, lest they trample them under their feet, and turn again and rend you (Matt. 7:6).

Beware of **dogs**, beware of evil workers (Phil. 3:2).

But it is happened unto them according to the true proverb, The **dog** is turned to his own vomit again; and the sow that was washed to her wallowing in the mire (2 Pet. 2:22).

> For without are **dogs**, and sorcerers, and whoremongers, and murderers, and idolaters, and whosoever loveth and maketh a lie (Rev. 22:15).

Man is created above the animals and to mimic animal behavior is undesirable. Job spoke of those sinners who through degenerate living acted and lived like animals. In Job chapter 30 we read:

> 1 But now they that are younger than I have me in derision, whose fathers I would have disdained to have set with the **dogs** of my flock.
> 2 Yea, whereto might the strength of their hands profit me, in whom old age was perished?
> 3 For want and famine they were solitary; fleeing into the wilderness in former time desolate and waste.
> 4 Who cut up mallows by the bushes, and juniper roots for their meat.
> 5 They were driven forth from among men, (they cried after them as after a thief;)
> 6 To dwell in the cliffs of the valleys, in caves of the earth, and in the rocks.
> 7 Among the bushes *they brayed*; under the nettles they were gathered together.
> 8 They were children of fools, yea, children of base men: they were viler than the earth.

This was the product of human devolution, brought on by generations of degenerate living.

At Brownsville Assembly we witnessed many falling under the power of the Spirit. There was dancing in the Spirit, gentle, holy, and joyous laughter. Others were groaning under conviction of sin. NO ONE WAS *DRUNK* IN THE SPIRIT. BUT MANY WERE *FILLED* WITH THE SPIRIT. We were not knocking back shot glasses of Holy Ghost whiskey at Joel's place, rather we were drinking from the fount of living waters. Never, never is drunkenness, in or out of the Spirit, advocated in God's Holy Word. Rather we are commanded *not* to be *drunk* with alcohol, *but* to be *filled* with the Spirit.

Here is a contrast, not a favorable comparison. On the day of Pentecost Peter declared:

> For these are **not drunken,** as ye suppose, seeing it is but the third hour of the day. **But** this is that which was spoken by the prophet Joel; And it shall come to pass in the last days, saith God, I will pour out of **my Spirit** upon all flesh (Acts 2:15-17).

Paul wrote to the Ephesian Church:

> And **be not drunk** with wine, wherein is excess; **but be filled with the Spirit** (Eph. 5:18).

> And he drank of the wine, and was drunken; and he was uncovered within his tent (Gen. 9:21).

Dr. Michael Brown is on the pastoral staff at Brownsville Assembly of God. In his book *Holy Fire* he says:

> Is the *emphasis* on "getting drunk" on God's new wine reflective of the heart and soul of New Testament Christianity? The question is not whether God sometimes overwhelms His people with an outpouring of the Spirit to the point that we are accused of drunkenness. Let the inundation come, and let the critics howl! The question is whether we should build our theology on the words of the mockers who say, "These men are drunk," instead of saying with Peter, "These men are *not* drunk" — and then, like Peter, bringing a withering word to both the critical and the convicted. Doesn't the New Testament urge us to be alert, sober, and watchful? Of course, we can never get enough of the joy of the Lord (at least, I can't!) and we can

never have too much of the Spirit. But we can major on the outward instead of the inward; we can miss the heart of the Word. . . .

Why not emphasize fullness instead of drunkenness? The difficulty is not so much with the nature of the manifestations. The difficulty is with our emphasis.

We spotlight the sensational and underscore the unusual, and then we wonder why people aren't focusing on Jesus. The bottom line is that the Church in this hour doesn't need more folly. Filling, yes; folly, no. Rejoicing, yes; revelry, no. We are called to go into all the world and make disciples, not drunkards.

The Church still has little or no prophetic voice to the nation. The outpouring of the Spirit has certainly drawn the attention of the media, and to some extent, the world *has* been touched. Backsliders have returned to the Lord and sinners have been saved. But the Church hardly has a voice. Someone must sound the trumpet! Those who have been awakened must in turn become awakeners. Who will call our nation to account?

For some, the "blessing" could become a curse. (There are churches that have completely bought into "the renewal" that are already in serious decline. Danger!) God forbid that we make the Spirit into a spectacle and turn holy excitement into Hollywood entertainment. If you concentrate on the laughter more than the Lord and on the shaking more than the Savior, take heed. You may get what you want. Instead of soaring with the Spirit you may end up slobbering in the Spirit. Instead of "soaking" you may find yourself sinking. Watch out![3]

Is It Old-Time Pentecost?

I was asked by an elder pastor, "Brother Lewis, is this revival old time Pentecost?" Yes it is, in every sense of the word. Compare it to the Day of Pentecost in the Book of Acts. Compare it to great revivals of the past. Compare it to the Pentecostal revival in the early 1900s. Every element of those revivals is present in this current revival. That includes both positive and negative aspects.

Pastor John Kilpatrick writes of various manifestations of the Holy Spirit, including falling on the floor, shaking, trembling, groaning, travailing, weeping, holy joy and laughter, being still or solemn, etc. In his book *Feast of Fire,* Brother Kilpatrick documents these manifestations with Bible passages and with historical references to previous profound revival movements.[4] Also see Michael Brown's *From Holy Laughter to HOLY FIRE* , chapter 10, "Jerkers, Jumpers, and 'Holy Disorder.' "[5]

Some of our churches are so dead and formal that an utterance in tongues or an interpretation or a prophecy *is not allowed in our public meetings.* On the morning I attended the worship service in Brownsville Assembly there was a powerful utterance in an unknown tongue, followed by the interpretation. No one on the platform treated it in an offhand manner, nor was there anything less than full respect for it. I testify that it was genuine, from the Holy Ghost. This is just one example.

Just like the Azusa Street Revival in 1906-1909, there were people from all walks of life, worshipping together in equality. There were people from all races. The Lord used a one-eyed black preacher, William Fox Seymour, to lead the early beginning of the revival. Sadly, in some places the Pentecostal revival was corrupted by racial discrimination. Even today we have churches that are predominantly white or predominantly black. Not every aspect of "old time Pentecost" was ideal. We should be more concerned for biblical revival, Book of Acts revival, than anything else.

In the Brownsville revival we could detect no discrimination. I saw people there from every social and economic environment. There were professional people, blue collar workers, artists, and white collar workers. We saw African-Americans, Orientals, Hispanics, Native Americans, and Caucasians, etc. In the revival there is no place for discrimination. We are all brothers and sisters in Christ. We are all equals before God.

Past revivals have never been without flaws. None have reached absolute perfection. The same is true of this current move of God. God's part is perfect, but the human vessels He uses are flawed. I feel sorry for critics who spend all their time examining flaws and never get into the stream of the moving of the Holy Ghost.

The leadership at Brownsville Assembly deals with excesses and abuses, as in the case of holy laughter. There are beautiful and comforting aspects of the joy of the Lord, one of which is holy laughter. But my observation is that raucous or disruptive manifestations of laughter are not tolerated.[6]

How Long Will It Last?

There is no question that the revival is spreading. I live in Missouri. Many pastors and members of our churches have visited Brownsville and have caught the vision for revival. They have carried the fire back to their local churches. The story is the same all over the nation. Delegations from many nations are carrying the revival home to their native shores. Some great revivals of the past have been local in scope. Others like the Pentecostal revival of this century have swept all over the world.

We hope that the current revival grows and lasts until Jesus comes back, bringing in a great harvest of lost souls.

I have been profoundly moved by evangelist Stephen Hill's book *A Time to Weep.*[7] I strongly recommend that you get a copy and read it.

We position ourselves "between the porch and the altar," knowing that today's tears of repentance and of intercession will bring an even greater harvest of souls.

> Bringing in the sheaves, bringing in the sheaves
> We shall come rejoicing, bringing in the sheaves.
> — Knowles Shaw

> Sing unto the Lord, O ye saints of his, and give thanks at the remembrance of his holiness. For his anger endureth but a moment; in his favour is life: weeping may endure for a night, but joy cometh in the morning (Ps. 30:4-5).

A Vision for Tomorrow

In the last days God will show many signs, wonders, and revelations through dreams, visions, and expanded understanding of the Word of God. While God's prophetic revelation is complete in the Bible, our illumination and understanding of that revelation is growing. We understand more about prophecy today than we did a year ago. Jesus said that certain things were spoken (as prophecies) so that when they were fulfilled the believer's faith would be strengthened (John 14:29). The Amplified Translation of Daniel 12:4 indicates that in the end times there will be an increase of knowledge. The Amplified Translation also reveals that understanding of the purposes of God in the latter times will increase!

> But you, O Daniel, shut up the words and seal the book until the time of the end. [Then] many shall run to and fro and search anxiously [through the Book], and knowledge [of God's purposes as revealed to His prophets] shall be increased and become great (Dan. 12:4; Amp).

The great prophecies of the end of the age are not all negative! The prophet Joel speaks of the glories of the era preceding the establishing of Messiah's Kingdom:

> And it shall come to pass afterward, that I will pour out my spirit upon all flesh; and your sons and your daughters shall prophesy, your old men shall dream dreams, your young men shall see visions: And also upon the servants and upon the handmaids in those days will I pour out my spirit (Joel 2:28-29).

This passage is quoted by the apostle Peter in his great sermon on the Day of Pentecost. He indicates a partial fulfillment at that time, and we can conclude that there will be a future fulfillment in the "end times." In the millennial Kingdom the prophecy receives its ultimate fulfillment. At any rate, we are most certainly living in a day when God is revealing many things to his servants. It is important to understand the nature of visions and wherein their value lies. In the last days knowledge will be increased.

Any personal revelation must be in agreement with the Bible. It will usually be a confirmation and/or an expansion of a truth revealed in the Holy Scriptures.

In the years from 1957 through 1960, God spoke to me in wondrous visions concerning the future destiny of the Church and of our nation. The Lord showed me that there could be a terrible persecution of the Church accompanied by a frightening loss of personal liberty. This was a matter of deep concern and I prayed for further information. What could be done to avert this destructive force from being unleashed on the Church and our free nation?

A Remarkable Vision

In August of 1973, Mrs. Lewis and I attended the General Council of the Assemblies of God. While there, we were approached by an old friend whom we had not seen for several years. Reverend O. Kenneth Brann said, "David, I have been trying to get a work going in a house in Elizabethtown, Kentucky. Could you come to our little church and help us?" Kenneth knew that my ministry involves holding teaching and evangelistic meetings in churches, colleges, etc. I told Brother Brann that after the council I did have a few days open, and could stop over in Elizabethtown for a few nights. It was while we were in that Kentucky town that God gave me one of the most unusual and powerful revelations I have ever received, outside the Bible itself. It changed the course of our lives and ministry. From that day on we began to emphasize the positive side of Bible prophecy. I had immediately written down everything the Lord showed me. We printed it up and gave it to the people. A spirit of revival broke out and soon afterward the congregation was able to build a lovely brick church.

In September of 1973, the Lord spoke to me by means of a vision in the night. It is clear and vivid in my mind right now as I write this. In the vision I was elevated high above the earth, looking down upon it. I saw many lights scattered over the landmasses of the continents. The Holy Spirit showed me that the symbol of the lights spoke of how the gospel light is shining forth, throughout the whole world. There were more lights in Russia and China than I would have expected. Some areas had only a few lights shining. These were areas where the gospel is not known or declared.

I praised God for the wonder of His creation, for our beautiful earth, and I praised Him for the going forth of the gospel. I felt very peaceful. I looked at the glaze of lights in the USA, Canada, some South American countries, and other areas. I felt a great thankfulness, and a sense of tranquility. I felt we could continue sending out the gospel to the dark parts of the world, thus completing the task of fulfilling the Great Commission.

Suddenly my emotions changed. I was uneasy. Some dark foreboding gripped my mind. Dark, thick, ugly clouds began to creep up around the horizons of the earth. They spread rapidly until they blanketed the whole world. Only a few lights feebly showed through. This symbolized a coming persecution of the Church. The Church was driven underground by the anti-God forces that even now work in the world. No longer could the Church openly hold services, broadcast over TV and radio, and pass out literature.

In horror I cried out, "Oh, God, must this be?" The Holy Spirit spoke in response to my tortured question and it was like thunder in my soul: "No, it is not inevitable. This is what will happen to the Church if the Church fails in its mission and task, and if there is not a real revival in the Church. If the Church is apathetic and continues in sin, materialism, and worldly pursuits, this is what will happen, but it can be prevented." I began to rebuke this manifestation of Satan's power, entering into spiritual warfare. I shouted at Satan, "Back off devil! You will not defeat the Church of the living God."

The clouds rolled back and I saw earth as at the beginning of the vision. I asked the Lord what we should do to prevent Satan's victory.

The answer came, "Let believers everywhere be united in prayer and faith." The scene changed one more time. Suddenly all the lights on earth were interconnected by beams of light making a lace work of light over the earth: I was looking at the Church united in prayer and intercession!

That was the end of the vision, but not the end of the time of anointed inspiration. I sat down and wrote out the prayer covenant concept which we call *Holy Spirit World Liberation.*

You can now meet with a worldwide prayer meeting in the Spirit twice each week as explained in detail in my book, *Smashing the Gates of Hell in the Last Days.*

Simultaneously believers can join together and hurl thunderbolts of Holy Ghost power against the citadels of hell.

God gave similar revelations to many other ministries and bands of believers. Now a mighty revival is breaking out across our nation and throughout the world.

Perhaps you are also aware of the intensification of Satan's resistance against the Church. Demons growl their malice. Hell is enraged. Satan will go to any lengths to stop us, but God is raising up an army of Holy Ghost anointed warriors. Many other prayer ministries have an emphasis similar to the *Holy Spirit World Liberation Front.*

We cannot change events of the future that are pre-destined through God's prophecies in the Bible. But we can change, through the power and guidance of the Holy Spirit, many things that will affect the quality of your life, liberty, and witness for God in the end times. Pray for the leaders of our nation (read 1 Tim. 2:1-6). Remember 2 Chronicles 7:14.

In Jeremiah 18:7-8 we are told that if God has pro-nounced a judgment (evil) upon a nation to destroy it, if that nation repents, then God will repent (change his mind) about the judgment He planned to bring upon them! Also see Jonah 3:9 (better yet, read the entire Book of Jonah). We will affect certain aspects of the future in cooperation with God if we identify with His plan and will, and enter into intercession.

We stand at the crossroads. The fury of hell is mount-ing. Men of evil breathe threats against the Church. Satan wants to destroy us. What you do about it is important. God cannot answer prayers that are not prayed. Will you be content merely to study prophecy as a spectator, or will you be a participant in the ongoing plan of God? Will He say to you one day "Well done [not just, "well thought"] thou good and faithful servant?"

An Example of Prayer in Action

I am sharing some of my personal experiences with you with the hope that it will strengthen your resolve to spend more time in prayer and intercession. Let me tell you about how God inspired Ramona and me to pray through on an urgent matter by giving me a revelation of what was going to happen to President Gerald Ford.

On August 20, 1974, God gave me a revelation by the word of knowledge that there would be an assassination attempt on the life of President Gerald Ford. On August 21 we asked the congregation of Melrose Park Community Church (Chicago area) to join us in binding the spirit of murder, as it was going to be directed against the president. On August 22 the revelation came to me very clearly again. We have a statement signed (dated August 22, 1974) by Rev. David Ulseth and Rev. Samuel Bush that the revelation was given at that time.

As Mrs. Lewis and I prayed over the matter we came to the conclusion that there would be two attempts to kill President Ford. The Lord had told us that if the people of God would pray, these attempts would fail. We shared this revelation with thousands of Christians in the year that followed, both in pulpits and on national TV. Time passed by. Finally, when the two attempts on President Ford's life failed (in Sacramento and San Francisco, California) we rejoiced to see prayer answered.

Lynette Fromm, one of the would-be assassins, was pictured on the front of *Time* magazine looking in amazement at the gun in her hand and crying, "It didn't go off!" When Billy Graham had a press conference in Texas a few days later, he said, "It was angels of God that prevented the president's death." Later, former President Ford said in a news conference, "I am convinced that it was divine intervention that prevented my death." He was recalling the two assassination attempts.

We believe God answers prayer. He will hear our heartfelt cries for revival in these end times. Please bear in mind that we never seek to change or thwart the will of God. We seek, rather, to comprehend His will and then we seek to implement His plan through intercession and Spirit-led action and witness.

As we near the year 2000 we must bind together to thwart the plans of the occultic New Agers. They want to effect a major shift in humanity's perception of reality. They call this the "paradigm shift." (See the Stonehenge chapter — 16). If we let them succeed, the churches and the revival will suffer because of it. We are approaching the pinnacle of end-days spiritual warfare. Fleshly programs and means will not prevail over the demonic invasion in the near future. But through prayer we can build a wall of defense against Satan's devilish plans.

Ramona and I are called to raise up a well-informed army of prayer warriors who will get involved in thousands of prayer meetings on December 31, 1999, which will begin at 8:00 p.m. local time in your area and continue until after midnight into the next century January 1, 2000. Will you pledge to pray the year 2000 in? Pastors will you mobilize your churches? Individuals will you hold a prayer meeting in your home? Computer people, will you help flood the Internet with announcements of the prayer time? Please write to me and let me know how you want to get involved. We plan, God willing, to be conducting a Prayer and Prophecy Summit Conference from December 28, 1999 to January 1, 2000. YOU ARE INVITED. Write us and we will start sending information via our publication *Prophecy Watch International* to you.

Write for more information which will help you understand these prayer concepts. The literature will also help you get involved in God's end-time victory program. Request a copy of the *Holy Spirit World Liberation* folder. The folder is available in English, Spanish, and French. We distribute them free of charge all over the world.

David A. Lewis
PO Box 11115
Springfield, MO 65808 USA
Phones 417-882-6470
TOLL FREE (from USA & Canada) 1 800-772-5687
E Mail: DALewMin@aol.com

Endnotes

[1] David Allen Lewis, *Smashing the Gates of Hell in the Last Days* (Green Forest AR: New Leaf Press, 1987).

[2] Ibid.

[3] Michael L. Brown, *From Holy Laughter to HOLY FIRE* (Foley AL: Together In The Harvest Publications, 1996), p. 24-25.

[4] Kilpatrick, John, *Feast of Fire* (Brownsville, FL: John Kilpatrick, 1995) p. 100-104.

[5] Brown, *From Holy Laughter to HOLY FIRE,* p. 121-140.

[6] Kilpatrick, *Feast of Fire,* p. 88-91.

[7] Stephen Hill, *Time to Weep, the Language of Tears* (Foley, AL: Together in the Harvest Publications, 1996).

YES! Put my name on the list for special information on the December 31, 1999, Midnight Prayer Meeting.

Name _____

Address _____

State/Prov_____ Zip or PC _____

Country_____Phone _____

FAX: _____

E Mail _____

____Send free catalogue of tapes, videos, books, publications by David Allen Lewis.

____Send information - Dec. 28, 1999-Jan.1, 2000 PROPHECY AND PRAYER CONFERENCE

SEND COUPON TO
David A. Lewis
P.O. Box 11115
Springfield, MO 65808
The United States of America

Phone: 417-882-6470
TOLL FREE (from USA & Canada) 1 800-772-5687
E Mail: DALewMin@aol.com

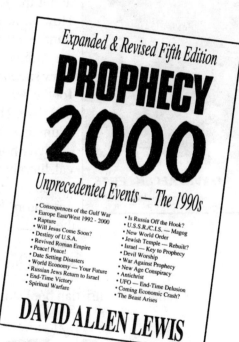